The Realpolitik of Evaluation

The Realpolitik of Evaluation shines a light on the divergent demands for evaluation. But what explains the "gap" between what those on the "demand" side expect in terms of evaluation results, and the "supply" of information provided by evaluators? Can anything be done to narrow this gap? What works and what does not work?

Examining these questions from both the demand and the supply side, experts describe ten different global examples of the gap between demand and supply of evaluation information in different contexts. In an attempt to bridge that gap, they effectively expose the biases behind supposedly non-partisan sources of evaluation information and highlight the pros and cons of attempts to bridge the gap through the use of third parties, enhanced stakeholder involvement, and the incorporation of social science models to strengthen Theories of Change (ToC).

The Realpolitik of Evaluation is an important book that poses questions at multiple levels of thinking. It will be of great interest to policymakers, program implementers, and project managers.

Markus Palenberg is the Founder and Manager of the Institute for Development Strategy (IfDS) in Munich, Germany, where he works as researcher, evaluator, and advisor. Over the last 15 years, Markus has conducted more than 40 research and consulting assignments in the public and private sector, specializing in evaluation of global programs and evaluating and advising on results-based management. He regularly serves as peer reviewer of research publications and advisor during the design phases of global programs, has published works on evaluation methodology, and has served on boards, executive committees and advisory panels for development programs and institutions.

Arne Paulson pursued a career in international development, working as an economist in a number of international organizations, including the World Bank, UNCTAD (Geneva), the International Energy Agency (Paris), and the Inter-American Development Bank (IDB), from which he retired in 2007. At the IDB, he worked in all aspects of evaluation, including ex-ante economic evaluation, ongoing monitoring of projects in execution, and ex-post evaluation of completed projects financed by the IDB. At the corporate level, he reported on the overall development effectiveness of IDB operations to the bank's board of directors and at international conferences.

Comparative Policy Evaluation
Edited by Ray C. Rist

The *Comparative Policy Evaluation* series is an interdisciplinary and internationally focused set of books that embodies within it a strong emphasis on comparative analyses of governance issues – drawing from all continents and many different nation states. The lens through which these policy initiatives are viewed and reviewed is that of evaluation. These evaluation assessments are done mainly from the perspectives of sociology, anthropology, economics, policy science, auditing, law, and human rights. The books also provide a strong longitudinal perspective on the evolution of the policy issues being analyzed.

The Realpolitik of Evaluation
Why Demand and Supply Rarely Intersect

Edited by Markus Palenberg and Arne Paulson

Routledge
Taylor & Francis Group
NEW YORK AND LONDON

First published 2021
by Routledge
52 Vanderbilt Avenue, New York, NY 10017

and by Routledge
2 Park Square, Milton Park, Abingdon, Oxon, OX14 4RN

Routledge is an imprint of the Taylor & Francis Group, an informa business

Library of Congress Cataloging-in-Publication Data
A catalog record for this title has been requested

ISBN: 978-0-367-43432-8 (hbk)
ISBN: 978-1-003-00516-2 (ebk)

Typeset in Times New Roman
by Wearset Ltd, Boldon, Tyne and Wear

Contents

Figures

Tables

Contributors

Per Øyvind Bastøe is Evaluation Director at the Norwegian Agency for Development Cooperation (Norad). Bastøe has broad experience in international development, evaluation, results management, and organizational change and has previously held senior positions in other parts of the Norwegian government administration, in the World Bank, and the Asian Development Bank. He has published several books and articles on development policy, evaluation, and organizational change.

Brian Belcher is Professor in the College of Interdisciplinary Studies at Royal Roads University (Victoria, Canada), where he holds the Tier 1 Canada Research Chair in Sustainability Research Effectiveness. Professor Belcher's research focuses on research effectiveness, research quality, and knowledge translation, primarily in the context of natural resources management and sustainable development. He is developing and applying theory and methods to understand and improve research effectiveness, research quality, and the societal impact of research.

Richard Boyle is head of research, publishing, and corporate relations with the Institute of Public Administration in Ireland. He has worked with the IPA since 1986. His research interests focus on public service reform and developing and implementing effective performance management and evaluation systems. He has researched and written extensively on evaluation and public service reform and has worked widely with Irish central and local government, the OECD, and the World Bank. He is a former board member of the European Evaluation Society and a founder member of the Irish Evaluation Network.

Christina (Tina) Christie is Professor of Social Research Methodology and Chair of the Department of Education at UCLA. Dr. Christie specializes in social program and policy evaluation. Her research focuses on the factors and conditions that influence evaluation practice in an effort to strengthen our understanding of evaluation as a method for facilitating social change. Christie has served as a lead investigator on over 30 grants and contracts funding evaluative research on education, child maltreatment, and health behavior programs. She is the editor of four books, has published over 50 scholarly articles and book chapters, and is co-editor of the book series Evaluation in Action. Christie is the former Director of the UC Evaluation Center, a seven-UC campus research center, and currently serves as co-Investigator on the National Institutes of Health, Coordination and Evaluation Center for The Diversity Program Consortium. Dr. Christie's awards include the American Evaluation Association's Marcia Guttentag Early Career Award (2004) and Distinguished Research on Evaluation Award (2019), and the American Educational Research Association's Research on Evaluation Special Interest Group, Distinguished Scholar Award (2018).

Agathe Devaux-Spatarakis manages and works on evaluation projects and strategic consulting assignments for French local and national authorities as well as research institutions. She has a PhD in political science and specializes in (theory-driven) impact evaluations and the assessment of innovations and experiments. Prior to this, Agathe was the scientific manager of impact evaluations of agricultural research at Cirad and a consultant at Euréval while pursuing her doctoral degree.

Pearl Eliadis is a human rights lawyer and practitioner who has successfully led complex, global projects on national human rights institutions, capacity assessment, and women's rights with institutional and multilateral clients. With more than 20 years' experience, Pearl also serves as adjunct professor at McGill University's Law Faculty and at the Max Bell School of Public Policy, where she is a member of the teaching faculty. She is a full member of the McGill Centre for Human Rights and Legal Pluralism and serves on several non-profit and advisory boards. She has published extensively on human rights and public policy.

David Gilchrist is Professor of Accounting at the University of Western Australia. He has held senior roles in the public sector, commerce, and the not-for-profit sector in Australia and has taught in a number of universities including the London School of Economics in the UK. He holds a visiting professorship at Hebei GEO University in the People's Republic of China. Gilchrist has published widely in relation to the government and not-for-profit nexus, human services policy, and sustainability. He was a lead author of the seminal report "Australian Charities 2013," an author of *The Three Sector Solution* published by the Australian National University Press, and an author of *Public Sector Accounting, Accountability and Governance* for Routledge.

R. Pablo Guerrero is an economist and former advisor at the World Bank. He has graduate degrees in economics and business and did postgraduate executive education at Harvard University. He is a former chief of evaluation at the Inter-American Development Bank and advisor to the Director-General of Evaluation at the World Bank. Among his contributions are the launching of the Evaluation Capacity Development Program at the World Bank, managing the World Bank's Secretariat for the Comprehensive Development Framework, and developing the World Bank's Strategy for Middle-Income Countries. He has done consulting work on country strategies and finance for the World Bank and, since the 1990s, has contributed to several books in the Comparative Policy Evaluation Series: *Evaluation Capacity Development*, *Success in Evaluation*, and *Doing Public Good?*

Sebastian Lemire is an associate at Abt Associates. Sebastian has over the past 15 years designed and implemented a broad range of evaluations – nationally and internationally. As a scholar-practitioner, his interests revolve around theory-based evaluation, alternative approaches to impact evaluation, and evidence reviews. Sebastian has published numerous articles and special issues on these topics in evaluation and policy studies journals. He currently serves as Associate Editor of the *American Journal of Evaluation.*

Ida Lindkvist is a senior advisor in the Evaluation Department at the Norwegian agency for development co-operation (Norad), working with the evaluation of Norwegian development assistance. Lindkvist holds a PhD in economics, having previously worked as a researcher on global health and published various articles and book chapters in this area. Lindkvist has recently taken a particular interest in results-based management, results-based financing, and the political economy of evaluation.

John Mayne is an independent advisor on public sector performance based in Ottawa and Bangkok. Over the last 15 years he has focused on international development evaluation and results-based management. He has authored numerous articles and reports, including several on contribution analysis and theories of change, and co-edited eight books on program evaluation. In 1989 and 1995, he was awarded the Canadian Evaluation Society Award for Contribution to Evaluation in Canada. In 2006, he was made a Canadian Evaluation Society Fellow. Dr. Mayne's current interests are on approaches in complex settings for strengthening impact evaluation and building useful theories of change.

Steffen Bohni Nielsen is Director-General at the Danish National Research Centre for the Working Environment. Previously, he has held positions as an Executive Director in local government, Senior Director in Ramboll Management Consulting, partner at PwC and Deputy Director at the National Board of Social Services. He has carried out an extensive number of evaluations, nationally and internationally and has worked as commissioner of evaluations. He has published articles in all major peer-reviewed evaluation journals on a variety of topics. He currently serves as Chairman of the Board of the Danish Society for Evidence-based Practices in the Human Services.

Olaf Rieper has an MA in sociology from the University of Copenhagen and a PhD from the Copenhagen Business School. He is currently an emeritus research director at the Danish Center for Social Science Research. He has conducted evaluations and research on public programs and organizations for Danish and Norwegian government agencies and for the EU Commission. The focus has been on welfare services and its organizations as well as on regional development programs. He has published on research methodology and on the evidence movement. Olaf has been working as a consultant in Ann Arbor, Michigan and in Lyon, France. He has been a co-founder of the Danish Evaluation Society and the first chairman of its board.

Francesco Mazzeo Rinaldi teaches evaluation research and programming courses in the Social and Political Science Department of the University of Catania, Italy. He is also currently Affiliate Professor at the KTH, Royal Institute of Technology, School of Architecture and the Built Environment, Stockholm. In the last 15 years he carried out training, research, and consulting activities on program and policy evaluation in several regional, national, and international public organizations in the domains of environmental, social, and R&D policy.

Daniel Suryadarma conducts applied economics research in the areas of education, poverty, and social policy. His work has appeared in peer-reviewed journals, including *American Economic Journal: Applied Economics* and *Journal of Development Economics*. His research has informed policy discussions at the Indonesian Vice President's Office, Indonesian Ministry of Education and Culture, Australian Aid Program, and the World Bank. Daniel is currently the Deputy Team Leader of the RISE Programme in Indonesia, an education research program managed by the SMERU Research Institute. Daniel is also an assessor for the Australian Research Council and a member of the Indonesia Young Academy of Sciences.

Peter Wilkins is an adjunct professor at The John Curtin Institute of Public Policy at Curtin University in Western Australia and works as an independent consultant. He has served as Western Australia's Deputy Ombudsman and prior to that had been WA Assistant Auditor-General Performance Review. He has worked in Australia, England, Canada, and Malaysia in roles including engineer, research fellow, public sector manager, and consultant. He has published widely in the fields of accountability, governance, performance, and evaluation.

John Young is the Executive Director of the International Network for Advancing Science and Policy (INASP) in Oxford, UK. He has spent the last 20 years doing research, evaluations, and advisory work on a wide range of topics including research policy linkages; policy engagement and influence; organizational and institutional development; capacity development, government service reform; monitoring evaluation and learning; and strategic communication in more than 20 developing and emerging countries. Before that he spent 20 years in Sri Lanka, Kenya, and Indonesia researching, developing, implementing, and testing new approaches to rural development and decentralized public services.

Foreword

Ray C. Rist

This is an important book for three reasons.

First, transposing refined economic terms like "supply" and "demand" to a new social science like evaluation creates more chaos and confusion than it does clarity and precision. This book documents such confusion and difficulty when it is clear that presumptions of clarity about these terms do not hold up when a transition has taken place. Paper after paper describes the gap between assumptions of what is to be understood by supply and what is presumed by "demand" when economics frames the discussion for evaluation. These terms take on different meanings when such a conversion takes place. Failing to recognize the change in meaning only breeds confusion and a lack of clarity. These papers make clear that evaluation is the discipline that suffers, not economics.

Second, these chapters also demonstrate that evaluation has not sorted out these terms in the context of its own terminology, as opposed to relying on economic understandings. A plethora of meanings is given to both terms by evaluators. Consequently, the gaps in understanding are real and not to be ignored. In these papers, one sees the confusion that evaluators generate about these concepts and the lack of congruence between these two terms. Multiple meanings are attributed to the term "supply" as well as to "demand." But having said this, it is to be noted that the "gold standard" glossary of 75 evaluation and results-based management terms provided by the OECD in 2002 includes neither word. Consequently, this entire discussion of supply-demand has thus far emerged and evolved within the evaluation communities in just the past 17 years.

Third, due to the complexity of the issue, this book does not venture a simple recipe for how to make supply meet demand. Rather the chapters illustrate on a case by case basis what can go right and what can go wrong. In addition, the book discusses in specific contexts what can be done to close the gap. Multiple contexts are presented here, and thus no one single way forward. Different evaluation questions beget different strategies for answering them. Think of a middle-range matrix. The editors posit that finding a solution that can stand up to the "realpolitik" challenge may involve acknowledging the multiple realities of supply and demand, as well as the gap that will continue to exist into at least the near future.

This is not only an important book; it is also provocative. It merits our time and attention. At one level, it calls into question the ongoing facile use of terms like supply and demand. We in evaluation simply need to up our game and start using language with more precision and care. At a higher level, this book calls into question a persistent fog in our thinking. It is intellectually sloppy to presume we all know what we mean by terms like "supply" and "demand." We do not. We must demand more of ourselves. Our profession depends on us to do so.

July 2019
Washington, DC

1 Introduction

Markus Palenberg and Arne Paulson

The discussions that led to this book began with a simpler view of the evaluation world – one in which the "gap" between the demand and supply of results information (highlighted in previous works in this series), was thought to reflect a simple lack of understanding between the demanders of evaluations, and the suppliers of evaluation information, about which "facts" were needed to support credible evaluations. In that context, it was hoped that a "tool kit" could be developed that would bridge the gap between demand and supply.

This view of the world may have been unduly simplistic. As our authors demonstrate in the chapters that follow, there are in fact many types of "demand" for evaluation (some of them more aspirational than pragmatic), while the suppliers of evaluation information may sometimes focus more on their own professional interests than providing useful information for improving policies and programs. The current political climate, which even suggests that "alternative facts" can be used as a convenient substitute for actual facts when desired, merely injects additional confusion into our view of reality and further widens the evaluation gap.

The purpose of this book, therefore, is really to: shine a light on the divergent demands for evaluation (some of which may be more apparent than real); expose the biases behind some seemingly non-partisan sources of evaluation information; and highlight the pros and cons of attempts to bridge the gap between demand and supply of evaluation information through the use of third parties, enhanced stakeholder involvement, and the incorporation of social science models to strengthen Theories of Change (ToC).

Policymakers, program implementers, project managers, and evaluators all feel under increasing pressure to "demonstrate results" in order to justify their respective actions.[1] Policymakers, for example, need to demonstrate to their constituencies that current government policies are indeed on track to achieve their objectives and merit public support. Program implementers, for their part, are eager to show that the sub-programs that underlie government policies are efficient and effective. Project managers at the field level are constantly being exhorted to prove that they are successfully "doing more with less." And evaluators – the ones who are actually in a position to supply evaluation information to support (or deny) the claims of higher-level authorities – are under pressure to supply evaluation results.

Thus, the demand for evaluation information about "results" is tiered at different levels, but how consistent are these demands with one another, and with data that is actually available from evaluators within the required time-frame and budget? Why is frustration continuously expressed by those who demand evaluation results when professional evaluators present them with their responses? What explains the "gap" between what those on the "demand" side expect in terms of results, and the "supply" of information provided by evaluators? Can anything be done to narrow this gap? What works and what does not work?

This book examines these questions from both the demand and the supply side.

The Demand Side

Results information is required from a range of different stakeholders for a range of different purposes. One useful categorization comes from literature on results-based management (RBM) and broadly differentiates between learning, decision-making, and accountability purposes (Binnendijk, 2001; Mayne, 2007a, 2007b; Kusek & Rist, 2004; Vähämäki, Schmidt, & Molander, 2011; UNDG, 2011; Vähämäki, 2017). These purposes can be summarized as follows:

- Learning: results information is used for personal and organizational learning of people and institutions designing, implementing, and experiencing the effects of policies and programs. Learning also takes place during monitoring, evaluation, and research processes.
- Decision-making: results information is used to inform decision-making processes of people and institutions responsible for policies and programs, with the aim of improving performance in achieving results.
- Accountability: results information is reported by people and institutions implementing policies and programs to legitimize their choices and resource use, and for ensuring support. Results information is also reported to those people and institutions involved with implementing policies and programs, and to those affected by them, to satisfy their respective learning, decision-making, and accountability requirements.

In addition, demand for results information can also be driven by less rational notions that can be understood in the wider context of the political economy in which public policies and programs are developed and operate. Demand can be insincere and rhetorical if not associated with a push for accurate reporting on outcomes and impacts of policies and programs. Or, demand can be created to promote product marketing for specific evaluation instruments.

The Supply Side

Information on the results of policies and programs is generated in different ways, for example through monitoring, evaluations, audits, and research. Accordingly, there are different types of providers of results information. Volume, type, and quality of results information produced by these means is influenced by many factors that can be sorted into two broad groups: institutional and methodological.

Institutional Factors

Institutional factors are, for example, the degree to which evaluation, audit, monitoring, and research activities are prioritized and supported financially and politically. Lack of financial support can lead to insufficient capacity for generating results information in terms of human resources, skills, and experience, and in terms of systems and processes. With insufficient support and funds, monitoring and evaluation cannot accurately map results of policies and programs in terms of coverage and quality.

Publicly financed institutions also exhibit incentive structures and pronounced organizational cultures that can foster or limit their ability to produce and make use of results information.

Another institutional factor is timing. Public institutions and programs follow political and budget cycles that may hinder longer-term processes aimed at generating results information. In many cases, efforts for generating results information are tied – financially and time-wise – to the programs being examined, possibly leading to short-termism and lack of information on outcomes and impacts occurring after programs have ended.

Methodological Factors

Apart from technical factors, generation of results information is influenced by methodological factors. Methodological factors are related to strengths and limitations of approaches and methods with which results information is generated.

For example, results-based management (RBM) frameworks focus on indicators that go beyond activities and outputs and encounter challenges with respect to regular monitoring and causal attribution. Welfare economics approaches, for example Cost-Benefit-Analysis (CBA), have successfully been applied to interventions in many sectors but encounter difficulties when benefits are difficult to quantify. Experimental approaches to impact evaluation such as Randomized Controlled Trials (RCTs) are useful for investigating causal mechanisms in specific contexts but struggle with broader application due to their inherent inflexibility. Other evaluation methodologies such as Contribution Analysis (CA), Process Tracing (PT) or Qualitative Comparative Analysis (QCA), and mixed method approaches have been employed successfully to investigate contribution claims and to understand complex causal relationships but are not widely applied and usually cannot answer questions on how much an intervention has contributed to intended results.

Book Outline: Exploring the Gap Between Demand and Supply

The authors of this book describe ten different examples of the gap between demand and supply of evaluation information in different contexts, and attempts made to bridge that gap.

Ida Lindkvist and Per Øyvind Bastøe question how genuine the demand for evaluation results really is at higher levels and in the public at large, when it comes to Norwegian development assistance. When contrasted with actual budget expenditures on evaluation, the authors conclude that much of the supposed demand for evaluation results is actually "inflated" or "fake" demand.

At the other end of the spectrum, Agathe Devaux-Spatarakis describes a situation in which the "suppliers" of evaluation information took control of evaluation planning for certain experimental social programs in France and succeeded in forcing project managers and program implementers into accepting Randomized Control Testing (RCT) as the only legitimate evaluation tool. RCTs however require controlled and stable conditions which was at odds with the need of program managers to adjust programs during implementation. In the end, most results information generated by RCTs was not used meaningfully.

Can an intermediary organization help in bridging the gap in expectations on the demand side, and what is practically feasible on the supply side? Richard Boyle reports on the experience of the non-profit Atlantic Philanthropies in the Republic of Ireland, where it aimed at prompting government engagement with results information in a more systematic way. These efforts met with some success until the charity began to wrap up its operations. Will those efforts continue to bear fruit without outside support? Or will government budget cuts of necessity reinforce the demand for evaluation results to demonstrate that remaining funds are wisely spent?

A somewhat different take on third-party involvement with government interventions and their evaluations is provided by David Gilchrist and Peter Wilkins in their chapter on the use of not-for-profit and voluntary organizations to deliver human services to support social policy objectives in South Australia. There were several reasons for adopting this approach, including the fact that it was seen as a cheaper source of service delivery, more flexible, and – because those organizations are closer to the communities in which they work – have more opportunities for identifying needs and demands, and for assessing the relative impact of programs. On the other hand, their analysis notes that the voluntary and not-for-profit organizations have been challenged with insufficient resources, increasing pressure to perform more with less in the face of changing funder priorities, and impacting their ability to pursue their mission. Despite these challenges, a key body in the public services sector concluded that a lot had been learned about the procurement of outcome-based services and the importance of involving service users as well as providers in the co-design and co-evaluation of services. The authors remain hopeful that voluntary organizations and governments will be keen to see the process through.

Olaf Rieper's chapter provides a detailed review of how an intermediary organization was usefully incorporated into the evaluation itself, of the Norwegian health care reform program in 2012–2015. The author, who was chairman of the intermediary organization (the Research Council of Norway) at the time, is in a unique position to describe the inner workings of the council, its Evaluation Steering Committee and advisory groups, and the organizational and cultural aspects which contributed to a seamless evaluation process with no significant gaps observed between what was expected, and what was obtained, from the evaluation. Although it is too soon to judge some of the long-term results of the health reform program, and despite the difficulty of separating out the impact of the health reform from other parallel initiatives, the author concludes that the Norwegian health reform evaluation provides a good practice example of how the involvement of an intermediary organization can harmonize expectations between demand and supply in the evaluation process.

Other chapters also emphasized the importance of stakeholder involvement in the design and evaluation of interventions. Francesco Mazzeo Rinaldi, for example, describes an evaluation done for the research and development (R&D) component of an EU-sponsored regional development program in Sardinia, Italy. The organizers of that evaluation included institutions at the national, regional, and municipal levels, various EU funds, and experts in the fields selected for evaluation, academics, and individuals from the public and private sector. The result was a highly complex evaluation setup designed to assure stakeholder participation, not only with regard to the planning and implementations aspects, but also in terms of the evaluation of the program. The author concludes that the complex arrangements helped reduce unrealistic expectations about the evaluations. Unfortunately, the failure to pay sufficient attention to the "supply" side of evaluation information – notably the lack of baseline data and inadequate data collection during implementation – made it impossible to answer even the most basic evaluation questions.

Brian Belcher, John Young, and Daniel Suryadarma report on another complex evaluation effort emphasizing stakeholder participation. Noting the high demand from funders, research users, research managers, and researchers themselves for better evaluations for improved accountability, decision-making and learning purposes, they describe and analyze the evaluation of CIFOR's Climate Change Research program. The chapter discusses the factors driving demand for results information and analyzes how its supply can be further improved. Given that multiple actors are involved and that the "results chain" incorporates long time-lags and numerous feedback loops, quantitative evaluation methods were judged not to be appropriate for many of the kinds of projects and programs that CIFOR undertakes. The evaluation consequently focused on demonstrating results in terms of: influencing international dialogue and behavior of national policymakers; use of research results by stakeholders; and frequent citation of CIFOR publications, books, and policy papers – each of which underscored the plausibility of their Theories of Change (ToC) model. The authors observed that the process of developing the ToC was, in itself, a valuable learning experience, and one which should be continued to further improve the model. They note that this iterative process necessarily involves a high degree of participation by staff of the organization and evaluators in the design, collection, analysis, and interpretation of data, and ultimately, in a common appreciation of results and recommendations.

Stakeholder involvement is also a key factor of Pearl Eliadis's chapter on successfully integrating a human rights-based approach into public policies and programs. Too often, she observes, human rights concerns are dealt with by superficially "checking boxes" in the approval process, without much thought being given to how particular subgroups of the population (in particular marginalized groups) will be affected. The author illustrates her point by contrasting two programs to promote accessible transit: the metro (subway) system in Montreal, Canada, and a snow-clearing program in Sweden. The former was designed on a "needs-based" approach that considered factors such as total population, existing transport infrastructure, percentage of the population covered by the service, and cost of service. However, little attention was given to one marginalized group within the population: persons with disabilities – who, because of economic disadvantage and social isolation, are particularly vulnerable to lack of access to public transportation. The result is that extensive investments have been made in Montreal's transport infrastructure which are now difficult – and costly – to remediate. In the Swedish case, on the other hand, an existing municipal snow removal program was deliberately reformulated to give priority to bus stops, pedestrian walkways, and bike paths, because a human rights-based approach was employed: gendered analysis showed that women were more likely to have to walk on snow-covered paths and take children to school and/or bus stops while men normally drove to work on cleared roads. The new snow removal scheduling was not only more equitable, but generated additional benefits connected with improving work productivity for women and reduced accidents involving pedestrians. The author concludes that a human-rights based approach narrows the gap between the supply and demand for results information by ensuring that the original design of programs incorporate human rights-sensitive information in both the development and evaluation stages of public policy.

Sebastian Lemire, Christina Christie, and Steffen Bohni Nielsen extrapolate even further on the importance of stakeholder involvement in theory-based evaluation. Incorporating social science (behavioral) theory more fully into program theory (theory of change), both substantiate the causal connection between a program and a set of desired outcomes and facilitates claims about how the program would work in different settings with potentially different target groups. Taken collectively, explaining why programs work is increasingly what evaluations are asked to do because it allows for a deeper and more robust understanding of program performance – which in turn can support further refinements and design improvements. In fact, the authors urge us to further extend the approach to "theory knitting," where one or more existing social science theories are used as the conceptual grounding for both the design of the program and underlying program theory. Based on a framework developed to support the systematic and transparent integration of social science theories into program theories, they apply this model to 57 evaluations and try to answer the following question: does theory knitting serve to bridge the gap between the supply and demand for results information? Their conclusion is that it does. If program theories build upon accepted causal mechanisms already established in social science theories, it may be sufficient to report on early results (which are easier to assess and understand), without having to argue about how these results will ultimately lead to outcomes and yet still give policy makers and budgetary authorities something "solid" to use for accountability and learning purposes.

John Mayne's chapter on realistic commissioning of impact evaluations rounds out the book, seeking to explore the gap between impact questions that can be asked and the answers that evaluations can realistically provide. He warns us that asking unrealistic or misunderstood questions about impact can only lead to unrealistic expectations for impact evaluation, and ultimately to weak evaluations. In simpler settings, the evaluation of interventions was based on a counterfactual view of causality: what would have happened without the intervention? But interventions designed to improve the wellbeing of citizens are becoming more complex and "messy." The goals of such programs have become increasingly ambitious (e.g., reducing poverty, empowering women) and multi-faceted, involving multiple actors and sectors, focusing on several target groups over a long time frame, and are influenced by a number of factors other than the intervention itself. These are generally not amenable to evaluation by the use of an explicit counterfactual. However, causality can still be demonstrated even in complex interventions, if one considers the "causal package" of the intervention, which includes the actions of various partners involved in the collective effort. Regardless of whether other external influences have been at work, if all of the factors in the causal package are necessary for the success of the package, then the intervention can still be said to be a contributory factor to the observed changes – even if it is not possible to quantify the size of the contributions being made. Under this conceptualization, impact evaluation questions should more appropriately focus on areas such as: what are the observed impacts; did the intervention make a contribution; how; were other influences at play; are results sustainable; will the intervention make a contribution in the future? In the current environment of complex interventions, such questions make more sense than traditional impact evaluation questions such as: to what extent did the intervention meet its objectives; or, has the intervention been effective? Mayne concludes by saying that commissioners of evaluations do not need to give up on getting robust information about interventions, including for accountability purposes, but they do need to think differently about what kinds of information they should ask for and expect to get.

Finally, in the last chapter of the book, R. Pablo Guerrero distills conclusions for evaluation discipline drawn from the preceding chapters. Viewed from a pessimistic perspective, the reader may wonder whether the "gap" between the demand and supply of evaluation information is inevitable – or even deliberate. Yet many of our chapter authors offer positive suggestions for closing the gap, including organizational arrangements to bring demanders and suppliers of evaluation information closer together, feedback during the evaluation process to strengthen and refine the underlying theory of change, greater stakeholder involvement to facilitate acceptance of evaluation results and recommendations, and measures to encourage greater public support for paying for, and paying attention to, evaluations. The question that readers are left to ponder is whether such efforts to close the gap still lead to evaluation results that are credible and meaningful.

Note

1 With results information we refer to quantitative and qualitative evidence of planned and achieved changes associated with policies and programs, as well as evidence about how those changes were achieved. In other words, results information covers both the "what" and the "how" of changes associated with policies and programs.

References

Binnendijk, A. (2001). *Results based management in the development cooperation agencies: A review of experience*. OECD.

Kusek, J. Z., & Rist, R. C. (2004). *Ten steps to a results-based monitoring and evaluation system*. The World Bank.

Mayne, J. (2007a). *Best practices in results-based management: A review of experience. A report for the United Nations Secretariat*. Focus International. Retrieved from www.focusintl.com/RBM043-2007%2007%20UN%20Best%20Practices%20in%20Results-Based%20Management.pdf

Mayne, J. (2007b). Challenges and lessons in implementing results-based management. *Evaluation*, *13*, 87–109.

UNDG. (2011). *Results-based management handbook: Harmonizing RBM concepts and approaches for improved development results at country level*. UNDG.

Vähämäki, J. (2017). *Matrixing aid: The rise and fall of "results initiatives" in Swedish development aid*. Stockholm Business School.

Vähämäki, J., Schmidt, M., & Molander, J. (2011). *Review: Results based management in development cooperation*. Riksbankens Jubileumsfond.

2 The Results Paradox in Norwegian Development Assistance

Ida Lindkvist and Per Øyvind Bastøe

The context of this chapter is the international development aid landscape. A landscape undergoing fundamental changes. Critical questions are being asked regarding the value of traditional long-term aid. At the same time, pressure is increasing to fund short-term initiatives related to security issues and refugees, especially in Europe. China, India, and other non-OECD development actors are gradually playing a more important role alongside private foundations and an increasing number of civil society organizations. The UN General Assembly recently approved the Sustainable Development Goals, with 17 goals, 169 targets[1] and 232 indicators.[2]

Norway is among the world's most generous development aid donors, maintaining a commitment to allocate 1 percent of the gross national income to aid. On international rankings, like the Commitment to Development Index (Center for Global Development), Norway has consistently come out among the best on the aid indicator score, although with a weaker overall score in 2017.[3]

Within this context, results orientation is considered an important tool to monitor performance and document achievements. The current (at the time of writing) Norwegian government, which has been in office since 2013, has repeatedly stated its intention to increase efforts to improve results measurement and systematic evaluations as a basis for budget decisions and to increase transparency on aid. References to results orientation are numerous in official aid publications, budget proposals, and policy papers. The Norwegian Agency for Development Cooperation (Norad) has published an annual "results report" for the last ten years reporting on a selection of Norwegian aid initiative achievements.

However, despite nurturing this image of transparency and focus on results, there is surprisingly little attention to development effects, limited interest for honest reporting, and it is difficult to determine whether evidence has been used as the basis for formulating development policies and making budget decisions. Several evaluations, reviews, and assessments of Norwegian aid have pointed to shortcomings of monitoring and evaluation of Norwegian aid, and to difficulties of finding relevant results information.

In this article we will explore this results paradox – the apparent discrepancy between the rhetoric on results and the real interest in showing results – and offer some possible explanations of why this occurs in the Norwegian development policy area.

Increasing Results Orientation in Development Assistance

Results orientation has been slowly adopted in international development assistance over the last 50 years. A starting point was the introduction of the Logical Framework Approach in 1969 in the US Agency for International Development (Rosenberg, Posner, & Hanley, 1970). Another influence came from management approaches in the private sector, like the "Managing by objectives" approach (Drucker, 1954). In other parts of the public sector, results orientation was a key element in the "new public management" movement in the 1980s and 1990s. In the development sector it gained momentum through the adoption of the Millennium Development Goals in 2000. Later, attention increased through the Monterrey Consensus in 2002, which stressed the need to mobilize financial resources more efficiently and emphasized development effectiveness as a core operational concept. Results orientation was translated into operational efforts through the Marrakech Roundtable on Results in 2004 and the Paris High-level Forum on Aid Effectiveness in 2005. Since then it has been accepted as a core concept in international development assistance.

In Norway, results orientation in central government activities emerged gradually through the 1980s and 1990s. One reason for the slower development of results orientation in Norway than in other OECD countries was the lack of an economic recession in Norway due to the abundant access to oil and gas resources. Unlike other OECD countries, the public sector in Norway was not regarded as requiring major reforms (Organisation for Economic Co-operation and Development [OECD], 1980).

However, in the mid-1990s, things started to happen: first with the establishment of a Performance Audit Department in the Auditor-General's Office in 1995 and then with the introduction of the Government Financial Regulations in 1997. These regulations require all parts of the state administration to formulate objectives for state funds, to monitor performance, and to evaluate and report on results (Øvrelid & Bastøe, 2002). In some ways the development aid area has been an exception to the general trend in the Norwegian government administration. Already in 1977, a department for evaluation and research was established and in 1993 a handbook on evaluation and results assessment was published (Ministry of Foreign Affairs [MFA], 1993). Despite these initiatives, there is little evidence of any visible effects related to results orientation within the development aid area.

A general criticism of results orientation in the development aid area has been that the concepts are primarily being used to express intentions of achieving results. Only to a limited degree have they been used as tools for documenting what has actually been achieved through the various programs and projects.

A more fundamental critique is that results orientation is an expression of modern management approaches and represents an "engineering approach" to problem solving. It allows complicated problems to be decomposed into manageable and well-defined sub-problems that can be controlled and addressed through planning. This linear way of dealing with complex problems is considered naive and unrealistic; the reality is much more complex and requires a dynamic approach to problem solving (Ramalingam, 2013).

A similar critique, albeit less severe, has been frequently raised when it comes to results measurement approaches in the public sector. Van Thiel and Leeuw (2002) argue that a narrow focus on output measurement can lead to several unintended consequences that may have negative influences on the performance of public sector initiatives.

We will not go into these fundamental concerns with results orientation in detail in this chapter, because they do not seem to play a role in the current situation in the development aid sector in Norway. We will limit our discussion to looking into possible reasons why the government, on the one hand makes strong and multiple arguments for an increased attention to results orientation, but on the other hand only half-heartedly supports strengthening of capacity to measure and assess results and rarely makes any use of results information for decision-making and budget allocations.

Data Presentation and Findings

We analyzed the results rhetoric by looking at the use of the word "results"[4] in government documents from 2013–2016. Specifically, we included budget proposals from the Ministry of Foreign Affairs (MFA) which is mandated with managing development assistance,[5] white papers on development assistance, foreign policy addresses to parliament, responses to these addresses from the parliament, and relevant reports from the Auditor-General.

We started by simply counting the number of times the word "results" appeared in budget propositions and listed types of results-related terminology. Furthermore, we categorized all phrases where the word "results" appeared (but not linked to specific results) and grouped them into the following: a) measurements of results, b) strategy for achieving results, c) simply stating the importance of results, and d) results-based financing. In addition, we conducted a simple analysis of how often (frequency per page) the word "results" was used in budget propositions for all ministries (year 2015/2016) and for the Ministry of Foreign Affairs for the last ten years.

A clear limitation to our approach was that it is possible to discuss results without referring to the word "results." For instance, the Ministry of Climate and the Environment may have a clear results strategy and a clear way to measure results without ever mentioning the word "results." It could, for example, simply discuss planned and achieved emission reductions. Another limitation was that the documents we conducted this analysis on covered areas other than development assistance. To deal with these limitations we analyzed two budget proposals from the Ministry of Foreign Affairs in their entirety.

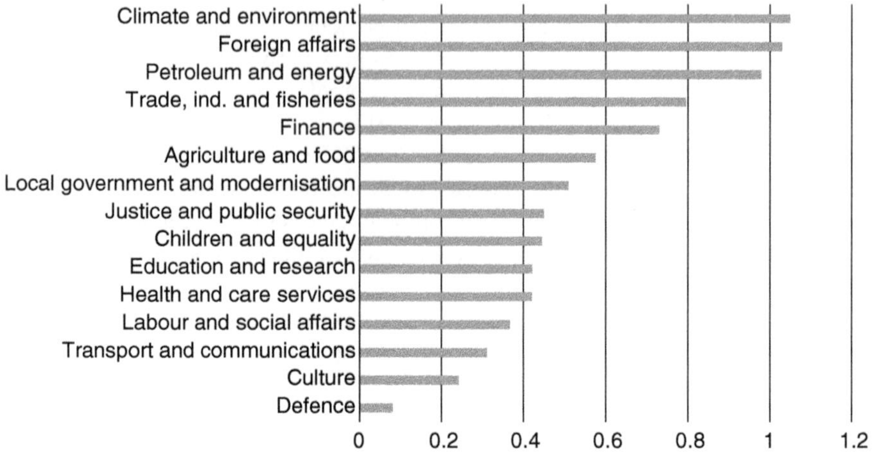

Figure 2.1 Average number of times the word "result" appears per page in Norwegian budget proposals for all ministries for the year 2015/2016.

From the simple word count of "result" we could see that in the budget proposals for fiscal year 2015/2016 (Figure 2.1), the word "result" was most frequently used by the two ministries managing most Norwegian development assistance, i.e., the Ministry of Foreign Affairs (MFA) and the Ministry for Climate and Environment.[6] In budget proposals to the parliament from these two ministries, the word result (more precisely words with the word stem result) appeared approximately once per page, in contrast to the Ministry of Defense where "result" was mentioned less than once in every ten pages.

From Figure 2.2 we can see that from fiscal year 2006/2007 and until 2015/2016, there was an increase in the mention of results in budget proposals from the Ministry of Foreign Affairs. In fact, in this period the number of times the word "result" was used doubled from about once every second page to once every page. While this does not necessarily imply an increase in results orientation, it clearly indicates more results rhetoric.

The budget proposals in fiscal years 2014–2015 and 2015–2016 contain 29 different terms that include the word stem result. Apart from the word stem (result/results) itself, the following terms were most frequent: results-based, results framework, results reporting/results reporting system, results achieved, results orientation, results monitoring, and managing for results.

As previously mentioned, quotes were organized into four different categories, with one of these being strategy, i.e., description of how results should be obtained.

Mentioned strategies for achieving better results (budget proposals from the Ministry of Foreign Affairs 2014/2015 and 2015/2016) were: concentration of funds (geographically and thematically); prioritizing effective partners; using evaluations and research to improve effectiveness; basing development policies

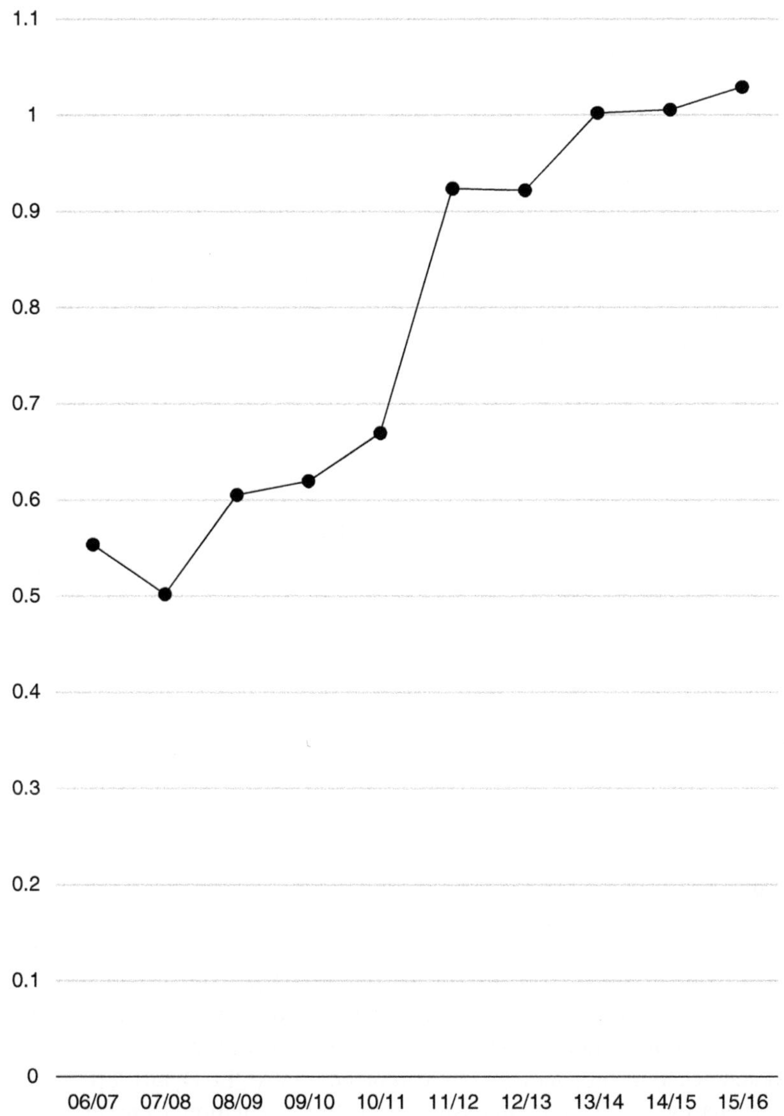

Figure 2.2 Average number of times the word "result" appears per page in budget proposals from the Norwegian Ministry of Foreign Affairs from 2006/2007 to 2015/2016.

on evidence; and supporting innovative projects/programs and making payments contingent on results. The introduction to the budget proposal to the parliament (2014/2015) notes: "The total budget for 2016 is 33.6 billion NOK and constitutes 1 percent of estimated GNI for 2016. But more important than volume is the work towards targeted, concentrated and more efficient use of aid to achieve better results."[7] (MFA, 2014/2015b, p. 12). This reflects the political platform[8] of the new government from 2013, which promises a "Results-oriented development policy with systematic evaluations with budgetary consequences, allowing for full openness about volume, execution and effects of Norwegian development policy."[9]

Result measurement appears to be an area of importance in the budget proposals and white papers. The ministry's budget proposal to the parliament stresses that great emphasis is placed on documenting results (MFA, 2014/2015b, p. 128). However, less information is included in budget proposals and white papers on how this should be done. That said, the Ministry of Foreign Affairs states that the Evaluation Department should document results, that multilateral organizations should have independent evaluation organizations to allow for verification of results, and that competence on results measurement should be strengthened in developing countries (MFA, 2014, p. 43). Furthermore, concentration of Norwegian development assistance is expected to result in improved results documentation. Finally, in budget proposal 2015/2016 the MFA states that all rules and regulations have been updated to allow for better results documentation,[10] and the ministry concludes that the majority of Norwegian supported aid projects demonstrate good results.[11]

When contrasting the results rhetoric in budget proposals with evaluations of results management, there seems to be a disconnect between rhetoric and reality. In the Evaluation Department's yearly report from 2011, Norad's Evaluation Director concluded that none of the evaluations or studies commissioned by the Evaluation Department could report sufficiently on outcomes or impact of Norwegian development assistance (Evaluation Department, 2011). In fact, in a comparative study of results management Lloyd, Villanger, and Poate (2014) concluded that the performance of Norwegian results documentation was poor (2014, p. 389).

Similarly, the Auditor-General's report on results orientation in Norwegian development assistance identified weaknesses in the ministry's results documentation which the report found could prevent results from being achieved (Auditor-General, 2011, p. 8). Furthermore, a peer review of Norway conducted by the OECD DAC found that while results were reported, "Norway has problems linking these outcomes to its broader development objectives" (OECD, 2013, p. 79).

In the evaluation of 2014 commissioned by the Evaluation Department in Norad, weak results documentation was attributed to the following:

- Current policies, systems, and procedures are too fragmented, insufficiently comprehensive, and do not provide the necessary guidance for staff.
- Training reaches too few staff, there are significant gaps in coverage, and there is little supporting material. Formal advice and quality assurance is too limited to be effective at ensuring evaluability.
- Implementation of a results focus fails to ensure evaluability, partly because there is little clarity about minimum standards, but also pressures of

time on staff, low priority by senior managers, and a lack of incentives to prioritize results.

- EVAL [Evaluation Department] -commissioned evaluations are not designed and managed in a way that ensures they measure and report on results. (Evaluation Department, 2014, p. xvii).

In interviews with staff, evaluators found that ministry leadership did not appear to prioritize results documentation. In the words of a staffer:

> You hear ministers and senior leaders talking about the need to show results, but it is another thing to make it happen. The practical implications of the results agenda are not recognized. The leadership [is] not willing to invest the time and resources needed.
>
> (Evaluation Department, 2014, p. 63)

In their recommendation to the ministry, the Evaluation Department offered two sets of recommendations: first to improve management and, second, to improve rules, guidelines, and courses available for staff. Recommendations for improved management included recommendations for: the leadership to strengthen their knowledge of, and prioritize, results management; introduce incentives promoting a results orientation; ensure that staff have the appropriate time and resource availability; assure quality in decentralized evaluations; and promote a culture for learning.

The second set of recommendations concerned rules, guidelines, and competence building. In the aftermath of the evaluation, the ministry appeared to have focused on this second set of recommendations[12] and in the budget proposal to the parliament it wrote: "External evaluations and reviews have identified weaknesses with the ministry's system to measure results of the initiatives supported. The ministry has introduced procedures to improve measurement and reporting of results, including skills upgrading initiatives for staff at all levels. A more systematic assessment of results frameworks for the initiatives supported is being implemented, in addition to stricter requirements for reviews and evaluations during the project period. This will contribute to better information about results achieved from Norwegian grants"[13] (MFA, 2015/2016, p. 23). Given the lack of mention of management it appeared that the ministry did not believe improvements in senior management itself was necessary. Finally, concentration of development assistance geographically and thematically was believed to allow for improved results documentation, possibly because economies of scale would allow for setting aside more time and resources for results documentation (MFA, 2014/2015a, p. 53).

In a recent doctoral thesis, Reinertsen (2016) argues that today's criticism of results orientation is not new and in fact mirrors the Evaluation Department's criticism in the 1980s. While it is too early to say whether the current changes implemented by the Norwegian government will improve results orientation, it is significant that 30 years of efforts appear not to have led to better results documentation.

Theories That Can Explain the Current Results Paradox

How can we explain the paradox that political leaders and senior management in relevant ministries have an outspoken commitment to a results agenda, demand results documentation, evaluations and learning, while the aid bureaucracy seems incapable of satisfying this demand? One answer, which we will get back to in the discussion which follows, is that it is not possible to document results at the level requested by policymakers. For now, we will leave this explanation aside and instead present explanations from the literature of political economy of evaluation and related literature on results-based management, for why donor agencies and even policymakers may be reluctant to prioritize a results focus.

We argue that this literature can be grouped into two categories: in the first category we have explanations asserting that demand for results is not genuine, the second category includes more practically oriented explanations, where the extent to which organizations focus on results is discussed in terms of whether the organization has specific features thought to be important for results-based management in place. The latter strand originates in organization theory and is to some extent characterized by resource optimism. An underlying message of this strand of literature is that while a focus on results may be challenging to implement, it is possible if the organization gets things right.

Genuine Demand for Results?

The first group of explanations focuses on preferences, i.e., a disinterest in results and incentives. Although such a disinterest in actual results may arise due to a disingenuous interest in development outcomes, it does not preclude altruistic intent, as both self-interested and altruistic agents can be disinterested in documenting results.

One of the most elaborate models within this category was developed by Martens (2002). Following Anthony Downs (1957), Martens argues that policymakers mainly care about being re-elected. Depending on which electorate policymakers cater to, they will be more or less interested in documenting the results of development assistance. Martens assumes that suppliers of aid projects are also motivated by self-interest and unless they are punished for poor performance, they will not exert optimal effort. Furthermore, he assumes that suppliers can exert some influence over policymakers. If policymakers and suppliers collude, policymakers may create unclear and “wooly” objectives and invest little in evaluation. As a result, suppliers will exert minimal effort and the electorate will not learn of failures, unless what Martens calls the pro-aid lobby is able to discover them. Unless the electorate is very pro-aid and the pro-aid lobby is very strong, the aid agency is unlikely to invest much in evaluation.

To make matters more complex, Lindkvist and Dixon (2014) argue that different types of altruism exist in the electorate. Inspired by Andreoni (1990) they differentiate between “pure altruism” and “warm-glow altruism,” and argue that if aid is more about feeling good (warm glow) than doing good (pure altruism), the electorate may be more interested in disbursements than in actually making a difference for beneficiaries. In fact, given the difficulty in fighting poverty in some contexts, the electorate may prefer to know less and not more about outcomes and impact.

Easterly (2002), inspired by Niskanen's theory of bureaucracy (Niskanen, 1968, 1994), argues that aid agencies produce glossy brochures and collude to hide bad projects to maximize budgets. In other words, the main motivation of bureaucracies is to maximize budget, and not the outcomes for beneficiaries.

Pritchett (2002) on the other hand argues that even altruistic agents[14] may oppose evaluation if they care more about the aid project than the electorate/taxpayers. The idea is that because advocates care more about the outcomes for beneficiaries, they have a higher tolerance than the electorate for funding some failed projects as long as they believe they are helping beneficiaries overall. Hence, to ensure funding, and keep the aid money flowing, they will avoid evaluations. However, with guaranteed funding they would prefer to evaluate projects to increase the overall effectiveness.

Also, evaluators may have a disinterest in demonstrating results. Michaelowa and Borrman (2006) demonstrate that the extent to which an evaluator will credibly document results also depends on the market they operate in. Together with Martens (2002), they demonstrate that employing external consultants does not necessarily solve the motivational problem described in the previous section. If the operations side commissions evaluations, their evaluations may be positively biased even when consultants are external. This will be particularly true if these consultants are heavily specialized in working for the agency and few other employers exist. Martens assumes that such evaluation consultants will adopt the incentives in the agency. He writes,

> Reputation effects and peer group pressure will ensure that these "independent consultants" temper their critical remarks. Evaluators operating as consultants have no incentive to reveal precise and controversial information. It makes their report vulnerable to heavy criticism and long-drawn discussions without any increase in their remuneration.
>
> (2002, p. 166)

In fact, even if the commissioning office is external to operations, and consultants are external, consultants may want to please agents at the operations side as these may aid the consultant in his work.

Lack of Resources

While a focus on results and results-based management have been in vogue in development agencies for decades, evaluations and research have demonstrated that a focus on results has been difficult to implement in practice. This literature originates in the theory of organizations and emphasizes culture, institutional design, and knowledge as crucial determinants for whether an organization is able to focus on results. Mayne (2007) sums up challenges in two categories: organizational and technical. Organizational challenges are mainly related to organizational culture and refer to existing assumptions/beliefs and values shared in the organization: is this an organization where we focus on outcomes? Are expectations about what one can achieve realistic? Do we know and agree with respect to what information we should collect, and so forth? An example of a shared belief or assumption is that disbursement of funds should not be delayed allowing for a costly/time-consuming evaluation of a program. If most staff prioritize like this, even though they are aware that results information is important, the organization may be skewed towards disbursement rather than maintaining a focus on outcomes. Technical challenges relate to existing knowledge and skills and to the quality of the monitoring and evaluation process and the extent to which this information is used in the organization. Examples of technical challenges include a difficulty in documenting and attributing changes in outcomes due to funding decisions, i.e., had baseline data been collected, had Monitoring and Evaluation (M&E) been an integrated part of the project, it would have been possible to document outcomes.

Van Thiel and Leeuw (2002) argue that getting the culture and the skills mix right is a continuous process. As the organization develops and if performance improves, monitoring and evaluation strategies too must evolve. In addition, getting the right balance between collecting accurate information and preventing distortive behavior is not easy. If the organization focuses too much on collecting data on outcomes, classic agency problems may occur such as motivational crowding out and crowding out of tasks. When outcome information has an influence on financial resource decisions, literature on results-based financing predicts an increased focus on outcomes which cannot easily be measured at the expense of outcomes more difficult to measure (also referred to as crowding out of tasks or multitasking – see Holmstrom & Milgrom, 1991). Furthermore, for individuals, when performance is linked to financial incentives, this may alter the individual's information from extrinsic to intrinsic (see Frey & Jegen, 2001), i.e., motivational crowding out.

The challenge with these "challenges" is that, on the one hand, Mayne (2007) finds that failing to address any one of them may undermine the system, while on the other hand addressing all of them simultaneously may be difficult. For example, Mayne concludes that it is important to avoid information overload and be selective in what information to collect, but to also take action to prevent distortive behavior. Van Thiel and Leeuw (2002) write that it is necessary to collect a variety of indicators to prevent distortive behavior, but that an over-focus on results reporting may also create such behavior and drive a wedge between results indicators and actual results. Furthermore, Mayne finds it important to hold managers accountable for the contribution to outcomes rather than actual outcomes, since they may have limited influence on actual outcomes. For their part, van Thiel and Leeuw (2002) state that accountability is key to ensuring accurate results information.

Discussion

We started the previous section with the assumption that the Norwegian aid administration can, but is for some reason unwilling, to document results at the level that is demanded by policymakers. This assumption may not be correct. Answering the question of whether aid is effective in general is one such example. It is simply not very meaningful, as it is akin to the question of whether doing good is effective; the answer will always depend on what you do and what you want to achieve. That said, we believe it is possible to provide a credible account of the effectiveness of programs, projects, and grant schemes, although project size may constitute a trade-off: providing credible results may be costly and for small projects the cost may exceed the benefit. To free up enough resources to ensure that results can be credibly documented, the organization might have to reduce the number of agreements, or sample projects for evaluation as described in section 4. This is precisely what the government has tried to do.

Disingenuous Demand (Not Really Interested in Documenting and Using Results)?

To sum up, several agents involved in development cooperation may not actually want to document the effects of development cooperation; demand is disingenuous (these included policy makers; the electorate is not directly affected by development cooperation and may prefer "feel good over do good"), the aid bureaucracy may prioritize maximizing budgets and aid disbursement over effectiveness, implementing partners may prioritize ensuring that funds keep flowing, evaluators may prefer to please any of the above to increase the chance to win future bids, and to ease the evaluation process. While we cannot conclude that demand for results is disingenuous, the following may indicate that a focus on results is not always what is prioritized: the budget for centralized evaluations is relatively low compared to budgets in comparator agencies in other countries and staff have, during focus group discussions, stated that the management did not prioritize results (Evaluation Department, 2014).

Lack of Resources (Competence, Skills, and Culture)?

Information on the results culture in aid administration is limited. However, we saw from the evaluation on evaluability that the pressure to disburse can trump careful consideration with respect to how results could be documented. The rule of thumb appears to be that "disbursement is more important than documenting results" (Evaluation Department, 2014, p. 66). This provides direction for the organization in terms of results focus, or the lack thereof. Furthermore, and on this we have less information, it is possible that beliefs about what constitute credible results are not the same across the organization. This could explain how it is possible for Norad to publish a result report every year, while the Evaluation Department in Norad in its annual report states that we cannot credibly report on results. This is to some extent also reflected in a recent evaluation on the quality of decentralized evaluations (Evaluation Department, 2017); the evaluators believed that a majority of evaluations failed to credibly document results, while grant managers believed evaluations were useful.

With respect to skills, credible documentation of results demands a high monitoring and evaluation skillset at several levels: grant manager level, quality assurance, and the management level. In the Norwegian aid administration, a large base of staff is considered generalists, and are not recruited for their skills in monitoring and evaluation. Furthermore, staff (in particular in the MFA) rotates, often every three years. Training in monitoring and evaluation is also rendered ineffective by poor attendance rates. Furthermore, even though evaluations occur at both centralized and decentralized levels, there is no entity with responsibility for quality assurance in decentralized evaluations.

Is Norwegian Development Cooperation Worse than Comparable Agencies?

The Norwegian case is not necessarily special. Savedoff, Levine, and Birdsall (2006) write that

> after decades in which development agencies have disbursed billions of dollars for social programs, and developing country governments and nongovernmental organizations (NGOs) have spent hundreds of billions more, it is deeply disappointing to recognize that we know relatively little about the net impact of most of these social programs.
>
> (2006, p. 1)

Not even the World Bank, used as an example to be copied, goes free of criticism: Martin Ravallion, a former World Bank economist writes that "Evaluation is generally weak and unbalanced, both before and after implementation. This reflects a lack of focus on the welfare outcomes of projects and policies" (2016, p. 83).

The short review of literature in the previous section suggested that aid agencies in general may experience an inflated demand for results, i.e., that the demand is not real. We agree with Gaarder and Bartsch (2014) in that aid agencies have a plethora of interest and objectives, and documenting results and welfare impacts on beneficiaries is only one of them.

Whether Norway is worse off with respect to a results focus is difficult to say, and the aid administration's practice of results-based management will itself be the topic of an upcoming evaluation.

Concluding Remarks

We argue that the existing results paradox, i.e., that the ministry responsible for development assistance repeatedly states that results matter while the aid administration is criticized for not being able to document results, is likely a result of both inflated demand and limited resources. This may however change. Traditional development assistance has long been protected from cuts due to the Norwegian commitment to donate 1 percent of GNI and increasing oil revenues. However, Norwegian aid is unlikely to maintain this protected position due to falling oil prices and a weaker currency. It is possible that this new situation will result in a real demand for a critical analysis of results through results documentation, as the need to prioritize will become imminent. Whether this occurs is likely to depend on which of the underlying causes for inflated demand predominates.

Notes

1 https://sustainabledevelopment.un.org/post2015/transformingourworld
2 https://unstats.un.org/sdgs/indicators/indicators-list/
3 www.cgdev.org/commitment-development-index-2017
4 Specifically, we searched for the Norwegian word «resultat», i.e., "result" as this word stem is present in most other types of results' words. For example: results framework, results orientation, results-based and so forth.
5 Other ministries also manage a smaller share of the development aid budget. The Ministry of Foreign Affairs is however responsible for the largest bulk of funds.
6 In-donor official development assistance funds for refugees managed by the Ministry of Justice and Public Security not included.
7 Bistandsbudsjettet for 2016 er på 33,6 mrd. kroner og tilsvarer 1 pst. av BNI- anslaget for 2016. Men enda viktigere enn volumet er arbeidet med å målrette, konsentrere og effektivisere bistanden for å oppnå bedre resultater (MFA, 2014/2015b, p. 12).
8 The political platform was a policy document released when the new government took office, stating the specific policies and objectives of the new governing coalition.
9 Translated from Norwegian; «Regjeringen vil: -Resultatorientere utviklingspolitikken, gjennomføre systematiske evalueringer med budsjettkonsekvenser og legge til rette for full åpenhet om omfanget, gjennomføringen og effektene av norsk utviklingspolitikk.» From www.regjeringen.no/no/dokumenter/politisk-plattform/id743014/
10 (p. 23) «I løpet av 2015 er alle regelverk for departementets tilskuddsordninger oppdatert, disse skal tas i bruk i 2016. Regelverkene har tydeligere krav til kvalitetssikring gjennom hele prosjektsyklusen, fra planlegging til avslutning. Dette innebærer mer systematisk vurdering av partnere og prosjekter før avtaler inngås, tettere oppfølging og kontroll av partner og prosjekt gjennom implementeringen av tiltak, og tydeligere krav til rapportering på resultater.» (MFA, 2015/2016, p. 23).
11 (p. 45) «En overveiende andel av Norges bistandsprosjekter viser gode resultater.» (MFA, 2015/2016, p. 45).
12 The recommendations from the Evaluation Department, and the management response can be found online: www.norad.no/en/toolspublications/publications/2014/can-we-demonstrate-the-difference-that-norwegian-aid-makes-/
13 Translated from Norwegian: «Eksterne evalueringer og gjennomganger har påpekt svakheter ved departementets system for å måle resultater av tiltakene som støttes. Departementet har iverksatt tiltak for å forbedre resultatmåling og resultatrapporteringen, herunder igangsatt kompetansehevende tiltak for medarbeidere på alle nivå. Mer systematisk vurdering av resultatrammeverk for tiltakene vi støtter er innført, videre stilles det økte krav til gjennomganger og evalueringer i løpet av prosjektperioden. Dette vil bidra til bedre informasjonen om resultatene oppnådd ved norske tilskuddsmidler.».
14 Pritchett calls them advocates.

References

Andreoni, J. (1990). Impure altruism and donations to public goods: A theory of warm-glow giving. *The economic Journal, 100*, 464–477.

Auditor-General. (2011). *Riksrevisjonens undersøkelse av resultatorienteringen i norsk bistand.* Oslo: Riksrevisjonen (Auditor-General).

Downs, A. (1957). *An economic theory of democracy.* New York: Harper and Row.

Drucker, P. F. (1954). *The practice of management: A study of the most important function in American society.* Amsterdam & New York: Harper & Brothers.

Easterly, W. (2002). The cartel of good intentions: The problem of bureaucracy in foreign aid. *The Journal of Policy Reform, 5*, 223–250.

Evaluation Department. (2011). *Evaluation of Norwegian development assistance. Yearly report.* Oslo: Norad.

Evaluation Department. (2014). *Can we demonstrate the difference that Norwegian aid makes? Evaluation of results measurement and how this can be improved. Evaluation Report 1.* Oslo: Norad.

Evaluation Department. (2017). *The quality of reviews and decentralized evaluations in Norwegian development cooperation.* Oslo: Norad.

Frey, B. S., & Jegen, R. (2001). Motivation crowding theory. *Journal of Economic Surveys, 15*, 589–611.

Gaarder, M. M., & Bartsch, U. (2014). Who cares about development outcomes? Market failures and the role of the evaluation function. *Journal of Development Effectiveness, 6*, 361–377.

Holmstrom, B., & Milgrom, P. (1991). Multitask principal-agent analyses: Incentive contracts, asset ownership, and job design. *Journal of Law, Economics, and Organization, 7*, 24–52.

Lindkvist, I., & Dixon, V. (2014). To "feel good," or to "do good?" Why we need institutional changes to ensure a results focus in Norwegian development assistance. *Journal of Development Effectiveness, 6*, 350–360.

Lloyd, R., Villanger, E., & Poate, D. (2014). Results measurement and evaluability: A comparative analysis. *Journal of Development Effectiveness, 6*, 378–391.

Martens, B. (2002). The role of evaluation in foreign aid programmes. In B. Martens, U. Mummert, & P. Murrell. (Eds.), *The institutional economics of foreign aid.* Cambridge: Cambridge University Press.

Mayne, J. (2007). Challenges and lessons in implementing results-based management. *Evaluation, 13*, 87–109.

Ministry of Foreign Affairs (MFA). (1993). *Evaluation of development assistance. Handbook for evaluators and managers.* Oslo: The Royal Ministry of Foreign Affairs.

Ministry of Foreign Affairs (MFA). (2014). *White paper: Report No. 25 to the Storting: Education for development.* Oslo: Ministry of Foreign Affairs.

Ministry of Foreign Affairs (MFA). (2014/2015a). *Meld. St. 10 Muligheter for alle – menneskerettigheter som mål og middel i utenriks og utviklingspolitikken.* Oslo: Ministry of Foreign Affairs.

Ministry of Foreign Affairs (MFA). (2014/2015b). *Prop. 1 S: Proposisjon til Stortinget (Budget proposition to the Storting).* In M. O. F. (Ed.), Affairs. Oslo: Ministry of Foreign Affairs.

Ministry of Foreign Affairs (MFA). (2015/2016). *Prop. 1 S: Proposisjon til Stortinget (Budget proposition to the Storting).* In M. O. F. (Ed.), Affairs. Oslo: Ministry of Foreign Affairs.

Michaelowa, K., & Borrmann, A. (2006). Evaluation bias and incentive structures in bi-and multilateral aid agencies. *Review of Development Economics*, *10*, 313–329.

Niskanen, W. A. (1968). The peculiar economics of bureaucracy. *The American Economic Review*, *58*, 293–305.

Niskanen, W. A. (1994). *Bureaucracy and public economics*. Aldershot, England & Brookfield, Vt., USA: Edward Elgar Publishing.

Organisation for Economic Co-operation and Development (OECD). (1980). *Strategies for change and reform in public management Paris: Organisation for Economic Co-operation and Development*. Paris: OECD.

Organisation for Economic Co-operation and Development (OECD). (2013). *OECD-development co-operation peer review: Norway 2013*. Geneva: OECD.

Pritchett, L. (2002). It pays to be ignorant: A simple political economy of rigorous program evaluation. *The Journal of Policy Reform*, *5*, 251–269.

Ramalingam, B. (2013). *Aid on the edge of chaos: Rethinking international cooperation in a complex world*. Oxford, UK: Oxford University Press.

Ravallion, M. (2016). The World Bank: Why it is still needed and why it still disappoints. *The Journal of Economic Perspectives*, *30*, 77–94.

Reinertsen, H. (2016). *Optics of evaluation: Making Norwegian foreign aid an evaluable object, 1980–92*. (PhD dissertation). University of Oslo, Oslo.

Rosenberg, L., Posner, L., & Hanley, E. (1970). *Project evaluation and the project appraisal reporting system*. USA: Agency for International Development. Fry Consultants Incorporated.

Savedoff, W. D., Levine, R., & Birdsall, N. (2006). *When will we ever learn? Improving lives through impact evaluation*. Washington, DC: Center for Global Development.

Van Thiel, S., & Leeuw, F. L. (2002). The performance paradox in the public sector. *Public Performance & Management Review*, *25*, 267–281.

Øvrelid, R., & Bastøe, P. Ø. (2002). Norway: Toward a results-oriented government administration? In J. E. Furobo, R. C. Rist, & R. Sandahl (Eds.), *International atlas of evaluation*. New Jersey: Transaction Publishers.

3 Behind the Scenes of the French Evidence-Based Policy Movement

Rise and Fall of an RCT-Driven Model of Evidence

Agathe Devaux-Spatarakis

The beginning of the new century witnessed a growing worldwide interest in impact assessment by evaluation methods, and a general call for Evidence-Based Policy (EBP) within international and national organizations (Donaldson, Christie, & Mark, 2009; Evaluation Gap Working Group, 2006). EBP movements call for policy initiatives to be more systematically supported by evidence, and they create opportunities for dialogue between those involved with the supply and demand for that evidence (Sanderson, 2002). The strategies of these movements are two-fold. First, they hope to act upon the supply side of evidence by improving the quality of studies produced; second, they attempt to foster the use of evidence by policy actors by institutionalizing a more systematic use of evidence in policymaking (Lee, 2004; Parsons, 2002). An overview of EBP movements around the world shows that their strategies vary depending on the characteristics of national evaluation suppliers, national institutions, and political culture (Rieper, 2009). Across countries, a diversity of methods for impact evaluation has been promoted, different types of suppliers of evaluation have been identified, and various types of knowledge synthesis are being delivered to policymakers.

Research literature in this field has extensively covered scientific debate on the most relevant methods of producing evidence, as well as on how to identify barriers and facilitate use of evidence by policymakers (Donaldson et al., 2009; Duflo, Glennerster, & Kremer, 2004; Sanderson, 2002; Solesbury, 2001). However, little attention has been given to the study of EBP movements themselves and to accounting for national choices of EBP in regard to standards of evidence, both on the supply and the demand side. This study expands upon this body of research by looking at the roots of EBP movements, their genesis, and emerging EBP coalitions.

This research[1] adopted a Political Sociology of Science[2] approach to account for variations in EBP models across countries (Frickel & Moore, 2006). This approach calls for devoting special attention to the individuals that participate in these movements, and the interests driving them to champion particular EBP models. It leads us to understand EBP movements as indeterminate processes under the influence of many actors, both from the supply and the demand side, pursuing various aims, with conflicting interests at times. Consequently, the hypotheses put to the test are: 1) that national EBP models emerge as consensuses between these actors which reflect their positions, and 2) that one can therefore also expect these consensuses to be subject to instability when there are shifts in the balances of power by the actors driving supply of and demand for evidence.

To test these hypotheses, the present chapter undertook a thorough study of the French EBP movement from 2005 to 2013. This movement is of particular interest in many regards. First, it was subject to rapid institutionalization, as only four years separate the first mention of EBP by a public official in 2005, and the creation of a dedicated national fund within the French government for this purpose in 2009. Second, because the French EBP model explicitly promoted the use of Randomized Controlled Trials (RCTs), despite the infrequent use of this method by French evaluators and scientists. Third, because the French EBP movement, although promising, has in hindsight led to very little use of evidence from impact evaluation, and has rapidly vanished from use by the central government, for reasons which we hope to clarify.

Data used in this research were collected in semi-structured interviews conducted with more than 50 high-level French administration officials, scientists who had conducted RCTs, and managers of pilot programs. These interviews were complemented by a literature review of approximately 200 scientific and administrative documents that were produced by members of the French EBP coalition. Finally, 15 in-depth case studies were conducted of RCTs implemented in France.

Evolution of EBP Models and the Role of RCTs in France

This first section presents why and how a coalition for EBP emerged in France, and how the actors involved influenced the shape of EBP. Studying the interests and strategies of individuals within this coalition helps explain not only the methodological choices of the French EBP movement, but also the limits this placed on its sustainability.

EBP Models as Results of Consensus Between a Coalition of Actors

One of the first puzzles this chapter tries to solve is how to account for the methodological hierarchy defined by the EBP movement in France. Our first line of enquiry turned to the literature on how RCTs became a gold standard for producing evidence, and why the evidence they produced was considered central for informed decision-making. RCTs are presented by their supporters as the most rigorous and least biased demonstration of causality, whereas other evaluators question their relevance in assessing many types of programs and call for methodological pluralism (LaLonde, 1986; Rubin, 1974). However, it is not the purpose of this chapter to engage in this methodological and epistemological debate that has animated the supply side of impact evaluation, i.e., the evaluators' community. Rather, this chapter aims to understand the drivers of choices made on the demand side for evidence, e.g., public officials. The literature describing the emergence of the use of new tools and instruments by public officials leads us to consider the scientific value of these tools and to study their genesis and their supporters (Le Galès & Lascoumes, 2004). The strong hypothesis of our study is that, beyond its scientific legitimacy, RCTs' supremacy is a dependent variable in the role that RCT suppliers played in the genesis of the EBP movement at a national level.

RCT legitimacy is historically linked to the methodological hierarchy of the evidence-based medicine (EBM) movement which emerged in the 1970s (Petrosino, 2013). The hypothesis underlying the extension to other fields is that if RCTs were deemed the most rigorous method for assessing drug treatment impact, it should also best address policy impacts (Duflo et al., 2004). Nevertheless, a closer look at the genesis of EBM reveals the determining role played in this methodological hierarchy by a lobbying coalition of evidence suppliers wishing to conduct RCTs. This is supported by the historical enquiry of H. Marks concluding that EBM's institutionalization in the United States and its methodological preference for RCTs stemmed mainly from the lobbying work of statisticians wishing to conduct RCTs (Marks, 1997, p. 32).

Once, this methodological preference took hold in EBM in the 1990s, it was then taken up by organizations such as the Cochrane Collaboration,[3] which conducted systematic reviews and meta-analyses and called for the development of RCT-based studies in order to strengthen its findings (Rieper, 2009). From this time on, evidence-based practices remained closely intertwined with RCT as a gold standard for obtaining credible evidence. A rapid overview of the American and British EBP movement encourages us to pursue this research agenda on EBP coalitions, particularly on the role of evaluation suppliers within those coalitions, their vested interests, and their contribution to the EBP doctrine for evidence.

The British EBP model was mainly championed by public officials; what we call the "demand side" for evidence. EBP was identified as a political resource to justify the New Labour shift in ideology, guided by the motto "What matters is what works" (Solesbury, 2001). The main challenges were seen to be the construction of knowledge management structures within the British government (Amann, 2000). The focus of EBP institutionalization in Britain was therefore not on the production of new evidence, but rather on the synthesis of existing studies and the improvement of communication between scientists and policymakers (Cabinet Office, 2000). Meanwhile, coalitions of suppliers of evidence created the Campbell Collaboration in 2000 (a sister organization of the Cochrane Collaboration) but were not originally at the source of the political initiative for EBP. Hence, in the British EBP documents of that time, RCTs are referred to as one of many tools of EBP and are not identified as the cornerstone of EBP's success (Cabinet Office, 1999, 2000).

By way of contrast, in the United States, an official "Coalition for Evidence-Based Policy" emerged from 2001 onwards. Its publications, and the members of its advisory board, demonstrate tight links between this coalition and RCT suppliers, and the focus of this movement was on the production of evidence by RCTs.[4] A study funded by the W. Grant Foundation closely monitored the work of the coalition and described its lobbying activities targeted towards the American administration, and its championing of RCTs (Martin, 2004). Without discussing these different initiatives and their impacts further, the main point is that this coalition was, apparently, mainly shaped by suppliers of RCTs and therefore promoted a model of EBP relying on the production of new evidence by this specific method. Its impact on the US Department of Education is one of the clearest examples of this tendency. The "What Works Clearinghouse" was created within the Institute of Education Sciences to gather evidence in the field of education using the Cochrane Collaboration's quality standards of evidence. Jon Baron, head of the EBP coalition, was nominated to be a member of the National Board for Education Sciences in 2004 and became the board's chair in 2011. In contrast, the demand side (i.e., the federal government), did not generally support RCTs or call for their use. Another report of the W. Grant Foundation based on interviews with public officials advised the coalition to drop the association of RCTs with "Gold Standards," as it could undermine the promotion of EBP amongst policy actors (Herck, 2009).

This brief overview suggests that, not surprisingly, EBM coalitions tend to focus on RCT-generated evidence if their main actors are suppliers of RCTs (the US example), and on institutionalization of new knowledge management systems within government without exclusive methods preferences if their main actors are public officials (the UK example). This hypothesis is now put to the test using primary data on the French EBP movement.

The Role of RCT Champions in the French EBP Movement

Determining the precise date when an EBP movement starts is not an easy task. Indeed, discourse regarding the improvement of policy through better use of expert knowledge has been a commonly stated political goal in France, on and off since the 1950s. We identify the first signs of the emergence of EBP in terms of three narratives: first, a call for the use of evidence in public policy programming; second, a plan for institutionalizing a new knowledge management system; and third, a strategy on how to gather or produce this evidence.

The first champions of EBP in France came from academics wishing to conduct RCTs. In 2004, a constitutional modification allowed the use of pilot programs, hitherto prohibited as a violation of the principle of equal access, to policies within the French territory. From that point onwards, as one of these academics expressed: "French statisticians who had been chomping at the bit for decades, were now eager to use RCTs."[5] Their challenge now rested on their ability to find project managers willing to assess their pilot programs using this method. At the same time, Esther Duflo, a well-known French economist heading the

Abdul Latif Jameel Poverty Action Lab (J-PAL) at the Massachusetts Institute of Technology (MIT) in the US, as well as other researchers, championed RCTs as a superior tool for producing evidence for international organizations, such as the World Bank. RCTs were also promoted by these individuals in France through the French Agency for Development, and the European Development Research Network (Duflo, 2005; Evaluation Gap Working Group, 2006).

On the demand side (public officials) the emergence of an EBP narrative can be traced back to a report of a national commission on disadvantaged families, published in 2005. The report recommended a new policymaking process, driven by results-based information obtained through experiments, for new solutions based on that evidence (Hirsch, 2005). This recommendation was the result of a meeting within this commission of a group of policy actors and high-level civil servants with a group of statisticians promoting RCTs. The recommendation was brought to the fore by the chairman of this commission, Martin Hirsch, who continued to play a central role in the French EBM movement. This chairman had accumulated experience as a high-level civil servant, as a member of several ministries' cabinets, as a public health institute administrator, and at that time, as the chairman of a charity foundation in France (Emmaüs). He stood out from other French public officials as being already familiar with using RCTs in evidence-based practices through his professional career as administrator of the European Agency for the Evaluation of Medicinal Products, which frequently used trials, and through his contacts with J. Gueron, the former president of the Manpower Demonstration Research Corporation (MDRC) (Hirsch, 2010).

Following his appointment to this commission, Hirsch's autobiography and press interviews reflect his willingness to support this new policy process (i.e., pilot programs assessed by RCTs), and to convene individuals willing to engage in EBP (Association des Journalistes de l'Information Sociale, 2006; Hirsch, 2010). In his own words, Hirsch "fought for experiments," and mobilized his scientific and political network to create a new independent agency in the image of the American MDRC, dedicated to fund pilot programs and their evaluations with RCTs (Hirsch, 2010). Members of the board of this agency published press releases and organized conferences presenting "social experiments" in the policy process to policy actors (Agence Nouvelle des Solidarités Actives, 2006; La République des idées, 2006). The group defined "social experiments" as a new bottom-up policymaking process, proceeding through small scale innovation, and rigorous evaluation by means of RCTs, followed by larger-scale roll-out (replication) in the case of positive evidence about the impact of those pilots. In a nutshell, they shaped an RCT-driven model of EBP.

Suppliers of RCTs also created new scientific organizations for implementing RCTs. In 2007, the Parisian Laboratory in Experimental Economy (LEEP) was created and Duflo founded a J-PAL Europe office[6] in the Paris School of Economics. The aim of these new structures was to give more international visibility to French economic research as well as to attract funding from the public and private sector (Paris School of Economics, 2012). Interviews with researchers working in these academic institutions revealed that RCTs were understood to be a means to reach these goals: they could be funded by public and private sources and their results could be published in highly regarded international economic journals.

Academics wishing to conduct RCTs also benefited from a privileged relationship with French Ministries. In France, statisticians are public officials and can work both within ministerial statistical departments and at universities. This allows them access to French administration technical services and makes them potentially influential advisors on methodological choices. As one statistician practicing RCTs recalled, "I knew them (Ministry of Employment) from my past work experience, they needed advice for impact evaluations, therefore, they had a sympathetic ear for my methodological advice (RCTs)." The first RCTs emerged from these relationships, particularly within the Ministry of Employment from 2006 onwards. A few experimental studies emerged from these initiatives, but they still lacked enough political support to be considered a national EBP movement. They found this support when Hirsch was nominated to a high position within the French government in 2007.

A Brief Period of EBP within the French Government

Following French presidential elections, Hirsch was appointed as Haut Secrétaire aux Solidarités Actives (High Secretary of Active Solidarities) within the French government. The president (Nicolas Sarkozy) called upon him to implement a new income maintenance program. In Sarkozy's conservative government, Hirsch, hitherto identified as a left-wing public actor, represented openness to new ideas, and new policymaking processes. The president gave him the mission to "reconcile citizens with policies by proving they [policies] can make a difference" (Sarkozy, 2007). Hirsch accepted the position under two conditions: 1) to test the new income maintenance program, preferably using RCTs, before generalizing it, and 2) to work independently, i.e., not under any ministry. Hirsch formed a small team of high-level public officials and scientific experts in favor of EBP and familiar with RCTs. Members of this group stated in public interviews that they were non-ideological and, in a way, isolated from the rest of the conservative government who referred to them as "a cult" (Dujol, 2010).

The national experiment with the new income maintenance program was advised by a scientific committee. Committee members were selected by Hirsch's team, sharing its inclination towards RCTs, and was conceived by M. Hirsch as the first embodiment of EBP in France (Direction de l'Animation de la Recherche, des Études et des Statistiques (DARES), 2008).

However, two attributes of RCTs did not receive political support. First, the notion of depriving the control group – a significant share of the target population of the program – of the program's assumed benefits was not popular among politicians. Given intensive media coverage of the new income maintenance program, they did not permit the use of this evaluation method. Second, the same political pressure prevented waiting long enough for evaluation results to inform decision-making. Instead, larger-scale roll-out of the program was approved only one year into the program and was evaluated by quasi-experimental methods, i.e., with a simulated rather than a real control group. Evaluators of these programs expressed their disagreement with the decision to roll out the program at that early stage and the head of the evaluation committee stated that "the results of the impact evaluation were not available when it was decided to roll-out the program." From available evaluation data, Hirsch nevertheless concluded that "this program has a rate of employment 30% higher than for non-beneficiaries" (Gomel & Serverin, 2009) in support of the French National Assembly bill rolling out this program. Overall, although this first national "experience" in experimental evaluation constituted a first step in propagating this EBP model and narrative, it was nevertheless perceived as a missed opportunity by many members of the EBP coalition because of the above-mentioned methodological weaknesses and the use of only intermediary results.

Going forward, Hirsch's team continued advocating the benefits of evaluating social experiments through RCTs to inform policymaking by policy actors. Conferences were organized gathering RCT champions such as the then director of MDRC, academics, directors of J-PAL such as E. Duflo and A. Banerjee, other prominent economists from MIT such as J. Angrist, and French scientists of the EBP coalition. The audience of these conferences were program managers and members of the French government and administration, representing the potential demand side of EBP. Hirsch called for the "strength of evidence" in his introductory plenary address and introduced subsequent speakers from the RCT supply community as the solution for building a new policymaking process (DARES, 2008).

As this way of conducting policy became more popular, Hirsch opened "a second front" for EBP with the creation of an Experimental Fund for Youth, with a state contribution of 150 million euro and additional contributions of 50 million euro by the private sector (Hirsch, 2010). This new organization was governed by a political and a scientific committee and reflected the institutionalization of the French EBP model. Its mission was to issue calls for proposals devoted to finding new solutions for disadvantaged youth segments. Applications were selected based on the relevance of the pilot programs, but also on their evaluation framework. It was made explicit within the methodological guidance issued by the scientific committee that pilot programs planning to be evaluated by RCTs would have strongly improved chances of being selected and funded (Conseil Scientifique du FEJ, 2009). Members of Hirsch's cabinet also organized matchmaking sessions, where program managers could meet RCT suppliers. Hirsch explained:

> we organized the "Meetic" of social experiment, saying: either you are researchers and academics who suggest methodological protocols and we will help you find policy actors willing to be a "testing ground"; or you are policy actors, companies or NGOs who wish to carry out pilot projects, and we will try to find researchers to help you render it evaluable under conditions enabling us to draw policy lessons from them.
>
> (DARES, 2008)

According to our analysis of the documents produced by this new experimental fund, the main emphasis of the EBP model was on the production of RCT-based evidence, while little attention was given to shaping a learning management system based on the use of the impact evaluations' results. This strategy reflected Duflo's hypothesis that "better" evidence, produced by RCTs, will systematically improve the use of impact evaluation results in program planning (Duflo, 2005).

Within four years, this small coalition was successful in building the first organization explicitly dedicated to EBP within the French government. The organization's main focus was the production and funding of RCTs to generate new evidence on pilot programs. Yet, this experimental fund also reflected the coalition's independence from ministries, resulting in a lack of political support within the French government. As it was not institutionally anchored to any ministry, its capacity to influence policymaking depended on Hirsch's direct influence within the French government. This political linkage was lost when Hirsch left the French government, and the experimental fund, in 2010. Without its principal political leader championing EBP, the fund was then mainly used for financing new pilot programs and less attention was given to the production of evidence through evaluation. This decline led many members of the scientific evaluation committee to withdraw, which eventually scattered the coalition. The

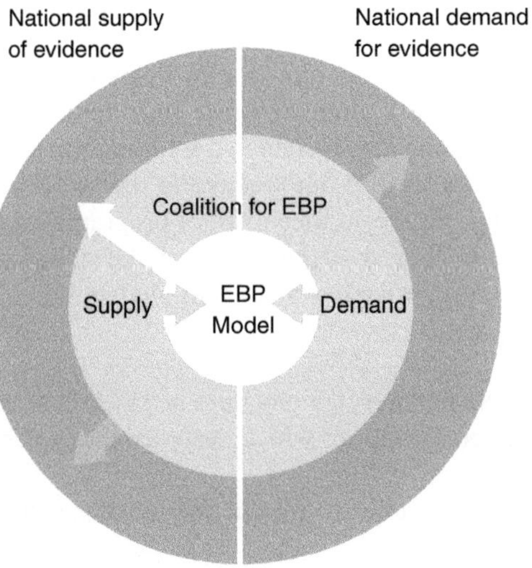

Figure 3.1 Graphic representation of the EBP movement in France.

Note

This diagram illustrates the French EBP movement in France. A small coalition made of actors of the demand and the supply side of evidence (in light grey) shaped an EBP model (in white) and attempted to gather support for EBP from each of these two sides (in dark grey). Yet this EBP model's agenda was mainly set on the supply side to generate evidence produced by RCTs, making the assumption that political use would follow.

attempt to institutionalize EBP in France was put aside, and members of the coalition opted for carrying on with RCTs only through their own personal connections with policy actors.

In short, this case study shows the close relationship that existed between supply and demand within the French EBP coalition. But the French EBP movement was only supported on the demand side by an independent group within the French government, with little political support at national level, since the majority of policy makers were against RCTs. After the departure of these outside actors, no further demand for evidence based on RCTs was voiced within the French government.

Yet, the "demand" for evidence did emerge at another level. Managers of experimental fund programs had high expectations for this evaluation method in demonstrating the impact of their pilot programs. Many experiments launched in the first year of the experimental fund were already underway; one-third of the pilot programs were evaluated by RCTs, and half of the overall evaluation funds had been dedicated to fund RCT-based evaluations.

We now turn to these experiments to better understand the match – or mismatch – between the demand for and supply of results information at the level of evaluations of individual program pilots.

RCTs Create a Mismatch Between Demand and Supply of Evidence for Impact Evaluation

Acknowledging how the French EBP model was shaped helps to understand the interests at stake around impact evaluation. It sheds light on the demand for – and supply of – evidence and helps us to understand how impact evaluation results were used. Since RCTs were promoted as the tool of choice for French EBP, our research focused on case studies of pilot programs evaluated by this method to understand how they met the needs of the demand side. Three groups of stakeholders were involved with impact evaluations of pilot programs:

- Sponsors: public or private actors funding pilot programs and their evaluation;
- Project managers: people and organizations which designed the projects and would implement them;
- Evaluators: individuals (mainly researchers) conducting impact evaluations.

According to our findings, the use of impact evaluation results depended mostly on the degree of interaction between these three groups and on the level of agreement they had on the focus of the evaluation, and to a lesser extent on the quality of the evidence produced. The following sections present the expectations held by each group when engaging in impact evaluation, and how those needs were later addressed by the evaluation results produced by RCTs.

Suppliers of RCTs: Academic Interest as Main Motivation

Before studying the use of impact evaluation results by program managers and policymakers, one must account for the nature of the evidence produced by those evaluations. The short history of EBP in France presented above showed that evaluation suppliers were also pursuing their own career and academic interests in conducting RCTs. First, as stated in publications and confirmed in our interviews, a key interest in this group was to apply this evaluation method and to gain experience in its application (Fougère, 2000; L'Horty & Petit, 2010). Since 2000, the rise of international academics' interest in impact evaluation among micro-economists has been well documented (Card, DellaVigna, & Malmendier, 2011; Levitt & List, 2008). One of the French statisticians we interviewed who conducted RCTs explained: "This method (RCTs) has become the norm in applied economics [...] If you want credible results, it is expected to give evidence by this method." French researchers not only wished to conduct RCTs themselves, but also to study behavioral mechanisms in order to bridge some knowledge gaps on specific issues debated academically. During interviews, these statisticians explained how they chose pilot programs for evaluation depending on the research questions they could address by conducting impact evaluations on this topic.

A couple of public servants working for the experimental fund complained about the fact that some academics or researchers seemed determined to apply RCTs even if conditions were unfavorable for this method. One interviewee expressed this as follows: "With some researchers, we were under the impression that applying the method (RCTs) was the most important [sic]. Whereas the aim of this call for projects was not to conduct pure scientific work but to improve social policies." Most academics interviewed account for this behavior by their hope, at the time, of convincing project managers to adapt their pilot project to RCTs' protocol requirements. Yet, these researchers eventually had to lower their expectations about the quality of evidence produced in these contexts. From the start of the experiment, some projects were not fit to be evaluated by RCTs: they were either too small to encompass enough beneficiaries to be statistically significant, too complex to be comprehensively evaluated by this method, or did not allow for strict randomization. Moreover, projects better adapted to RCTs at the onset could become unsuitable later because of low adoption rates, or because of modifications made to the intervention during implementation – both conditions strongly hindering proper implementation of RCT evaluation protocols.

As a result, only a few RCTs of pilot programs met the criteria necessary to be considered credible evidence by the scientific community. Almost all the results had to be strengthened by additional statistical analysis, or new data collection, to increase their internal validity. In the end, no RCT reviewed for this chapter led to a clear-cut recommendation favoring larger-scale roll-out of the evaluated pilot program, and evaluators frequently called for more experiments to draw definitive conclusions. The interests of these scientists were focused more on learning about behavioral mechanisms common to many programs based on long-term cumulative evidence from evaluating diverse programs, rather than on improving the approach of a particular program. One of them explained this in an interview as follows: "This is not an evaluation method shaped to assess if a program works or not. It is an evaluation to answer the question what should we do? What is the problem? We have an interest in mechanisms, in testing hypotheses."

These experiences allowed researchers to better define conditions for producing evidence with RCTs. It generally appeared that the best evidence was produced when evaluators actively contributed to the design of the project. When collaborating with project managers, evaluators managed not only to establish implementation controls to reduce bias, but also to shape the intervention itself in order to better address a given scientific question. Some experiments blurred the lines between the supply and demand side of evidence. Evaluators sometimes approached project managers in order to find a field for experimentation or mechanisms of interest for scientific debate, and at least they co-constructed the experiment with project managers. According to our analysis of interviews with evaluators, their ideal project with respect to evaluation was a very simple and time-specific intervention, mobilizing one simple technical mechanism, with beneficiaries who were easy to reach and to monitor, involving low levels of media and political interest, and with low stakes for project managers. Commenting on such conditions a statistician interviewed explained: "Here we have the opportunity to experiment, not just to be evaluators, but to choose things, to set variables, to interact with people implementing in the field. We are more proactive, more beforehand."

As a result, from the supply-side perspective of researchers implementing RCTs, the best evidence was produced when projects strictly followed their protocols, with no adaptation of the program during the evaluation period. Yet, these requirements overlooked the policy environment of "social experiments" and the particular conditions and interests for learning of implementers and policymakers. Studying the "demand side" of impact evaluations entails first defining which groups of stakeholders constitute this demand. In the RCTs under study, two groups with different demand expectations emerged: program managers conducting pilot programs, and policymakers or sponsors funding impact evaluations.

Incompatibility Between Program Managers' Learning Needs and RCTs

The expectations of program managers leading them to design pilot programs to be evaluated by RCTs were manifold. Many project managers viewed the experimental fund as an opportunity to access funds to carry out innovative programs in times of budgetary cuts. Their main interest in collaborating with RCT evaluators was to increase the chances that their project would be selected for funding. One of the members of the experimental fund recalled this as follows:

"It was the price to pay to prove that they were right, to fund their project. [...] it was a blessing in disguise." The impact of these funds varied depending on the size of the organization, but to some small NGOs it amounted to more than half of their overall annual budget. Project managers generally had two expectations of RCT evaluation results: 1) to gain insights on the project in order to improve its design and implementation in the field, and 2) to demonstrate the project's impact in order to secure sustainable funding for larger-scale implementation after the experimental phase was over.

Eventually, during the experiment process, their learning expectations and needs diverged from the evaluation design of RCT. When project managers started collaborating with evaluators, they often had not clearly understood the requirements of RCT evaluation protocols regarding project design. Many pilot projects were too complex to be rigorously assessed by RCTs, as they were tailored to offer comprehensive solutions for disadvantaged youth. They involved many stakeholders and were aimed at hard-to-reach beneficiaries. Projects also did not follow strict plans since project managers were used to – and expected to be able to – adjust implementation of innovative approaches "as they went" in accordance with the obstacles or opportunities encountered during implementation. Project managers were accustomed to "learning by doing" and therefore adapted the pilot programs while they were in their experimental phase in order to maximize impact. Hence, in many cases, and as other observers have noted in other contexts, pilot projects only began to stabilize by the end of the experiment (Patton, 2010). This led many project managers to discredit RCT results since they only focused on how the project was originally designed and ignored many of its modifications. One evaluator acknowledged this disconnect during an interview: "What were they (project managers) actually doing in the field? We've never managed to figure it out." Project managers expected a comprehensive contextualized assessment of their pilot projects, whereas the impact evaluations that were conducted often focused on the one dimension of the project that could be best monitored and randomized.

The timeline of the production of impact evaluation results was often misaligned with the program managers' needs. Evaluators issued evaluation results, at the earliest, six months after the end of the pilot program. In some cases, given the various breaches of RCT protocols and the time it took to come up with remedial analysis, this period extended to one or two years. In contrast to the supply timeline, pilot projects demanded evidence much earlier. They were funded only temporarily by the experimental fund, and no learning-based management system had been defined for using evaluation results. Consequently, program managers whose organization partly depended on these subsidies expected evidence before the end of the experiment in order to secure future funding. This led them to only use intermediary results, when those were in favor of the project, or to even conduct surveys on their own to gather additional data they considered necessary. As a result, decisions to roll out pilot programs were often not grounded in evidence from impact evaluations but reflected political windows of opportunity or political influence wielded by project managers.

Another reason possibly explaining the scarce use of impact evaluation results by program managers was that evaluations were funded and imposed upon them by the experimental fund. Therefore, our attention now turns towards the political committee of the experimental fund as well as other public officials influencing decisions for or against roll-out of pilot programs.

Cherry-Picking of Evidence

Studying evaluation use entails turning the focus of analysis towards institutions or public officials who decided to fund these pilot projects and their evaluation. Yet, in the cases under study, political turnover hindered this inquiry. By the time impact evaluation results were issued, the Experimental Fund for Youth had little influence on decisions for roll-out. Although results of experiments were made public, it remained unclear which institution – and how – should take them on board. No systematic learning management system was established and in only a few cases were RCT results used at all. To proceed with this analysis, we conducted follow-up studies of all pilot projects to trace if they were rolled out, maintained at the same level, or suppressed after their evaluation.

Overall, it appears that political interest in impact evaluation has been opportunistic rather than systematic. As highlighted earlier, one of the main interests was to fund experiments in order to prove the efficiency of reforms. Hence, selective attention was given to those evaluation results backing political agendas. Because politicians rarely stayed in office in the same position for more than a few years, interest in some pilot projects could fade when new elections shifted interest to other issues. Although these characteristics of the political environment are well known, looking at practical cases demonstrates how the quality and usefulness of the evaluation evidence produced had little influence on actual decisions taken.

Many local experiments were rolled out nationally before their impact evaluation results were published. Pilot programs were viewed as innovative interventions, to test different ways of implementing a program rather than experiments that needed to be scientifically assessed. Consequently, some pilot programs were rolled out nationally after only one year of the experimental phase and only based on intermediate evaluation results and, in other cases, entirely without proper evaluative evidence. It appears that other factors were more important; for example the degree of alignment with political agendas and the influence project managers themselves had on programmatic decision-making. Given frequent breaches in RCT evaluation protocols and difficulties of evaluators to deliver clear-cut answers on the overall impact of the interventions, the quality and usefulness of the evidence produced remained limited, and politicians cherry-picked evidence that supported the reform agendas they promoted.

Three impact evaluation results were explicitly used to back political decision-making at a national level and were portrayed as examples of good practice in evidence-based policymaking. A closer look at that evidence – and at who used it in what way – leads us to question this judgment.

The first case concerned a local pilot program aimed at involving parents in their children's schooling. The decision to roll out the pilot project nationally was based on positive intermediate results after only one year of the two-year pilot program experiment (Ecole d'Economie de Paris, 2011). The decision to fund the program nation-wide was taken by a high-level civil servant within the Ministry of Education who was also the former project manager of this pilot experiment. During an interview, this public official explained the factors leading to this roll-out:

> After one year, we could already see the virtues of this pilot, one of them being its low cost and the other its positive impacts [...] I personally advised the Minister on rolling out the program and he accepted. [...] We took our decision on the basis of the first evaluation but the fact that I became a "bee" going from my former job to the department of education was a particular case.

The second case was an experiment in the use of anonymous CVs in employment applications funded by the French government and conducted by the national employment agency. This pilot aimed at testing a measure passed by means of a bill passed five years earlier by the former government, but which had not yet been implemented. Surprisingly, results from this experiment showed that the use of anonymous CVs increased discrimination in hiring rather than reducing it. However, researchers who had conducted the evaluation questioned the validity of these negative results: companies participating in the study had been aware that they were being tested, and could have experienced a Hawthorne effect[7] (Behaghel, Crépon, & Le Barbanchon, 2011). Nevertheless, the French president at the time (Sarkozy) used these RCT results to terminate the program and to back his decision to not implement this bill. In this case, our hypothesis is that that negative evaluation results, even though questionable, were welcomed as useful "scientifically"-based political arguments.

The third case was a pilot that consisted of organizing a boarding school for disadvantaged students. Two opposite decisions emerged from this experiment that was assessed by RCTs. First, although no results were yet available, the president at the time (Sarkozy) decided to expand the program even in the absence of scientific evidence (Cour des comptes, 2014). Second, after new presidential elections, the subsequent president (Hollande) terminated the program, stating that it was inefficient even though final evaluation results still had not yet been published. Eventually, the evaluation concluded that this pilot program had an overall positive impact on students but at a very high financial cost (Behaghel, De Chaisemartin, Charpentier, & Gurgand, 2013; Beyer, 2013).

These three cases exemplify weaknesses of an EBP model driven by suppliers of evidence and relying only on the strength of RCTs to foster EBP amongst policy actors. The lack of genuine demand for evidence and of understanding of what kind of evidence can be produced by RCTs led, in France, to a failure to meet learning expectations by project managers, and opportunistic or non-use of evidence produced by RCTs by politicians in power.

Conclusion

This study of the French EBP movement sheds light on the processes leading to the emergence of supply and demand for RCTs in France in the context of relatively narrow and small social programs. Within the Experimental Fund for Youth, for example, between 2009 to 2012, only 15 percent of pilot programs were eventually evaluated by RCTs, yet those RCTs absorbed 50 percent of the overall evaluation budget of the fund. It is an example of a supply-driven coalition favoring construction of an EBP model, mainly relying on the hypothesis that better evidence produced by RCTs would foster wider policy use. This scientific coalition rapidly found support from one main politician, who managed to build an institution dedicated to EBP and institutionalize the model through the Experimental Fund for Youth. Yet, the loss of this political support, with the departure of this individual, ultimately led to the decay of the EBP movement in France.

At a micro-level, this review of the implementation and use of RCTs reveals discrepancies between the learning interests on the demand and the supply sides for the evidence produced by this method. The RCTs that were conducted produced evidence that, due to implementation difficulties, rarely met academic standards. Policymakers ended up cherry-picking convenient results rather than integrating evidence systematically into their decision-making.

More broadly, this review raises general questions about the interaction between supply and demand for impact evaluation using RCTs. Since impact evaluation calls for scientific evidence and rigorous conduct of evaluations by properly trained evaluators, can these new suppliers of evidence satisfy their academic interests without overlooking the needs of the demand side? What degree of influence should suppliers of certain evaluation methods have on the shape of pilot programs in order to fulfill their research program and protocols?

When asked to define “intelligence,” Alfred Binet, inventor of the IQ test, reputedly replied “Easy: intelligence is what my test measures;” from what we summarized in this chapter, we should be careful that when asked to define “impact” the answer does not become “Easy, it is what RCTs measure.” Well, this has not been shown since RCTs were never properly implemented, so whatever they measure seems spurious and subject to what the “supplier” provides.

Notes

1 This study is based on PhD research conducted in France between 2010 and 2014 and funded by a joint grant between the Centre Emile Durkheim (Institute of Political Science of Bordeaux) and the evaluation consulting group Euréval.

2 The new political sociology of science was summarized by Frickel and Moore as follows: “The centerpiece of the NPSS project as we see it is the analysis of institutions and networks as they condition the availability and distribution of power in the

production and dissemination of knowledge" (2006, p. 19). This program of inquiry gives particular attention to unequal distribution of power and resources, rules and rulemaking, and the dynamics of organizations.

3 The Cochrane Collaboration was founded in 1993. It was developed to promote and organize the conduct of systematic reviews of all relevant randomized controlled trials of healthcare.

4 For instance, J. Gueron of the MDRC and R. Boruch, author of randomized experiments for planning and evaluations are on its advisory board (Coalition for Evidence-Based Policy, 2007).

5 Interviewees were guaranteed anonymity in return for candid answers and therefore are not identified. We try where possible to account for their work position.

6 On its website, The Abdul Latif Jameel Poverty Action Lab (J-PAL) is presented as: "a global research centre working to reduce poverty by ensuring that policy is informed by scientific evidence. Anchored by a network of 158 affiliated professors at universities around the world, J-PAL draws on results from randomized impact evaluations to answer critical questions in the fight against poverty." It holds offices in all continents.

7 The Hawthorne effect refers to the process where human subjects of an experiment, or pilot program change their behavior, simply because they are aware that they are being studied.

References

Agence Nouvelle des Solidarités Actives. (2006). *Revue succincte d'activité, 1.*

Amann, R. (2000). Foreword. In S. M. Nutley, P. C. Smith, & H. T. O. Davies (Eds.), *What works? Evidence-based policy and practice in public services*. Bristol: The Policy Press.

Association des Journalistes de l'Information Sociale. (2006). Martin Hirsch – Président d'Emmaüs France et de l'Agence nouvelle des solidarités actives – Petit-déjeuner. *Association des journalistes de l'information sociale.*

Behaghel, L., Crépon, B., & Le Barbanchon, T. (2011). *Evaluation de l'impact du CV anonyme, synthèse et rapport final, 97*. France: Paris School of Economics, CREST, J-Pal.

Behaghel, L., De Chaisemartin, C., Charpentier, A., & Gurgand, M. (2013). *Internats d'excellence: les enseignements de Sourdun*. France: Paris School of Economics, J-PAL Europe, Institut des Politiques Publiques.

Beyer, C. (2013). Vers la fin des internats d'excellence. *Lefigaro*. Retrieved from www.lefigaro.fr/actualite-france/2013/04/11/01016-20130411ARTFIG00350-vers-la-fin-des-internats-d-excellence.php

Cabinet Office. (1999). *Modernizing government white paper*. London: Center for Management and Policy Studies.

Cabinet Office. (2000). *Adding it up, improving analysis and modelling in central government*. London: Performance and Innovation Unit.

Card, D., DellaVigna, S., & Malmendier, U. (2011). The role of theory in field experiments. *Journal of Economic Perspectives, 25*, 39–62.

Coalition for Evidence-Based Policy. (2007). *Hierarchy of study designs for evaluating the effectiveness of STEM education project or practice.* Washington, DC: Coalition for Evidence-Based Policy. Retrieved from http://coalition4evidence.org/wp-content/uploads/2009/05/study-design-hierarchy-6-4-09.pdf

Conseil Scientifique du FEJ. (2009). *Guide méthodologique pour l'évaluation des expérimentations sociales à l'intention des porteurs de projets, 22.*

Cour des comptes. (2014). *Rapport public annuel: Des internats d'excellence à ceux de la réussite: la conduite chaotique d'une politique éducative et sociale.*

Davies, P. (2004). *Is evidence-based government possible*? A Jerry Lee lecture given by Philip Davies, PhD at the 4th Annual Campbell Collaboration Colloquium in Washington DC, February 19, 2004.

Direction de l'Animation de la Recherche, des Études et des Statistiques (DARES). (2008). *Colloque sur les expérimentations pour les politiques publiques de l'emploi et de la formation, 168*. Paris.

Donaldson, S. I., Christie, C. A., & Mark, M. M. (Eds.). (2009). *What counts as credible evidence in applied research and evaluation practice*? Los Angeles: SAGE.

Duflo, E. (2005). Evaluer l'impact des programmes d'aide au développement: le rôle des évaluations par assignation aléatoire. *Revue D'économie Du Développement, 19*, 185–226.

Duflo, E., Glennerster, R., & Kremer, M. (2004). *Randomized evaluations of interventions in social service delivery*. MA: Massachusetts Institute of Technology. Retrieved from http://stuff.mit.edu/afs/athena/course/other/d-lab/DlabIII06/random-eval.pdf

Dujol, J. B. (2010). Un jeune au service des jeunes. *Les Echos, 11.*

Ecole d'Economie de Paris. (2011). *Quels effets attendre d'une politique d'implication des parents dans les collèges, évaluation de l'impact de la Mallette des parents*. Fonds d'expérimentations pour la jeunesse.

Evaluation Gap Working Group. (2006). *When will we ever learn? Improving lives through impact evaluation*. Center for Global Development.

Fougère, D. (2000). Expérimenter pour évaluer les politiques d'aide à l'emploi: les exemples anglo-saxons et nord-européens. *Revue Française des Affaires Sociales.*

Frickel, S., & Moore, K. (Eds.). (2006). *The new political sociology of science: Institutions, networks, and power*. Madison: University of Wisconsin Press.

Gomel, B., & Serverin, E. (2009). Expérimenter pour décider? Le RSA en débat. *Document de Travail Centre D'étude de l'Emploi, 119.*

Herck, M. (2009). *The coalition for evidence-based policy: Its role in advancing evidence-based reform, 2004–2009*. New York: William T. Grant Foundation.

Hirsch, M. (2005). *Au possible, nous sommes tenus. La nouvelle équation sociale, 15 résolutions pour combattre la pauvreté des enfants* (p. 116). France: Ministère des solidarités, de la santé et de la famille. Commission familles, vulnérabilité, pauvreté.

Hirsch, M. (2010). *Secrets de fabrication*. Paris: Grasset.

La République des idées. (2006). La nouvelle critique sociale, Grenoble, du 12 au 14 Mai 2006. *La République des idées*. Retrieved from www.repid.com/La-nouvelle-critique-sociale,7.html

LaLonde, R. J. (1986). Evaluating the econometric evaluations of training programs with experimental data. *The American Economic Review, 76*, 604–620.

Le Galès, P., & Lascoumes, P. (2004). *Gouverner par les instruments*. Paris: Presse de Science po.

Levitt, S., & List, J. (2008). *Field experiments in economics: The past, the present, and the future*. Cambridge, MA: National Bureau of Economic Research.

L'Horty, Y., & Petit, P. (2010). *Evaluation aléatoire et expérimentations sociales (Document de travail No. 135)*. Noisy-le-Grand, France: Centre d'études de l'emploi, Conservatoire national des arts et Metiers (CNAM).

Marks, H. M. (1997). *The progress of experiment: Science and therapeutic reform in the United States, 1900–1990*. Cambridge, UK & New York: Cambridge University Press.

Martin, B. H. (2004). *The coalition for evidence-based policy: Its impact on policy and practice*. New York: William T. Grant Foundation.

Paris School of Economics. (2012). *La lettre: Spéciale 5 ans. n°8.*

Parsons, W. (2002). From muddling through to muddling up – Evidence based policy making and the modernization of British government. *Public Policy and Administration, 17*, 43–60.

Patton, M. Q. (2010). Developmental evaluation: Applying complexity concepts to enhance innovation and use. New York: Guilford Press.

Petrosino, A. (2013). Reflections on the genesis of the Campbell collaboration. *The Experimental Criminologist, 8*, 9–12.

Rieper, H. (2009). The evidence movement, the development and consequences of methodologies in review practices. *Evaluation, 15*, 141–163.

Rubin, D. B. (1974). Estimating causal effects of treatments in randomized and non-randomized studies. *Journal of Educational Psychology, 66*, 688–701.

Sanderson, I. (2002). Evaluation, policy learning and evidence-based policy making. *Public Administration, 80*, 1–22.

Sarkozy, N. (2007). Lettre de mission de M. Nicolas SARKOZY, Président de la République, adressée à M. Martin Hirsch, Haut commissaire auprès du Premier ministre, aux Solidarités actives contre la pauvreté.

Solesbury, W. (2001). *Evidence based policy: Whence it came and where it's going.* Queen Mary, University of London: ESRC UK Centre for Evidence Based Policy and Practice. Retrieved from www.kcl.ac.uk/sspp/departments/politicaleconomy/research/cep/pubs/papers/paper-01

4 Influencing the Supply of and Demand for Results Information in Government

Can Outsiders Help? A Case Study from Ireland

Richard Boyle

In this chapter, the authors examine the evolution of evaluation in public investment programs in the Republic of Ireland, highlighting the seeming inverse relationship between the demand and supply of results information, and the strength of the local economy. The late 1980s and early 1990s represented the "golden age" for evaluation in Ireland when EU structural funds supported a significant portion of public expenditures but carried with them requirements for evaluating those programs. Subsequent improvements in public finances in the 1990s and 2000s relaxed the demand for evaluation and it played a decreasing role in informing public policy. Until 2008, that is, when the financial crisis caused a resurgence of interest in demonstrating that government policies generated "value for money." A private philanthropic organization, Atlantic Philanthropies, stepped in to rebuild the public sector's evaluation infrastructure within a time-bound framework and met with some success. But, the chapter questions, how sustainable will these efforts be now that the philanthropy's mandate is running out?

Background: Factors Influencing the Supply and Demand of Evaluation Information in Ireland

As in many countries, governments in Ireland have invested significant time and effort into producing better results information about government policy and programs. Demand for evaluation to support the production of results information in Ireland has varied over the years, both in intensity and in where the demand comes from. Similarly, the supply of evaluation has fluctuated, both in terms of the quality of evaluative information being produced and with regard to the capacity to conduct evaluation (Boyle, 2014).

Historically, a "golden age" for evaluation in Ireland was when EU structural funds support was a significant element of expenditure in the late 1980s and early 1990s. There was an associated requirement from the European Commission for evaluation of the programs supported by the structural funds. Results information became more prominent, and there was some evidence of enhanced supply of and demand for evaluations and use of findings to influence resource allocation decisions (Hegarty, 2003).

As the Irish economy grew rapidly in the 1990s and early 2000s, the demand for evaluation reduced as the pressure to engage in detailed scrutiny of public expenditure decreased. As structural funds support dwindled, the external pressure to evaluate coming from the European Commission also lost influence. While some results information was still being produced, there was limited evidence of it being influential with regard to the reform of spending programs (Department of Finance, 2004).

In response to the global fiscal crisis from 2008, and the major economic downturn in Ireland, the control and management of public expenditure has been a topic of much debate and concern. This has prompted developments aimed at re-growing policy evaluation capability within government, in the context of a wider public service reform initiative which includes a commitment to apply evaluation techniques to deliver "value for money" (as it is colloquially known) in public expenditure with more emphasis on results information (Department of Public Expenditure and Reform, 2011). These new measures include:

- The use of evaluations in periodic comprehensive reviews of expenditure (CRE), including both departmental-based and thematic evaluation reports;
- The introduction of an Irish Government Economic and Evaluation Service (IGEES) being developed as a cross-government service to enhance the role of economics and value for money analysis in public policymaking;
- Changes to the program review process, known as the Value for Money and Policy Review (VFMPR) process, including more targeted reviews, alignment with the expenditure allocation process, and greater involvement for parliament in the selection and assessment of reviews;
- The introduction of focused policy assessments (FPA), more narrowly focused assessments designed to answer specific issues of policy configuration and delivery and complement the VFMPR process;
- The introduction of a Public Spending Code to bring together good practice guidance on evaluation and appraisal;
- The creation of an Irish Government Economic and Evaluation Service Network to help build capacity.

Another interesting development has been an enhanced role for philanthropies in promoting evaluation of policies and programs they jointly fund with government. The Atlantic Philanthropies and the One Foundation, for example, are two "giving while living" limited-life philanthropies that have placed building evaluation and organizational learning capacity as a central element in their grant giving.

This latter point provides the main focus of this chapter, examining in particular the role of The Atlantic Philanthropies (a major philanthropic organization (www.atlanticphilanthropies.org) – hereinafter referred to as Atlantic) in prompting government engagement with results information in a more systematic way, and their influence on both the demand for and the supply of results information in government.[1] The Atlantic Philanthropies were founded by entrepreneur Chuck Feeney, who decided in 1982 to establish the philanthropy and become a champion of "giving while living," maintaining that people of wealth should use it to better the world during their lifetimes. In 2002 it was decided to limit Atlantic's life to a fixed term and to close their portfolio in 2020. By then Atlantic will have invested nearly $8 billion in programs and people, in the USA, Bermuda, Cuba, South Africa, Vietnam, Australia, Northern Ireland, and the Republic of Ireland (referred to as Ireland in this chapter).

Atlantic has worked closely with government in Ireland in co-funding a number of programs and projects based around alternative models of service delivery. For example, since 2012 Atlantic has supported 19 co-investments with government in Ireland: Atlantic's $110m investment in the areas of children and youth, dementia, and disability has been matched by $290m in public funding. Atlantic has collaborated with government at all stages, on a programmatic basis, from project inception to evaluation. They have been one of the pioneers internationally of philanthropies working closely with government to achieve their goals.

As part of this partnership, they have put particular emphasis on supporting the strengthening of both the demand and supply sides of evaluation in government to promote the production of results information and enhance the evidence base for policymaking. As well as supporting service delivery, Atlantic funding has the intention of foregrounding the evidence or research base to provide better information for decision-makers on policy selection, design, and implementation.

This chapter, based on research work commissioned by Atlantic, examines how successful this approach has been. It is based on a documentary analysis of government policy and evaluation papers, combined with a small number of case studies and a range of extensive, semi-structured interviews including members of Atlantic, selected grantees and, primarily, a range of officials from selected government departments and agencies. A total of 26 interviews were carried out (of which 16 were with senior policymakers). As part of this process, a number of interviews were conducted with "bellwethers" – influential people in the public sector who are thought leaders whose opinions about policy issues carry weight and predictive value (UNICEF, 2010, p. 34). The emphasis is on taking a critical look at whether or not the emphasis placed on the generation and use of results information has impacted on government practice, and the prospects for longer-term evaluative capacity building in government.

These approaches were used to provide evidence to support or refute a theory of change established for the study (see Figure 4.1). This theory of change was designed to show how the interventions of Atlantic were intended to influence government policy with regard to public service reform.

Atlantic has put significant effort into supporting evidence generation and gathering with a view to enhancing the evidence base used to inform policy development. With regards to the program for children, for example, which covers over 120 grants and an investment of approximately $170 million aimed at improving the health and development of children, Little

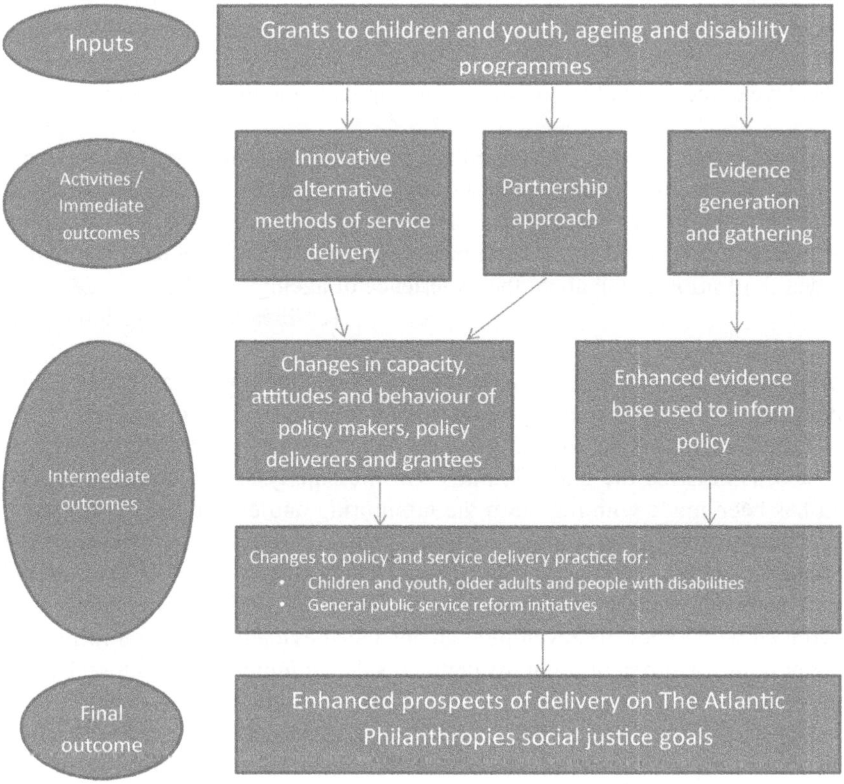

Figure 4.1 Theory of change for The Atlantic Philanthropies influence on government policy regarding public service reform.

and Abunimah (2007, p. 61) note in relation to both the Republic of Ireland and Northern Ireland:

> In designing the programme, many influences were brought to bear but two stood out strongly. First, it was clear that there was potential to bring a new perspective to ideas around community engagement. Second, it was considered that government expenditure would not be swayed by community engagement alone – that there was a need for high-quality evidence. The hypothesis was that governments on the island would take notice if rigorous and independent evidence showed that innovations for children and young people were having an impact on health and development. The marrying of community engagement and serious evaluation was never going to be easy, especially on an island where, as far as can be ascertained, there had previously only been a single experimental evaluation of a programme intended to improve children's health and development."

With regard to the program addressing ageing issues, covering approximately 110 grants and a total investment of around $200 million aimed at enhancing the rights of older people to health and economic security, Cochrane, McGilloway, Furlong and Donnelly (2013, p. 14) indicate the effect of limitations in the evidence base on the development of policy for the ageing population in the early 2000s:

> … it has been argued that overall, there has been a low level of awareness of ageing as a core government policy issue (O'Neill, Twomey, & O'Shea, 2009, p. 283). The subsequent lack of planning and provision for an ageing population has been further hampered by a lack of national datasets, with a dearth of information about the experience of ageing in Ireland.
>
> (O'Shea & Conboy, 2005, p. 4)

The following sections of the chapter examine the supply side and demand-side implications of Atlantic's engagement with government on the production and use of results information, the influence on policy development and implementation, and summarize the main findings. On the supply side, significant investment has been made with regard to the monitoring and evaluation of programs; the development of longitudinal studies and robust indicator sets, the building of academic capacity in research and evaluation, and the creation of institutional mechanisms to connect evidence with practice. These initiatives have been undertaken with a view to developing an enhanced evidence base to inform government policy and practice. On the demand side, an important aspiration behind the investment in evidence was that policymakers would make use of this evidence base to inform thinking about policy development and investment decisions. And that policymakers would subsequently demand similar results-oriented information in the development and assessment of future policies and programs. Atlantic hoped to build capacity amongst policymakers with regard to the production and use of results information. This was part of their goal of developing leaders and champions in the public service who would mainstream the learning from the co-funded programs after Atlantic's exit.

Enhancing the Evidence Base: Influencing the Supply Side of Results Information Provision

Atlantic has put effort into building robust evaluation practices that encourage the provision of results information in the programs they support, including the use of methodologies including randomized control trials (RCTs) and quasi-experiments, so as to better illustrate what works and what does not, and direct investment to those services shown to be more effective. As noted above, the use of RCTs in social interventions was relatively unheard of in Ireland with regard to social programs prior to this. Yet now over 20 RCTs, supported by Atlantic, have been undertaken to help show what works and what does not. These were often accompanied by process evaluations also supported by Atlantic to provide information on how the results were achieved. In contrast to the experience outlined by

Devaux-Spatarakis (this volume), RCTs were not put forward as the primary or only source of evaluative information, but as one of a number of methods to produce data. There was no pressure either from academics or from practitioners to "privilege" RCT data over other sources of data.

A particular benefit noted from the evidence generation was the creation of Irish cases that have been researched and documented (interviewees noted that this applies not only to RCTs but to other results-oriented evaluation reports of various projects such as evaluations of an Age Friendly Cities and Counties program and of the development of individualized supports for people with disabilities). This is seen as a big plus by many policy makers. Lesson drawing has taken place, and continues to take place, using evidence from abroad, but this can face challenges and resistance based on differing views as to the applicability of cases drawn from abroad in an Irish context. Having "home grown" cases of the evidence of policy impact was seen by a number of policymakers interviewed as important when persuading them as to the voracity of particular policies and programs.

Also, on the supply side, Atlantic aimed at improving the relevance and quality of results information for many of the grants they co-funded with government, by insisting on the creation of an independent expert advisory panel to advise on the evaluation of the grant, including the provision of results information. Atlantic would use their contacts to ensure that international experts in the field were brought in as members of the panel as appropriate. This ensured that the evaluation plans were informed by leading-edge thinking, and government officials working with these expert panels were exposed to this thinking and expertise.

Two particularly important initiatives supported by Atlantic to enhance the supply of evidence with a particular focus on results are the development of a longitudinal data set on ageing (TILDA), and the establishment of an institution dedicated to evidence generation and dissemination, the Centre for Effective Services.

TILDA: The Establishment of a Longitudinal Study Data Set

Atlantic has made a considerable commitment to supporting the development of research capacity in government and academia with regard to the policy fields of ageing and children. Of particular prominence is the Irish Longitudinal Study on Ageing (TILDA) (jointly funded by Atlantic, the Department of Health and Irish Life, a life assurance and pensions company). TILDA is a nationally representative survey of over-50s in Ireland carried out over a number of "waves" so as to provide data and trends over time.

Cochrane et al. (2013) note the intended benefits of creating a data source that provides information over time using the example of TILDA:

> While it is difficult to determine a direct link between Atlantic's investment and the general growth of ageing research across various institutions in Ireland,

> it seems likely that high profile, cross disciplinary and inter institutional initiatives supported by Atlantic, such as the Irish Longitudinal Study on Ageing (TILDA), have done much to establish ageing as a research priority across the country. Importantly, TILDA will continue to provide a vital piece of knowledge infrastructure that will improve the evidence base for planning, policy and research into the future ... The ability to identify policy related issues, such as the need for regular health assessments, and to track any subsequent effects of policy changes, are significant benefits of this study.

In the view of several of those interviewed, some of the work associated with TILDA would have happened anyway without Atlantic involvement, but more slowly. TILDA would not have been a priority of the Department of Health, so the contribution of Atlantic was significant in getting it up and running. One interviewee (a former secretary general of a government department) noted the importance of TILDA for the long-term development of the country but commented that from a government perspective it was not necessarily urgent or top of the agenda, i.e., if it was between keeping a hospital open and putting money into TILDA, governments are always going to choose the former. This reflects a view that was expressed in other interviews; that the urgent overrides the important in political decision-making, and that Atlantic funding had provided some degree of counterbalance to this.

Centre for Effective Services

The Centre for Effective Services (CES) is an independent, not-for-profit centre established in 2008. CES operates on an all-island basis in both the Republic of Ireland and Northern Ireland with the aim of promoting the development of an evidence-informed approach to policy and practice with those working with children, families, and communities. It had a staff of 32 and expenditure of approximately \$3.1 million at the end of 2015. The work of the centre is jointly funded by Atlantic and the Department of Children and Youth Affairs. It describes itself as part of a new generation of intermediary organizations working in the areas of evidence translation and implementation science. It operates as a body whose "work focuses on enabling dialogue and collaboration across the research-policy-practice boundaries" (Wimbush, 2014). Other similar organizations include the Norwegian Centre for Child Behavioural Development, the Netherlands Youth Institute, and the Dartington Social Research Unit in the United Kingdom.

With regard to influencing government policy and public service reform, the aim was that CES would work with policymakers to provide evidence as to program effectiveness, support implementation, and highlight what does and does not work, and how to improve, with a view to securing improved outcomes. CES uses a range of different evaluation methodologies, both quantitative and qualitative, and employs staff skilled in evidence generation and implementation science.

As well as directly providing a supply of results information for policymakers, CES has taken a role in building capacity amongst policymakers to help them better understand evaluation. For example, they have provided training programs for staff of the Department of Children and Youth Affairs in policy and program evaluation.

Linking Results Information and Policy Outcomes: Influencing the Demand Side for Results Information

Some reference has been made earlier to the role that evidence generated with the support of Atlantic has played in influencing the demand for results information. This section covers the issues in more detail, with an explicit focus on how the results information generated is feeding into the policy and reform process and how it informs demand.

A demand-side initiative pursued by Atlantic was the identification and development of champions of the use of evidence of results information and evaluation within government agencies. A small number of influential individuals at high levels in government departments and agencies (assistant secretary and principal officer in the Irish civil service) in areas where Atlantic were targeting, such as the Department of Children and Youth and the Department of Health, were identified as key individuals to work with, and to support, through for example, in some instances funding of their attendance at international conferences or seminars at which evidence-informed approaches to policymaking were being discussed. The idea was to ensure a cadre of people committed to the generation and use of results-based information within government. This approach worked well with the individuals concerned, in that they have been active in their support for evidence-informed policy development and demanding results-orienting information. But their numbers are small and could not be categorized as a critical mass capable of generating wider change across the system.

As well as this relatively informal approach to influencing demand, an important general point is that Atlantic and government developed a formal means of working with regard to the co-funded initiatives that aimed to help institutionalize demand for results information in the process. A memorandum of understanding (MOU) is agreed and signed by both Atlantic and government agency senior personnel for each initiative which provides the framework for the partnership. This MOU is seen as important in clarifying expectations. The focus on performance and outcomes in the MOU is viewed as particularly helpful in providing a clear sense of direction for the partnership. Having clear, performance-oriented agreements between government and Atlantic was seen as a plus by policy makers, reflecting the more "formal" side of the collaboration. The MOU would include statements setting out the expected outcomes, activities, and evaluation plan, along with reporting requirements and timelines. While in practice this MOU was applied flexibly, to allow for changing circumstances, it provided a backdrop and formalized the demand for evaluation in a way that institutionalized demand for results information into the project or program being developed.

There are also examples of the approach to results information generation promoted by Atlantic, and the evidence itself, feeding into policy documents produced by government and intended to help shape future demand for results information and reform efforts associated with the policy. For example, the Better Outcomes Brighter Futures policy framework for children and younger people (Department of Children and Youth Affairs, 2014) makes a number of references to the need for rigorous results information, influenced by the work jointly supported by government and Atlantic, such as:

> Ensuring that the road to a better future for Ireland's children is not just paved with good intentions means basing investment in evidence-based policies. … Through our investment in the Prevention and Early Intervention Programmes and other initiatives, we have emerging Irish evidence as to what works in supporting children and young people and their parents to achieve better outcomes. This is guiding decisions on where we put our money. The evidence tells us that investment in early years care and education reaps significant dividends throughout a child's life and to society as a result of better outcomes. The evidence confirms the importance of parents particularly in the early years of a child's life and the importance of friendships as children grow into adolescence.
>
> (p. ix)

Another example of government institutionalizing the demand for results information to help assess the effect of policy, influenced by Atlantic engagement on the issue, is illustrated by the fact that the national positive ageing strategy will be tracked by a Healthy and Positive Ageing Outcomes Initiative (HAPAI) focused on providing evidence as to the effectiveness and efficiency of the strategy. Its activities include:

- Formulation of key national indicators of older people's Healthy and Positive Ageing, using research and data already developed especially by TILDA, as well as the Central Statistics Office, and the Health Service Executive's Health & Wellbeing Directorate;
- The establishment of a research fund to commission additional one-off research to fill identified gaps in existing data required to cover all indicators, relevant to the design or configuration of future services and supports for older people;
- Publication of a biennial "State of the Nation's Older Persons" report, topic reports, etc., linking the changes in older people's wellbeing to policy development;
- Cascading of national data to the county level, supplemented by local data collection, and compilation of County Reports in selected counties;
- A physical activity communications program targeted at older people.

Of course, there is no guarantee that just because results information and its importance are cited in policy statements it will be used in practice. It is a necessary but not sufficient condition. But it is an important first step in getting the demand for results information embedded in the landscape of policy and service delivery.

This point is further illustrated by the example of TILDA, where the view of those interviewed who were familiar with TILDA suggested that its impact in its early stages had been greater in the academic field than with policymakers. Interviewees noted that plans had subsequently been put in place to integrate evidence from TILDA more closely into government policy development. For example, TILDA is seen as a key component of the Healthy and Positive Ageing Outcomes Initiative to provide results information to help measure the implementation of the national positive ageing strategy. A dedicated member of the TILDA team is involved in extracting data with which to monitor progress towards the goals and objectives of the strategy and this information will be provided directly to a steering group of government officials assessing the project. This points to the need, when developing demand for results information, for structured government engagement with such results information databases. It is not enough just to ensure that results information is provided, but to take steps, as in the TILDA example cited here, to ensure that policymakers engage with the evidence produced.

The government's general public sector reform plans also include examples of a more structured approach to developing demand for results information to influence policy (Department of Public Expenditure and Reform, 2014). The government is committed to developing a number of results-oriented practices in the context of a revised budgetary and expenditure framework. Evaluations are to be conducted to inform the periodic comprehensive reviews of expenditure. An Irish government economic and evaluation service (IGEES) has been introduced to enhance the role of value for money analysis in policymaking. A public spending code has been developed and a public service evaluation network created to help provide guidance and build capacity. All these initiatives are aimed at supporting the institutionalization of both demand for and the supply of results information (and other forms of evidence). The degree of influence of Atlantic on these developments is unclear, and many other factors have influenced them, not least the imperatives of the fiscal crisis. But interviews with officials indicated that the evidence generation work of Atlantic and its grantees had certainly been a significant contributory factor in determining the evolution of this approach to building demand for more and better results information across government.

Influencing Policy Practice

Ultimately, the aim of Atlantic's joint funding with government of service delivery programs, and their push to enhance the supply of and demand for results information, is to inform and influence policy practice. The intention is to encourage the development of policies that best address the needs of targeted groups (disadvantaged children, people with dementia etc.) and to build the capacity and capability of policymakers to better assess and develop policies.

An example of the effect of providing more robust results information on practice is provided by the experience of the Childhood Development Initiative (CDI) in West Tallaght, Dublin, a joint initiative of the Department of Children and Youth Affairs and The Atlantic Philanthropies. CDI supports the delivery of a range of early intervention and prevention programs to improve outcomes for children living in disadvantaged areas. Amongst the projects supported by CDI were Mate-Tricks and Doodle Den. Mate-Tricks was an after-school program designed to promote pro-social behavior amongst children aged 9–10. The evaluation included a randomized controlled trial to measure the effects of the program on child outcomes and a process evaluation that investigated its implementation. The evaluation found that even though it was implemented well and was positively received by participants, Mate-Tricks did not achieve the changes in outcomes and behaviors which it was designed to support (O'Hare, Kerr, Biggart, & Connolly, 2012). It was decided not to continue with the initiative. If the process evaluation had been the sole evaluation, the likelihood is that the program may have continued, given it was well-received by participants. It was the focus on results as shown by the RCT that prompted the decision to discontinue the program.

Doodle Den aimed at improving literacy outcomes for young children in a disadvantaged community through an after-school literacy program. Using a randomized control trial, the evaluation found improvements in children's overall literacy ability. The evaluation also found that Doodle Den led to improved concentration and reduced problem behaviors in school, an increase in family library activity, and in the child's reading at home (Biggart, Kerr, O'Hare, & Connolly, 2012). The cost of the program was also found to be reasonable, providing good value for money. Since completion of the evaluation, CDI has continued the delivery of Doodle Den in the seven participating schools. It has also been extended to a number of other locations in Ireland.

While the example above shows direct use of results information arising from Atlantic's support for evaluation, on the less positive side, several policymakers interviewed mentioned that they felt the approach adopted by Atlantic to evidence generation and gathering could at times be seen as over-burdensome and overly academic in nature. There was a perceived need amongst some of the interviewees for shorter research or ongoing research briefs more attuned to the demands of the policy environment, where politicians may be reluctant to wait for the results of long-term results-oriented evaluations. Much of the research and evaluation work was carried out by academics in third-level institutions. These academics are driven, in terms of career development, to produce reports for high impact academic journals. By their nature, such reports take time to produce and are often not easily accessible or readily digestible by policymakers.

With regard to RCTs, while the contribution they had made was generally welcomed, policymakers tended to stress that they needed to be mixed with other methodological approaches, such as case studies, that were less costly and timelier in terms of influencing policy. This emphasizes a point made by Devaux-Spatarakis (this volume) that the timeline of the production of impact evaluation results through such means as RCTs can be misaligned with program managers' needs. Several interviewees made the point that there are often limited windows of opportunity to influence political thinking with regard to policy, and if evidence is not available at these times, it can be hard to incorporate it later. Inevitably, methods such as RCTs take some time, sometimes over a number of years, before results are demonstrated. And RCTs alone do not demonstrate the factors that influence the results achieved (hence the need for accompanying process evaluations). Against this, where there are different services and different models being applied, it can be difficult to select where to do an impact evaluation and where to do a more rapid assessment.

A couple of interviewees also felt that in some cases there is a danger that the emphasis on evidence gathering and results-based reporting might make service deliverers more risk averse. The knowledge that they would be judged on specified results might make them less inclined to take risks and innovate.

These more negative points reflect a wider international debate on the relationship between research, evidence, and policy (see for example Nutley, Walter, & Davies, 2007; Ruane, 2012). And they were made in a general context where the evidence-informed approach promoted by Atlantic was seen as welcome and important. It was more a question of trying to get the balance right between rigorous evaluations that may take some years to produce results, and more rapid assessment techniques that give indications of progress that can be used by policymakers in discussions with politicians on policy development. Both are seen to be needed.

The CES experience further illustrates some of the challenges associated with getting results information used in the policy process. There were mixed views emerging from the interviews regarding the effectiveness of CES, particularly in its early years of existence. In general terms, its work with regard to children's programs with the Department of Children and Youth Affairs (a new department established in 2011) has been consistently well-received and regarded as influential. The production of the Ten Years of Learning report (Rochford, Doherty, & Owens, 2014) summarizing learning from the prevention and early intervention initiative was cited as an example of this, feeding as it did into the Better Outcomes Brighter Futures policy statement and the development of the ABC program, an area-based program targeted at improving outcomes for children, young people, and their families in disadvantaged areas. A confluence of a new department open to new ways of working and to evidence generation and a new body such as CES provided a good platform for positive collaboration. CES was also seen to have expertise in this area and to be good at capturing relevant results information and reporting on it in an accessible manner.

In contrast, early experience with CES in working with public officials in the Department of Education and in the sphere of community development were less well-regarded by policy makers. The work done was seen as being of limited use from a policy perspective and was not seen to display particular knowledge of or expertise in the policy fields concerned from the perspective of some interviewees. As a result, it failed to connect with the people best placed to effect reform as they regarded the research as being of limited quality and value. There was also a general concern amongst several policymakers interviewed, essentially for organizational rather than methodological reasons, about outsourcing policy knowledge and expertise, which they felt might be better located within government to build up capacity there rather than with a separate body such as CES.

An independent review of CES found that CES itself also had some difficulties in working with government departments arising from the common experience in the public sector of organizations taking on new mandates on the election of new governments, and changing personnel:

> The shifting roles and remit of Departments across the public service … have created a quite different landscape with changing personalities to one that previously existed. This has hindered the development of inter Departmental relationships and the ability of CES to secure medium-to-longer term commitments to a shared work agenda.
>
> (Prospectus & McMurray, 2012, p. 6)

This review of CES further found mixed views in relation to the effect of CES on strengthening a results orientation in government departments:

> A number of stakeholders questioned if CES has had any real impact in moving key policy makers and service providers to adopting an evidence-informed approach. Whilst it was widely accepted that it is most likely too early to make a definitive call on this at this point in time, it was argued that few noticeable shifts and commitments from the various Government Departments to an evidence-informed approach had been achieved. Findings from the online questionnaire however highlighted that the majority viewpoint held was that CES had significantly supported the case for evidence-based policy and practice.
>
> (Prospectus & McMurray, 2012, p. 9)

CES responded to these concerns and there was a general recognition in the interviews for this study, three years after the evaluation was published, that the relationship with CES across a number of government departments had become more productive. One policymaker noted that there was a need for a bridging mechanism between academics and policymakers, and that CES had helped get alignment between them, providing some understanding between the two worlds; a role seen as important in ensuring effective knowledge brokerage (Lenihan, 2015; Wimbush, 2014). At the start, CES were seen as closer to the academic world, but they now have a better balance.

Genio, an organization funded by Atlantic and government to develop better ways to support disadvantaged people to live full lives in their communities (particularly people with disabilities, mental health difficulties, and dementia) provides a further example of generating results information that is influencing policymakers with regard to the development of new practices in public sector reform. Data from internal and external evaluations carried out and commissioned by Genio showed that personalized supports for people with disabilities, mental health problems, and dementia produce better outcomes for the people supported, irrespective of their impairments and level of functioning, than for those who continued to live in congregated settings or in group homes. The evidence also showed that overall, personalized supports were much less costly for the same people than when they resided in congregated settings (though there were a few cases where the arrangements resulted in higher costs). As Healy and Keogh (2014, pp. 79–80) note:

> Providing evidence was … seen as important, particularly to inform budgetary allocations … In terms of assessing the case for this new paradigm, there is a need to test whether it is more beneficial for service users and also if it is more cost-effective. Evidence was seen as central to this new paradigm, and that therefore there was a need to "walk the walk" on this. Having hard evidence of impact was also seen as important to enlisting the support of the Department of Public Expenditure and Reform and private funders.

In part based on the evidence produced, the Department of Public Expenditure and Reform has been a supporter of the Genio approach and has promoted its role in public service provision and encouraged similar initiatives elsewhere in the public service as part of its wider public sector reform agenda. Of course, if the positive results evidenced had not also been achieved in a more cost-effective manner, there is a question as to whether the degree of buy-in from the Department of Public Expenditure and Reform would have been as great, as an important part of the department's remit is the control of public expenditure. Results information alone is unlikely to be enough to sway support for practice change amongst key influencers who have an expenditure and value for money remit, such as in the Department of Public Expenditure and Reform. But undoubtedly interviewees noted the fact that the evidence showed both positive outcomes and greater cost-effectiveness and was a major contributing factor in winning support from senior officials in the department, and demand for more results information along the lines developed here.

Summary and Conclusions

In recent years, philanthropic organizations in several countries have begun to play an increasing role with regard to the development of social policy and practice by government. There is significant debate internationally on the respective roles of philanthropy and government and the attitudes of one to the other (Harrow & Jung, 2011). The economic downturn, combined with factors such as the growth in "philanthrocapitalism" is leading to a reconfiguration of the roles and responsibilities of governments, civil society, and the private sector with regard to social policy. Increasingly, there is a move towards more partnerships and collaborations between philanthropies, non-governmental organizations, and government. But this presents challenges to all sides as to how to make the collaboration work, and what they want to achieve out of the collaboration.

This chapter has examined one aspect (the development of results information) of one example of collaboration between The Atlantic Philanthropies and the Irish government. Its main focus has been to explore to what extent the collaboration has led to the enhancement of the supply of, demand for, and use of results information on the part of the Irish government.

A number of positive developments emerge from the collaboration. A central benefit of Atlantic involvement has been the additional rigor brought to bear within parts of government with regard to what constitutes good quality results information and what information it is realistic to ask for. Rigor is a word that came up spontaneously in a number of the interviews. A level of analysis has been undertaken that would not have happened otherwise. The creation and existence of Irish cases where there is strong results information providing evidence of what works and what does not is viewed very positively by policymakers.

On the supply side, work supported by Atlantic has fed into wider government public sector reform initiatives with regard to enhancing the results information base, such as the comprehensive reviews of expenditure, longitudinal studies of children and older people, and the operation of the Irish government economic and evaluation service. The importance of results information generation and gathering has been promoted. It was a widespread view of those interviewed that the evidence bases created will remain and provide frameworks for analysis into the future and for the production of guidance for practitioners.

The creation of an intermediary organization, in the form of the Centre for Effective Services, jointly funded by Atlantic and government, is an interesting institutional response to the challenge of building effective supply of results information by creating a body dedicated to the creation of results information and other evaluative data. It has an explicit cross-departmental and indeed cross-national remit and can show some successes in the provision of results information, particularly in the field of children's policy.

On the less positive side, at times the approach to results information generation and gathering was seen as over-burdensome and overly academic in nature. Policymakers favor shorter, focused research pieces more attuned to the demands of the policy environment. To this end, Atlantic is seen as being more successful in having built research and evaluation expertise in academia and NGOs than it has been within government itself. The Centre for Effective Services has received a mixed response in some government departments, and some officials feel that such expertise should more appropriately sit within government departments than in an independent organization so that expertise is developed within government rather than outsourced.

On the demand side, arising from the Atlantic-government collaboration there is a greater awareness amongst some officials of the possibility of testing program expenditure and determining if it is effective, and if not, of shifting resources elsewhere where they may be more productively used. Some "champions" of results information have been created at senior levels in some government departments, providing leadership on this issue. However, it should be noted that several interviewees (as well as a vast body of literature) suggest that shifting expenditure on a large scale remains a challenging and politically sensitive task, despite what results information may show with regard to what works and what does not.

In terms of the central theme of this book, there is some evidence that the collaboration between Atlantic and the Irish government has helped to reduce the gap between the demand for and supply of results information. Key elements of Atlantic's particular contribution have been:

- The creation of data sets and reports that would not have existed otherwise;
- The development of the use of rigorous evaluation techniques in Ireland in the sphere of social programs;
- Development of capacity in results information generation and analysis;
- Structuring of demand for results information through the use of outcome-oriented MOUs and related documents;
- Influencing the views of some key policymakers on the benefits of results information and implementation science in informing policy development and implementation.

A central question, given Atlantic is a time-limited philanthropy whose last grants were given out in 2018, is whether there will be a lasting effect on results information generation and use by government after they have gone? The experience of the dismantling of large elements of the evaluation infrastructure following the diminution of the European Commission role in supporting structural funds evaluation in Ireland provides a cautionary tale in this regard. Some elements of the work, particularly on the supply side, will almost certainly remain. The longitudinal studies are likely to continue. The creation of the Irish Government Economic and Evaluation Service provides an infrastructure for the continuation of much of the learning on results information within government departments. The demand side is where the greater challenges are likely to present themselves. Without an outside body such as Atlantic or the European Commission to prompt demand for the use of results information, and if the economy continues to improve, past history would suggest that the pressure for an examination of the results achieved by government programs is likely to reduce. The prospects would seem to depend more on institutionalizing demand if the gap between supply and demand of results information is to continue to close.

Note

1 Much of the information for this paper arose from a research study by the author funded by The Atlantic Philanthropies titled "Influencing Government Policy and Practice." The aim of this study is to examine the extent to which the approach adopted by The Atlantic Philanthropies of working with government to influence government policy and practice, with a particular focus on public service reform, can be considered innovative and successful.

References

Biggart, A., Kerr, K., O'Hare, L., & Connolly, P. (2012). *Evaluation of the effectiveness of the Childhood Development Initiative's Doodle Den literacy programme*. Dublin: Childhood Development Initiative (CDI).

Boyle, R. (2014). *The state of policy evaluation in Ireland.* State of the Public Service Research Paper No. 14. Dublin: Institute of Public Administration.

Cochrane, A., McGilloway, S., Furlong, M., & Donnelly, M. (2013). The role and contribution of philanthropy to the lives of older people in Ireland. *The International Journal of Ageing and Society*, *2*, 13–23.

Department of Children and Youth Affairs. (2014). *Better outcomes brighter futures: The national policy framework for children & young people 2014–2020*. Dublin: The Stationery Office.

Department of Finance. (2004). *First formal report to the Minister for Finance by the Expenditure Review Central Steering Committee: Expenditure review initiative*. Dublin: Department of Finance.

Department of Public Expenditure and Reform. (2011). *Public service reform*. Dublin: Department of Public Expenditure and Reform.

Department of Public Expenditure and Reform. (2014). *Public service reform plan 2014–2016*. Dublin: Department of Public Expenditure and Reform.

Harrow, J., & Jung, T. (2011). Philanthropy is dead: Long live philanthropy? *Public Management Review*, *13*, 1047–1056.

Healy, J. A., & Keogh, F. (2014). Exploring a model of public services reform – A case of the Genio organisation. *Administration*, *62*, 55–90.

Hegarty, D. (2003, June 26–27). *Framework for the evaluation of the structural funds in Ireland.* Paper prepared for Fifth European Conference on the Evaluation of the Structural Funds, Budapest.

Lenihan, A. T. (2015). Institutionalising evidence-based policy: International insights into knowledge brokerage. *Contemporary Social Science*, *10*, 114–125.

Little, M., & Abunimah, A. (2007). Improving outcomes for children in the island of Ireland: The role of philanthropic investment. *Journal of Children's Services*, *2*, 60–68.

Nutley, S. M., Walter, I., & Davies, H. T. O. (2007). *Using evidence: How research can improve public services*. Bristol: The Policy Press.

O'Hare, L., Kerr, K., Biggart, A., & Connolly, P. (2012). *Evaluation of the effectiveness of the Childhood Development Initiative's Mate-Tricks pro-social behaviour after-school programme*. Dublin: Childhood Development Initiative (CDI).

O'Neill, D., Twomey, C., & O'Shea, E. (2009). Ireland. In E. Palmore, S. Kunkel, & F. Whittington (Eds), *The international handbook on aging* (pp. 283–296). Santa Barbara: Praeger Pubs.

O'Shea E., & Conboy, P. (2005). *Planning for an ageing population: Strategic considerations*. Dublin: National Council on Ageing and Older People.

Prospectus, & McMurray, A. (2012). *Centre for Effective Services review of outcomes and impact 2008–2011*. Dublin: Centre for Effective Services.

Rochford, S., Doherty, N., & Owens, S. (2014). *Prevention and early intervention in children and young people's services: Ten years of learning*. Dublin: Centre for Effective Services.

Ruane, F. (2012). Research evidence and policymaking in Ireland. *Administration, 60*, 119–138.

UNICEF (2010). *Advocacy toolkit*. New York: UNICEF.

Wimbush, E. (2014). Reshaping evaluation to enhance utilization in Scotland: The role of intermediary bodies in knowledge-to-action strategies. In M. Läubli Loud & J. Mayne (Eds.), *Enhancing evaluation use: Insights from internal evaluation units* (pp. 83–112). Thousand Oaks, CA: Sage.

5 Evaluation One Step Removed

The Government/Not-for-Profit Performance Nexus

David Gilchrist and Peter Wilkins

It has been the case for a number of decades that governments have increasingly relied upon not-for-profit and voluntary organizations (NFPOs) to deliver human services related to their social policy objectives. Governments have taken this road for a number of reasons, including that it is seen as a cheaper form of service delivery, it is more flexible, and because NFPOs are closer to the community thus having more opportunities for identifying need, demand, and for assessing the relative impact of programs (Gilchrist & Butcher, 2016; Mendes, 2008; Productivity Commission, 2010; Wilkins & Gilchrist, 2016).

The continued growth in the level of service commissioning by governments also raises some political and public policy issues as governments have become increasingly tied to the sector (having gradually reduced their capacity for service delivery over time as a result of the transition of publicly provided services to publicly funded, NFPO-provided services). Notwithstanding this increasing reliance, governments have sought to reduce expenditure, control service delivery, and enjoy the political capital that arises from such activities. On the other side of this nexus, NFPOs have been challenged with poor resourcing (Zhai et al., 2017), increasing pressure to perform more with less, the buffeting of funder priorities impacting the NFPOs' capacity to pursue their mission as they see it, and an almost universal view that market-style funding arrangements will result in better outcomes for service recipients (Center for Law and Social Policy, 2014; Garton, 2009; Gilchrist & Wilkins, 2016; McGregor-Lowndes, 2008; Roth, 2011).

Whatever the pressures, the funding of services provided by NFPOs is, largely, provided by the public purse and so there has always been, and will continue to be, a need to account for the provision of these resources. Equally, there has been a growing concern that the provision of the more traditional acquittal[1] style information does not effectively provide the necessary transparency, accountability or planning information which assists all interested parties, including service users, to assess NFPO operational impact. Increasingly then, NFPOs and governments have been under pressure to report their outcomes and undertake evaluations rather than the more traditional reporting arrangements that have included the reporting of outputs and the provision of audited accounts to government funding agencies (Buckmaster, 1999; Shergold, 2016; Victorian Auditor-General, 2010). In this context, both intended and unintended impacts need to be considered (Gilchrist & Butcher, 2016).

To identify the challenges and opportunities in evaluating outcomes and impacts where there is a nexus between independent bodies, this chapter examines interactions between NFPOs and government agencies in one state of the Australian federation – Western Australia. The experience in this jurisdiction is particularly informative because the Western Australian government established a policy – and developed infrastructure for its implementation – intended to re-shape the relationship between the not-for-profit sector and the state government in order to redesign the governance and acquittal framework away from inputs and outputs management, and toward outcomes reporting. This was intended to support better service delivery evaluation and flexibility in service procurement and delivery, both driven by the client's preferences.

Much has been written about the need for change in the relationships between governments and NFPOs and, in particular, on NFPO funding (Barraket, 2008; Frances & Cuskelly, 2008; Gilchrist & Knight, 2014; Gilchrist & Wilkins, 2016; Office of the Auditor-General (Western Australia), 2000, 2003 & 2013; Productivity Commission, 2010; Public Accounts Committee Western Australia, 2000; Wilkins & Gilchrist, 2016). However, it is the experience and challenges faced by commissioning government agencies that has not been well examined to date. This chapter focuses on this perspective. It considers the demand for impact-related evaluation and comments on the supply of these evaluations. Overall, the recent active policy environment has reinvigorated the commissioning agencies but inhibitors to achieving the policy objectives have been encountered. These include both institutional and operational inhibitors.

The chapter is presented in five sections (including this introduction). In the next section we describe the main features of the government's policy initiatives and in a following section we summarize the results of a series of evaluations of these initiatives principally from the government commissioning perspective (Gilchrist, 2016). The results of these evaluations are then discussed in a further section in the context of the broader literature and in the final section we draw conclusions regarding impact evaluation where there is a nexus between independent bodies.

Western Australian Policy Initiatives

The Western Australian government established the "Delivering Community Services in Partnership Policy" (DCSP) in 2011 which saw the establishment of the Partnership Forum – a body consisting of senior bureaucrats and NFPO executives – meeting regularly with a view to enhancing client-centric service delivery, increasing resources to the NFPO sector, and creating an outcomes evaluation environment. The shift to outcomes evaluation replaced an antiquated acquittals process in place up to that time.

The DCSP stated that:

> [p]rior to commencing any funding or contracting activities, Public Authorities must have regard to the desired impact or change they are seeking to achieve within the community … [and] are encouraged to recognize the valuable contribution that the not-for-profit community sector plays in the delivery of Community Services and should work towards collaboratively defining and articulating community outcomes.
>
> (Government of Western Australia, 2011, p. 7)

The style of funding arrangement developed out of the DCSP has also been referred to as "Individualized Funding and Person Centered Care." The intention is that the funding be provided to the service user and that a quasi-market funding arrangement allows the service user (either actually or figuratively) to make decisions about what services they receive, when they receive them, and from whom they are supplied. Ultimately, it is expected that the outcomes achieved as a result will be significantly improved over those achieved under previous funding arrangements. As can be imagined, this change was significant and challenged both NFPOs and the commissioning government agencies because the implementation required changes in policy, process, and practice away from traditional methods of commissioning, acquittal, and service delivery.

While this quasi-market style of funding arrangement has gained significant traction in Australia (and across the Anglophone world), it also presents significant challenges. These challenges include that outcomes can be very difficult to identify, quantify, and report. Further, the time required to achieve human services outcomes does not always conform to the annual reporting process that aligns with government reporting and appropriations. Costs associated with outcomes reporting can be significant and the assurance of reported data adds additional cost to the traditional audit process (Gilchrist & Knight, 2014). These challenges are faced by NFPOs, who have to develop outcomes reporting processes, and commissioning government agencies, who have to contract for, assess, and react to outcomes reported.

Evaluation is to play an important role in the change process. The DCSP stated that:

> [c]onsistent with the Partnership Principles and the requirements of the Policy, Public Authorities must have a review and evaluation system in place that will meet accountability requirements, preserve the integrity of processes, aid in maintaining the Public Authority's knowledge base and contribute to the identification of areas for improvement. There is a need to review the outcomes of each agreement against the original service objectives – the outcomes of which, should feed into the next round of needs assessment.
>
> (Government of Western Australia, 2011, p. 14)

The government instructed all its agencies involved in commissioning NFPOs to provide human services delivery to implement the requirements of the DCSP. It also established a unit within the Department of Finance with responsibility for oversight of the transition, to provide training and resources to both the Public Sector and the NFPO sector in order to support implementation, and to provide ad hoc advice. The forum also established a sub-group focused upon the evaluation of the implementation of the DCSP Policy as well as an additional sub-group focused on service commissioning.

An important consideration in the success of the intended shift to an outcomes-based relationship between agencies and NFPOs is the commissioning agencies' capacity (or lack of) to implement the requirements of the DCSP, and to re-engineer their processes and foci to ensure person-centered, outcomes-focused evaluation arrangements successfully replaced the previous arrangements.

While there was considerable angst and some commentary warning of the challenges ahead if the government pursued the DCSP (Rainnie, Fitzgerald, Gilchrist, & Morris, 2012) by and large, the NFPO sector and the public sector approached the new policy in good faith. International experience was examined with the intention of informing practice (Gilchrist & Knight, 2014). However, from the NFPO sector's perspective, the transition was probably made more palatable with a significant injection of funding by the state government. To maintain a supplier-sustainable price for service purchases, the government provided top-up funding in order to meet systemic underfunding identified via the Partnership Forum (Gilchrist & Knight, 2013a, 2013b).

Evaluation of the Policy Initiatives

Overall, the adoption of the DCSP Policy was intended to increase the sustainability of the NFPO sector, reduce administrative burden, and build capacity for increased work to be transferred from the government sector to the NFPO sector. It was also aimed at ensuring service users were in control of the services they accessed, and that accountability and evaluation arrangements were centered upon the outcomes achieved rather than the outputs created.

As such, the evaluation process was aimed at assessing, on an annual basis, the extent to which the above had been achieved to date. In undertaking the evaluation of the DCSP Policy, focus was placed on outcomes achieved in relation to the following areas which were also the central foci of the policy itself: a) NFPO sustainability, b) DCSP Policy implementation (principally in relation to the establishment of outcomes-based contracts and increased service delivery), and c) the impact of the DCSP Policy on NFPOs and agencies.

Of course, there were a number of practical impediments to the immediate and universal rolling out of this policy. These included: that old-style contracts were still to run their course, the new DCSP contracts not being implemented until contracts were renewed; some agencies experimented with a small number of funded NFPOs in order to consider the practical aspects of identifying and reporting outcomes thus delaying the full roll-out; and agencies needed to build capacity themselves to be able to respond effectively to the policy.

Evaluations were carried out for each of the three years from 2012 to 2014. The principle focus here is on the results for the evaluation of the 2014 year (Knight & Gilchrist, 2015). This is because the 2012 evaluation results constituted baseline data while the 2013 evaluation results only added an additional year. Focusing on the 2014 results allows us to consider both the position at a point in time and the trajectory based on the three-year trend.

In evaluating the implementation and impact of the DCSP relating to commissioning agencies, it is necessary to articulate the areas where the policy was intended to create benefits relating to evaluation. First, implementation of the policy and outcomes contracting is important as we would expect that old-style contracts were gradually replaced with new style contracts with a central theme being the placement of outcomes reporting at the center rather than outputs reporting. We would also expect that contract terms would be extended in order to meet efficiency objectives also described in the policy as extending contract periods to reduce transaction costs under the relatively more expensive outcomes reporting regime. Second, we would expect that agencies would have built the necessary capacity in terms of outcomes contracting skills amongst commissioning staff, and that the necessary infrastructure would have been established in order to manage contracts and assess program outcomes under the new contracting regime.

DCSP Policy Implementation and Outcomes Contracting

In terms of contracting in accordance with the DCSP, agencies needed to be transitioning the contracts they had issued to procure human services from NFPOs from traditional contracting models including acquittal processes and outputs reporting, to contract frameworks that identified, quantified, and reported upon outcomes achieved.

Approximately half (6 out of 13) agencies indicated that more than 80 percent of their contracts issued conformed with the DCSP Policy. Agencies reported transitioning contracts to comply with the DCSP Policy as service agreements were renewed. The progress made by agencies mostly reflects the number of contracts they have with service providers that have longer terms, with some agencies reporting that they were waiting for five-year contracts to expire.

However, there are other elements that also affected the extent to which agencies were able to comply. For instance, the state disability agency's transition to the DCSP Policy was being affected by national Individualized Funding arrangements and the roll-out of a new National Disability Insurance Scheme (NDIS).[2] The Child Protection Agency was also affected by Commonwealth/state funding arrangements in that it had a number of contracts still under the older Funding and Purchasing Policy Framework as they were jointly funded by the state and Commonwealth and these contracts are subject to ongoing negotiations about future funding.

As at June 30, 2014, approximately two-thirds (66 percent) of contracts were reported by agencies to comply with the DCSP Policy which was a substantial increase from a year earlier when approximately one-quarter (27 percent) complied.

However, NFPO responses indicated that approximately two-thirds (65 percent) believed that the initiatives had not resulted in any change to services or that they could not tell if services had improved. They indicated that in most cases, service providers self-evaluate and report on their performance, and that budgets for evaluating performance were often very small or non-existent (Knight & Gilchrist, 2015).

Defining, measuring, and monitoring performance against outcomes was reported to be a significant challenge. Agencies reported that nearly all contracts under the DCSP still contained quantitative output elements, with only a few stating that they had more than half of their contracts with clearly defined outcomes or that included statements on the quantitative outcomes to be achieved. In nearly all cases, agencies relied on NFPOs to self-report against contract specifications.

Additionally, agency comments highlighted the ongoing challenges with specifying outcomes. For instance, one commissioning officer commented:

> The difficulty in defining outcomes varies dependent on [the] type of services being procured. Evaluating performance against outcomes is even more difficult, particularly evaluating [the] on-going impact of service provision compared with perceived impact at time of exit. Some services have outcomes that seek long term behavior/attitude changes that are difficult to measure or [are] resource intensive to measure. Evaluation of these outcomes also requires longitudinal studies that are resource intensive and generally not undertaken by the Department. For services in joint State/Commonwealth funded programs the Outcomes and Outcome Indicators/Measures are sometimes predetermined in the bilateral agreement.

This comment raises significant questions about how rigorously agencies are applying the term "outcomes" in their responses to the evaluation surveys and whether the DCSP sets an unrealistic requirement for across-the-board outcome-based contracting, at least in the medium term.

Commissioning is costly for agencies and one objective of the DCSP was to introduce longer-term contracts in order to reduce contracting costs to both agencies and NFPOs. In this study, agencies commented that they are seeking to extend the term of service agreements and, in most cases, agencies reported using three-year contracts, with two one-year options to extend.

Approximately one in ten (11 percent) of service agreements had a term of less than three years and over half (54 percent) were for a term of either three to five years or for longer than five years.[3] However, there were situations in which short-term contracts needed to be used. For example, during the transition to the National Disability Insurance Scheme, the disability services agency was not able to extend contracts beyond June 30, 2016, the intended commencement date of the new scheme. Agencies also reported using shorter-term contracts as an interim measure in order to align individual agreements with those in other program areas.

In the context of open tender commissioning guidelines, agencies reported that they made significant use of the "Preferred Service Provider" status (PSP) of many of their NFPO contract partners in order to contain the costs of the commissioning process under the DCSP, notwithstanding that one goal of the DCSP is to encourage more open tendering. PSP status is used in preference to open tendering in order that long-established relationships with providers are able to be used to efficiently contract while reducing supply-side risk that may accrue from open tendering and appointing unknown/inexperienced providers. Such long-term relationships also prospectively allow for the redesign of contracts under the DCSP to be negotiated more effectively as the parties are well known to each other.

The extent to which agreements are awarded on a PSP basis varied greatly across agencies. Agencies reported seeking to increase the use of open tendering where possible, but there are many sound reasons for using a closed or PSP commissioning arrangement for human services. These include: to maintain service continuity and efficiency; in acknowledgement of the need for some service users to maintain a strong relationship with their providers in order to achieve better outcomes; and due to the lack of alternative viable providers. These factors are more prevalent in some service areas and locations than others.

Agency Capacity

Agencies commented that responding to changes in commissioning policy had been a main focus over recent years and had involved restructuring and redrafting tender and contract documents to ensure compliance. Increased costs were incurred across all of these activities as a result of the allocation of additional staff and because the challenges faced were often outside of the experience of those officers involved.

Agency staff have continued to participate in a wide range of training activities and most agencies reported that all relevant staff had received some initial training. In 2014, six of the reviewed 13 agencies rated their staff's current understanding of how to implement the DCSP Policy as "very good," five as "good" and one as "fair."

Agencies also reported strengthening their approaches to managing contract information and, while these changes reflect a maturing of contract management and use of contracts data, and improvements in data availability, it was observed that limits to the information collection approaches continued to hinder the collection of accurate and comparable data necessary to fully evaluate the implementation of the DCSP Policy. For instance, the range of data contained in databases had not changed significantly between 2012 and 2014.

Few agencies reported collecting information on the service outcomes to be achieved. In most cases, this data was recorded within the individual service agreement files rather than in a consolidated form, thus reducing agency capacity for aggregate, whole-of-program reporting.

Service agreement information was predominantly used for tracking contract end dates and commissioning cycles, and most agencies used it to plan future commissioning. Agencies continued to comment that the DCSP Policy has increased the amount of time required to procure and manage services. In most cases, agencies saw positive outcomes from the increased requirements, but felt under pressure to achieve the WA Government's policy objectives within the resources available. The increase in administrative burden arose from both the procedures required and the need to specify and measure outcomes, which can be particularly challenging for some services.

Evaluation of the DCSP Policy

The need for the continued independent evaluation of the implementation and impacts of the DCSP is well understood by the Western Australian parliament. A condition of voting the appropriation providing significant funding increases to NFPOs providing human services, in a parliament supporting a government with a very small majority, was that the government would undertake an evaluation of the DCSP annually for five years. It is hoped that this level of transparency will allow agencies, NFPOs, and other stakeholders to honestly appraise the impact of the DCSP and to respond to challenges in a meaningful and effective way to ensure, above all else, that the opportunity for outcomes reporting is enhanced with regard to the provision of human services in Western Australia.

The Western Australian Initiatives in Context

The reporting by agencies that they are moving towards outcome-based contracting is an encouraging indication that they have recognized the importance of this change. However, the responses indicated that they have not specified clearly defined outcomes on a consistent basis, which, in turn, indicates that there is a substantial gap between the policy and what is being achieved. A reported case demonstrates this neatly.

Case Study of the Nexus Between WA Agency and NFPO Outcomes and Evaluation

The state government child protection agency reported its performance in relation to out-of-home care under an outcome "Children and young people in the CEO's care receive a high quality of care and have much improved life chances." While this captured an outcome element focused on improved life opportunities, the effectiveness indicators reported do not address this aspect of the outcome statement. Instead, the agency reported two effectiveness indicators for 2014–2015 that related to the stability of placements and that principles for the placement of Aboriginal children established by legislation were met (Department for Child Protection and Family Support [CPFS], 2014, pp. 43–44).

Budget papers for the agency indicated that for 2015–2016, a revised reporting approach would include four effectiveness indicators, one based on compliance with the statutory principles for the placement of Aboriginal children (as above), another on meeting set timeframes for undertaking comprehensive care planning, and two capturing two aspects of the children's perceptions of their care relating to whether they felt safe and felt supported in their care arrangement (Government of Western Australia, 2015, p. 421). Notwithstanding such a review of their reporting, it is still evident that this does not address directly the improved life opportunities component of the outcome statement.

The agency observed that a pilot has been conducted of delegated case management for children in long term, stable placements with community sector organizations and which would be the subject of a joint evaluation "... inform[ing] the expansion of this pilot" (CPFS, 2014, p. 23).

It also reported in a completed evaluation that had reviewed a program that had supported 965 families (2,852 clients) in its first two years that the service had diverted families from the child protection system and engaged them with more appropriate support services at an earlier stage. The evaluation also identified opportunities to improve the network to enhance service delivery to clients (CPFS, 2014, p. 28).

Challenges Regarding Outcome Specification

The Western Australian experience appears to be similar to that across the country. This is illustrated by a survey of not-for-profit CEOs in 2014 which found that only a minority (28 percent) believe there were clearly defined outcomes in the social system in Australia, and even fewer (15 percent) believe that there were effective measures of these outcomes (PricewaterhouseCoopers, 2014).

The capacity for a service agreement to be defined in terms of outcomes varies widely. In many cases, the outcome from a community service (such as counselling, child protection, or disability services) cannot be easily specified or quantified and/or it can take years or even decades for the outcome to become apparent.

To some extent, the use of longer-term contracts is an enabler that helps to overcome the challenge of long-duration outcomes. Nevertheless, these issues represent a key methodological inhibitor to further progress the implementation of outcome-based contracting.

A review of the effect of government-funded outcome-based contracts in public human services has also observed that the outcome metrics used to date have not aligned well with the desired outcomes (Tomkinson, 2016).

In methodological terms, there is no doubt that the evidence points to real challenges experienced by agency commissioning staff. The lack of experience and capacity in this area meant that methodological challenges such as the identification of suitable outcomes, timeliness of outcomes development, timeliness of contracting, and the reporting timeframe were all inhibitors to the replacement of outputs reporting for outcomes reporting.

As such, another important enabler is access to relevant evaluation skills to ensure that concepts around outcomes are well understood and relevant issues can be addressed. While the evaluations of the DCSP Policy identified that agency staff skills were improving, they did not specifically identify if this included skills for accessing, conducting, and assessing outcome and impact evaluations.

The Supply of Evaluations

An overview of evaluations conducted for Western Australian human services is provided by an assessment of better practice programs by the Western Australian Commissioner for Children and Young People (CCYP). Criteria across three domains were used to assess the evidence: Evaluation effectiveness; Supporting evidence/theory, Replicability; and Innovation and cultural reach. The CCYP observed that while there was widespread advocacy for evidence-based practice in child and family welfare programs and service provision, there was a

> … dearth of research evidence in certain areas of child and family support. In cases where there is a lack of evidence supporting an initiative, and yet an initiative is clearly necessary, actions may need to be based on limited evidence, expert opinion and "practice wisdom," or the best available theory.
>
> (Commissioner for Children and Young People [CCYP], 2012, p. 101)

Across two reports there were a total of 63 programs operating in WA (CCYP, 2014). Forty-six of these were rated as Best Practice Programs (Table 5.1), the remainder being designated "Promising Programs" because they were assessed as showing "promise" in terms of their benefits for young people's wellbeing but their evaluations (although positive) did not meet the criteria established for the study by the Australian Institute of Family Studies (AIFS).

Three wellbeing domains (Education, Subjective Wellbeing, and Behaviors and Risks) provide almost two-thirds (30 out of 46) of the Best Practice Programs. Although unevenly distributed across the domains, the number of programs

Table 5.1 WA-based Best Practice Programs (CCYP 2012 and 2014)

Education	*Material Wellbeing*	*Family and Peer Relationships*	*Subjective Wellbeing*	*Behaviors and Risks*	*Other*	*Total*
13	4	5	9	8	7	46

listed indicates that some community service programs can be evaluated effectively.

A review of progress with outcomes measurement in the WA community sector identified the use of a proprietary approach to mapping outcomes (Outcomes star) by five NFPOs in areas such as accommodation and outreach services in the mental health sector (Adams, Flatau, Zaretzy, McWilliam, & Smith, 2015, p. 10). Similarly, Results-Based Accountability (RBA) was reported to be used by six NFPOs including one that had implemented RBA in over 60 services and had assisted over 20 organizations with RBA.

In addition, another was reported to have been funded by the Department of Local Government and Communities to trial RBA with nine community organizations (Adams et al., 2015, p. 11). It was also observed that changes to a procurement process by the government drug and alcohol agency represented a "... clear example of a policy effort to focus attention on measuring and achieving outcomes in the drug and alcohol sector" (Adams et al., 2015, p. 16).

A related survey of outcomes measurement in the Western Australian community sector found that the majority of organizations surveyed believed that they understood their outcomes well (73 percent) and that they measured outcomes (72 percent). Furthermore, of those that measure outcomes, the majority (71 percent) measured outcomes for all (31 percent) or most (40 percent) of their activities. However, customer satisfaction surveys and case studies or interviews were the most commonly used data, with organization-specific questionnaires used by approximately half (51 percent) of respondents. Concern was expressed about the low use of longitudinal data, it being critical to assessing the impact of programs over time.

The survey also found considerable differences in capacity for outcomes measurement between smaller and larger organizations, with almost half (47 percent) of larger organizations using technology-assisted data collection whereas less than one in six (15 percent) of smaller organizations did so. Further, almost one in five larger organizations had access to external measurement consultants (19 percent) compared with slightly over one in ten smaller organizations (11 percent). Similarly, almost one in five metropolitan organizations had access to external measurement consultants (18 percent) compared with slightly less than one in ten non-metropolitan organizations (9 percent). There were also differences in favor of larger and metropolitan organizations in relation to access to specialized data collection staff and having a research and evaluation unit (Flatau, Adams, & Seivwright, 2016).

There has been a broader recognition of the need for better human services outcomes information. For instance, the New South Wales Auditor-General has reported that the Department of Family and Community Services has measures for out-of-home care that focus mainly on outputs rather than wellbeing outcomes for children. This is reflected in NGO contracts, which include only one measure: the percentage of successful adoptions and restorations to their birth family, which could be viewed as an outcome measure. The Auditor-General identified that having baseline information on children's health, education, and welfare would allow a reference point from which to track changes in their wellbeing and that they would also enable NGOs to be accountable for their contribution to these outcomes. Potential wellbeing measures were identified as including children attending and completing schooling, having fewer health problems, and participating in sports and social activities.

Similarly, the New South Wales Government has supported a longitudinal study of children in care. It is following over 4,000 children and young people throughout their time in out-of-home care – measuring their physical health, cognitive and learning abilities, and socio-emotional wellbeing (Department of Family and Community Services [NSW], 2015).

Likewise, a survey of NFPO directors rated third and fourth of the top three things they could do better to have the most impact as performance monitoring and evaluation of individual services/programs (Australian Institute of Company Directors, 2016).

Barriers to Further Progress

More generally, the commissioning aspects of the DCSP constitute considerable change which was not necessarily within the workforce skills base. Lack of financial resources meant that training was not as substantial as it could have been, although agencies did report that they had taken advantage of centrally organized training established by the Department of Finance. The fact that this agency was tasked with establishing training for both the NFPO and government sectors suggest that both sectors were recipients of the same message, thus reinforcing the DCSP.

Notwithstanding these barriers, other institutional and, to a lesser extent, operational inhibitors, have been found to be important in inhibiting progress. The institutional inhibitors additional to workforce skills are financial, infrastructural intergovernmental, and operational.

Financial Inhibitors

The cost of commissioning, monitoring, and acquitting is high. It is arguable that this is also appropriate given that funding levels provided to the NFPO sector by the Western Australian government are considerable and this funding needs to be accounted for as it is public funds. However, the drive to implement the DCSP in government agencies within the parameters of current resourcing levels means that the agencies were stretched and were meeting the requirements of the policy by increments over time rather than immediately. For instance, some agencies reported increasing their commissioning staff establishment to the detriment of other areas of operation in order to meet the requirements of the policy. The agencies reported that they continued to use the Preferred Service Provider status in order to truncate the contracting process and to allow for better communications between commissioner and contractor during the establishment phase – this practice provides an interesting example of agencies choosing not to align with the DCSP encouragement of open tendering.

Infrastructural Inhibitors

The setting up of a central office intended to drive the implementation of the DCSP from both the government side and the NFPO side was an important piece of infrastructure that, over time, is likely to maintain momentum, build necessary infrastructure (such as contracts, models, and reporting arrangements), and to report to central government with respect to the implementation of the policy.

The effectiveness of the Department of Finance as a central agency and the capacity for government as a whole to report progress with regard to the DCSP was inhibited by the lack of administrative infrastructure within commissioning agencies. Of particular interest here is the lack of capacity for collecting and reporting data relating to contracting arrangements at an aggregate agency level. Poor database establishment and management will likely affect the capacity of agencies to demonstrate their effectiveness in relation to the DCSP.

More generally, it is reasonable to question whether the approach of establishing a compact between government and NFPOs provides a sound basis to establish an outcome-focused approach. While a review of compacts across the country indicated that they were not in general sustained, the DCSP differed from approaches elsewhere as:

> … the government and the sector have eschewed a bilateral compact in favor of a comprehensive policy statement; and a centre-right government appears to have succeeded in negotiating a settlement with the sector where a centre-left government demonstrably failed.
>
> (Butcher, 2015, p. 309)

Intergovernmental Inhibitors

Intergovernmental issues have also been identified as significant inhibitors. The Australian Federation has an impact on the implementation process for the DCSP. In Australia, there is a persistent and significant vertical fiscal imbalance between the Commonwealth (federal government) and the states and territories. This results in the states receiving Commonwealth funding for human services delivery (amongst other things) and in NFPOs being funded directly by the Commonwealth.

The intentions of the state government with respect to enhancing outcomes reporting may be frustrated by agreements with the Commonwealth that establish differing funding arrangements. The arrangements for this funding can obviate against the DCSP and the impact of the NDIS is a case in point.

For instance, the Commonwealth disability agency (the NDIA) does not have any outcome reporting requirements and it does not necessarily even want a relationship with service providers, believing that market pressures will focus service providers toward outcomes. The NFPOs involved do not report any information – outcomes or otherwise – to the Commonwealth disability agency although they have been required to report this kind of information for the funding provided for services commissioned by the state disability agency.

Concluding Remarks

In the context of the broad review of outcome-based contracting in public human services it was observed that there may be both "… a lack of capacity in the public sector to build and define outcome-based contracts for service, as well as a lack of capacity within delivery organizations to negotiate and deliver them" (Tomkinson, 2016, p. 13).

Both of these areas of capacity need to be taken into account by public sector managers charged with the implementation of outcome-based contracts. They also need to be taken into account when considering the timeliness of change and the practicalities related to redesigning the focus of contracting in complex, publicly funded human services that have operated in a particular way for three decades or more.

On the demand side for evaluation, the Western Australian experience identifies that there are significant practical impediments to achieving change toward an effective outcome reporting framework. These include: in relation to agency staff skills, staff numbers, the building of adequate contracting databases, the time it takes to contract for outcomes, system redesign, and the impacts of multiple jurisdictional interests within a federation.

On the supply side for evaluation, similar impediments manifest themselves. Lack of skills and experience, lack of financial capacity, infrastructural deficiencies, and lack of funding available for investment directed to strengthen the role of evaluation all conflate to challenge NFPOs.

Practical elements also act to impede both the demand and supply of evaluation in this area. For instance, human services are complex and lack the homogeneity useful in standardizing contractual arrangements. This lack of homogeneity also restricts the aggregation of evidence and reporting at a corporate level. Further, the realization of human services outcomes can take more than a reporting year to manifest – some can take decades and some generations. This reality conflicts with the important need of public sector agencies to acquit funding on an annual basis and for the risks associated with value for money imperatives as well as the need to ensure policy outcomes are achieved within a timeframe that is politically palatable.

With these institutional and operational inhibitors in play, advancing our understanding of the impacts of government-funded human services delivered by third parties remains more of an ambition than an achievable goal. Addressing the inhibitors in a coordinated fashion through a firmly embedded and broadly-based partnership between governments and NFPOs is essential if substantial progress is going to be made in achieving this goal.

Notes

1 In Australia, an "acquittal" is a written account of how grant funds received for a particular purpose have been spent.
2 The National Disability Insurance Scheme (NDIS) was established in 2012 and constitutes Australia's first national scheme focused on the provision of services to people living with disability. As such, it is a Commonwealth (or federal) scheme replacing previously state-funded schemes.
3 This data has not been compared with 2013 due to inconsistencies in agency reporting.

References

Adams, S., Flatau, P., Zaretzy K., McWilliam, D., & Smith, J. (2015). *Measuring the difference we make: The state-of-play of outcomes measurement in the community sector in Western Australia.* Bankwest Foundation Social Impact Series, No. 3. Western Australia: Bankwest Foundation.

Australian Institute of Company Directors. (2016). *NFP performance and governance study: Australia's NFP sector | Raising the bar 2016.* Sydney, AUS: Australian Institute of Company Directors. Retrieved from http://aicd.companydirectors.com.au/~/media/cd2/resources/advocacy/research/pdf/05365-nfp-governance-and-performance-study-2016-web-v2.ashx?la=en

Barraket, J. (Ed.). (2008). Strategic issues for the not-for-profit sector. Sydney: University of New South Wales Press.

Buckmaster, N. (1999). Associations between outcome measurement, accountability and learning for non-profit organizations. *International Journal of Public Sector Management, 12*, 186–197.

Butcher, J. (2015). Australian sub-national compacts with the not-for-profit sector: Pathways to cross-sector cooperation. In J. Wanna, E. A. Lindquist, & P. Marshall (Eds.), *New accountabilities, new challenges*. Canberra: ANU Press, The Australian National University.

Center for Law and Social Policy. (2014). *Social impact bonds: Overview and considerations.* Washington DC: Center for Law and Social Policy. Retrieved from www.clasp.org/resources-and-publications/publication-1/CLASP-Social-Impact-Bonds-SIBs-March-2014.pdf

Commissioner for Children and Young People (CCYP). (2012). *Building blocks: Best practice programs that improve the wellbeing of children and young people – Edition One*. Subiaco, Western Australia: Commissioner for Children and Young People. Retrieved from www.ccyp.wa.gov.au/media/1141/report-building-blocks-edition-one-february-2012.pdf

Commissioner for Children and Young People (CCYP). (2014). *Building blocks: Best practice programs that improve the wellbeing of children and young people – Edition Two.* Subiaco, Western Australia: Commissioner for Children and Young People. Retrieved from www.ccyp.wa.gov.au/media/1142/report-building-blocks-edition-two-july-2014.pdf

Department for Child Protection and Family Support (CPFS). (2014). *Annual report 2013–14.* East Perth, Western Australia: Department for Child Protection and Family Support. Retrieved from www.dcp.wa.gov.au/Resources/Documents/Annual%20reports/Annnual%20Report%202014.pdf

Department of Family and Community Services [NSW]. (2015). *First large-scale study into kids in care.* Ashfield, New South Wales: Department of Family and Community

Services. Retrieved from www.facs.nsw.gov.au/about/media/releases/archive/first-large-scale-study-into-kids-in-care

Flatau, P., Adams, S., & Seivwright, A. (2016). *The practice, prevalence and funding of outcomes measurement in the community sector: Findings from the Outcomes Measurement in the Western Australian Community Sector survey*. Centre for Social Impact. Retrieved from www.csi.edu.au/media/uploads/Bankwest_SIS_5.pdf

Frances, N., & Cuskelly, M. (2008). *The end of charity: Time for social enterprise*. Sydney: Allen and Unwin.

Garton, J. (2009). *The regulation of organized civil society*. Oxford: Hart Publishing.

Gilchrist, D. J. (2016). Partnerships between government and the third sector at a sub-national level: Experience of an Australian sub-national government. In J. R. Butcher & D. J. Gilchrist (Eds.), *The three sector solution: Delivering public policy in collaboration with not-for-profits and business*. Canberra: Australian University Press.

Gilchrist, D. J., & Butcher, J. R. (2016). Introduction. In J. R. Butcher & D. J. Gilchrist (Eds.), *The three sector solution: Delivering public policy in collaboration with not-for-profits and business*. Canberra: Australian University Press.

Gilchrist, D. J., & Knight, P. A. (2013a). *2013 evaluation of the sustainable funding and contracting with the not-for-profit sector initiatives and associated procurement reforms*. Perth: Government of Western Australia.

Gilchrist, D. J., & Knight, P. (2013b). *Annual funded sector report, report prepared for the Disability Services Commission*. Perth: Western Australian Government.

Gilchrist, D. J., & Knight, P. (2014). *Community employers, person centered care and individualized funding – Final report*. Perth. A joint report undertaken with community employers, WA.

Gilchrist, D. J., & Wilkins, P. (2016). Social impact bonds – The role of evaluation. In R. Pablo Guerrero, & P. Wilkins (Eds.), *Doing good? Private actors, evaluation and public value (comparative policy evaluation)*. New Brunswick: Transaction Publishing.

Government of Western Australia. (2011). *Delivering community services in partnership policy*. Department of Finance.

Government of Western Australia. (2015). *2015–16 Budget paper No. 2 – Budget statements Volume 1*. Government of Western Australia.

Knight, P. A., & Gilchrist, D. J. (2015). *2014 evaluation of the sustainable funding and contracting with the not-for-profit sector initiatives and associated procurement reforms*. Perth: Government of Western Australia.

McGregor-Lowndes, M. (2008). Is there something better than partnership? In J. Barraket (Ed.), *Strategic issues for the not-for-profit sector*. Sydney: University of New South Wales Press.

Mendes, P. (2008). *Australia's welfare wars revisited: The players, the politics and the ideologies*. Sydney: University of New South Wales Press.

Office of the Auditor-General (Western Australia). (2000). *A means to an end: Contracting not-for-profit organizations for the delivery of community services*. Office of the Auditor-General for Western Australia. Retrieved from https://audit.wa.gov.au/wp-content/uploads/2013/05/report2000_03.pdf

Office of the Auditor-General (Western Australia). (2003). *Contracting not-for-profit organizations for delivery of health services*. Office of the Auditor-General for Western Australia. Retrieved from https://audit.wa.gov.au/wp-content/uploads/2013/05/report2003_02.pdf

Office of the Auditor-General (Western Australia). (2013). *Sustainable funding and contracting – Component I funding to the not-for-profit sector*. Office of the Auditor-General for Western Australia. Retrieved from https://audit.wa.gov.au/wp-content/uploads/2013/09/report2013_13-Component-1-Funding.pdf

PricewaterhouseCoopers. (2014). *PwC-CSI community index 2014.* Centre for Social Impact. Retrieved from www.csi.edu.au/media/uploads/PwC-CSI_Community_Index_2_-_October_2014.pdf

Productivity Commission. (2010). *Contribution of the Australian not-for-profit sector, research report*. Australian Government Productivity Commission.

Public Accounts Committee Western Australia. (2000). *Accountability and not-for-profit organizations. Report No 49.* Parliament of Western Australia.

Rainnie, A., Fitzgerald, S., Gilchrist, D. J., & Morris, C. L. (2012). Putting the public first? Restructuring the West Australian human services sector. *International Journal of Employment Studies*, *20*, 104–125.

Roth, L. (2011). *Social impact bonds, e-Brief, New South Wales Parliamentary Library Research Service*. Parliament of New South Wales.

Shergold, P. (2016). Three sectors, one public purpose. In J. R. Butcher & D. J. Gilchrist (Eds.), *The three sector solution: Delivering public policy in collaboration with not-for-profits and business*. Canberra: Australian University Press.

Tomkinson, E. (2016). Outcome-based contracting for human services. Evidence Base. *ANZSOG Journal*, *1*.

Victorian Auditor-General. (2010). *Partnering with the community sector in human services and health.* Victorian Auditor-General's Office.

Wilkins, P., & Gilchrist, D. J. (2016). Accountability for the public policy contribution of not-for-profit organizations: Who is accountable to whom and for what? In R. Pablo Guerrero & P. Wilkins (Eds.), *Doing good? Private actors, evaluation and public value (comparative policy evaluation)*. New Brunswick: Transaction Publishing.

Zhai, L., Watson, J., Gilchrist, D. J., & Newby, R. (2017). Nonprofit vulnerability: An exploratory study. *Financial Accountability and Management*, *33*(4), 1–18.

6 The Role of an Intermediary Organization in a Large Evaluation

The Case of the Norwegian Health Care Reform

Olaf Rieper

This chapter tells the story of the Norwegian way of organizing large-scale research-based evaluations of public policy through the Research Council of Norway. The aim of such an intermediary organization is to establish an arm's-length distance between the unit that demands the evaluation and the suppliers (the evaluators), and to ensure that mutual expectations for evaluation information are met. The example described here concerns the evaluation of a large public sector reform within health care, the so-called Coordination Reform. The Norwegian way of organizing large-scale evaluations embedded in a research council is seldom seen in other countries.

The chapter will address the question of whether such a mediating organization in between the commissioner of an evaluation and the evaluators can help to better match demand for and supply of results information drawn from evaluation, and how it influences relevance and usefulness of the evaluation.

The author of the present chapter was the chairman of the Evaluation Steering Committee appointed by the Research Council of Norway – and this case study is based on my participation and observations throughout the four years of the evaluation process (2012–2015), on minutes of the committee meetings, and other documents which all are available on the homepage of the Research Council of Norway (RCN) website (www.forskningsradet.no). Thus, the story includes the chairman's reflections and observations, and is based on public documents. Members of the steering committee and the academic secretary of RCN have commented on an early draft of the chapter.

Thus, I will reflect upon such questions as: did the intermediary organization (Research Council and the steering committee) fulfill the role of preventing or mediating potential conflicts between the commissioner and the evaluators? Did the intermediary organization add any value to the evaluation in terms of the relevance, quality, and usefulness for the commissioner? What weaknesses were observed? The counterfactual question – what would have happened without this organization in between – cannot be answered in any stringent way in this chapter, only by commonsense reflections.

The Health Care Reform in Norway

In January 2012 Norway introduced a national health care reform (called the Coordination Reform – *Samhandlingsreformen*) whose primary intention was to achieve a better integration (coordination) between the hospitals at the regional level, and the health care and rehabilitation efforts of local governments (the municipalities).

Parallel efforts to the Norwegian Coordination Reform can be found elsewhere. The other Nordic countries, the UK, and the Netherlands have all introduced similar reforms. In fact, Denmark's Structural Reform of 2007 served as a model for Norway. Despite many differences in the general structure, the UK and the Netherlands have in recent years also decentralized part of their health-care tasks to the local level (Grimsmo & Magnussen, 2015).

In Norway, the government (Ministry of Health and Care Services, HOD) initiated a large-scale evaluation of the reform, to be conducted during its first four years (2012 to 2015). The evaluation was to address implementation aspects as well as the results obtained. A number of other large-scale reforms have been launched in Norway in the last decade and evaluated using the same general organizational setup within the RCN; for example the so-called NAV reform (the reform of the Norwegian labor and welfare administration) from 2005, was also evaluated within a similar organizational setup within RCN and a meta-evaluation of that evaluation was conducted afterwards (Forskningsrådet, 2014, in English; Hansen, Breidahl, Furubo, & Halvorsen, 2017). RCN has a very broad sphere of action in that it encompasses all subjects and disciplines and all aspects of society, from basic research to research-based innovation and commercialization.

The Evaluation and its Organization

The evaluation of the Coordination Reform was already mentioned in a policy document (Helse- og Omsorgsdepartementet, 2011a) in which it was stated that the reform should be evaluated.

The purpose of the evaluation was mostly formative (designed to improve, if necessary, the implementation of the reform according to plan), but not exclusively so. In fact, the evaluation aimed both at informing the present reform and future policy. Timely information about the implementation of the reform was to be delivered to the HOD in order to be able to make necessary adjustments to the implementation of the reform. But information about the effects (results) of the reform (both intended as well as unintended effects) were also to be collected, and the evaluation was to provide knowledge for future use in adjusting the policy instruments of the reform.

The evaluation focused on several of the main policy instruments of the reform: the cooperation agreements between the local governments and the hospitals owned by four regional health authorities; financial instruments; cohesive patient pathways (also called clinical pathways or integrated care pathways);

public health and prevention measures; inter-municipal cooperation; information and communication technology (ICT) as a means of coordination; and emergency inpatient units in local governments. More about these policy instruments will follow.

Six evaluation projects together covering these issues were selected with a total budget of 34 million NOK (approximately 4.5 million euro).

Organizational Aspects

The main message of this chapter is that organization aspects of evaluation do matter – in terms of aligning the information needs of the commissioner of the evaluation (in this case the ministry (HOD)), with what evaluators can provide. Therefore, the organization of the evaluation is described in more detail below.

As mentioned above, the Research Council of Norway has been used by ministries in Norway in several large-scale evaluations. The general role of the Research Council in that regard is to create an arm's-length distance between the authorities (often ministries) that commission the evaluations, and the evaluators. The authorities are responsible for the implementation of reforms or programs, while the task of evaluating the reform or program is entrusted to the Research Council which sets up a steering group for that purpose. The steering group has a high degree of autonomy and advises the Research Council on the evaluation mandate and is responsible for selecting the evaluation teams. In research-based evaluations the aim of the Research Council is also to contribute to developing research competencies and strengthen research teams in areas where it is needed. However, the general model of this organization varies somehow across ministries and evaluations, as well as over time. The organizational set up for the specific evaluation of the Coordination Reform is described below.

At the time the Coordination Reform was launched (in the fall of 2011) HOD asked the Research Council of Norway (RCN) to administer the evaluation. The RCN appointed an Evaluation Steering Committee (ESC) which was tasked with formulating the evaluation mandate and calls for tender of the evaluation projects, selecting the evaluation teams, monitoring the implementation of the evaluation projects, and writing a summary report of the evaluation results. The aim of this organizational set up was to assure a neutral and unbiased evaluation, keeping special interest groups at arm's length, including political pressures to influence the evaluation. Another main reason for selecting the RCN as the chosen intermediary was that the evaluation had to be research based, and RCN was known to have a high level of research expertise. Thus, the Coordination Reform evaluation was to be conducted using far more research competencies than ordinary evaluations. At least in the countries I know of, it is unusual to have an autonomous committee such as the ESC embedded in a research council endowed with such a high level of scientific credibility. This was also pointed out in the meta-evaluation of the NAV reform (Hansen et al., 2017).

Experience and Competence

The eight members of the Evaluation Steering Committee were appointed by the RCN and included international public health and evaluation experts from Sweden, Norway, and Denmark (because they would be able to read documents in Norwegian). They were selected mainly on the basis of their research competence and did not represent any special interest groups. Second, the staff of the RCN had long experience in running large evaluations; they had former experience and contacts with the HOD during other evaluations; their professional orientation was towards formative evaluation and utilization-focused results. Third, the members of the ESC, even if they came from different professional backgrounds, adapted constructive working modes, drawing on and mutually respecting the different professional backgrounds of its members, and they were part of informal networks within and between university departments and research institutions in public health and evaluation, as well as other relevant actors. Moreover, three of the Norwegian members currently or previously had jobs in the Norwegian health sector, so that in the ESC there existed not only a high level of research competence, but also first-hand knowledge of practices in the Norwegian health care sector. A different composition of an evaluation steering group – one with less expertise and less independence – might have been less qualified to judge the quality of the evaluation projects and less able to mediate, in a balanced way, between the ministry and the evaluators.

Implementing the Evaluation

Selection of Steering Committee Members

As previously indicated, the members of the ESC (including the chairman) were appointed by the RCN and the selection of individual members assured that the committee was focused on the practical use of evaluation results in a broad public health perspective, based on a high degree of knowledge about the Norwegian health sector. Moreover, the scientific (research) part was also considered to be important, and most of the members also had outstanding scientific qualifications.

Of the eight members, four had job experience in health care, while the other four were from the social sciences. Seven of the members had advanced academic qualifications and were attached to universities. In my professional judgment, this composition of the committee added to its independence and maintained a broad public health perspective (rather than only medical).

Formulation of the Evaluation Mandate

The formal framework of the tasks of the ESC was defined in a letter of commission from the HOD to RCN (Helse- og Omsorgsdepartementet, 2011b). The letter itself was very short – three pages – but stated the main issues to be covered by the evaluation and noted that the ESC should formulate a more detailed evaluation mandate in cooperation with the HOD. I believe this was a crucial point in reducing the potential gap between what the HOD expected from the evaluation, and what the evaluators were actually doing. If the mandate had been fully formulated by the HOD alone and/or by interest groups, there would have been a risk (in my point of view) that the mandate could have missed a broader perspective on the themes for the evaluation. Some of the main issues brought to light were the decision to add a point about ICT-supported cooperation in health care in the mandate, and reconsideration of the kinds of effects of the reform that could be evaluated during the three- to four-year timeframe. These were important issues and I believe that they helped to clarify and perhaps even change the expectations of both sides as to the evaluative information that could realistically be obtained. Otherwise, most of the original issues mentioned in the letter of commission were included by the ESC.

Thus, it was agreed that the evaluation should focus on a number of policy instruments in the reform, including:

- Financial instruments (municipal co-financing of specialist health care services, municipal financial responsibility for patients ready for discharge, government subsidies for municipal emergency inpatient units, and government subsidies for municipalities to finance their expanded areas of responsibility). The policies of co-financing and financial responsibility were intended to make it "profitable" for municipalities to invest in public health and preventive health care and thereby avoid hospitalizations, and to "bring home" patients ready for discharge as soon as possible and care for them in a more cost-effective manner.
- Health professional instruments such as the development of models for cohesive patient pathways (also known as clinical pathways or integrated pathways, which are a tool to manage the quality of health care across sectoral borders) informed by user experiences, and the development of higher medical competencies in local governments. Included in this set of instruments were also better public health promotion and preventive health services in local governments, e.g., by employing local preventive health coordinators.
- Organizational instruments, e.g., better cooperation between local governments; establishing multidisciplinary professional teams; more user/patient involvement in decision-making; and organizational models for the use of ICT and knowledge sharing among hospitals, local governments, and local government departments.
- Formal agreements between the Regional Health Authorities and local governments, to define the legal framework for dialogue and action.

Although the overall evaluation was to address all sets of instruments, not all instruments were expected to be covered by each evaluation project. Thus, the evaluators could choose and argue for specific instruments to be evaluated.

The evaluation mandate of almost ten pages (Helse- og Omsorgsdepartementet, 2011a), formulated by contributions from the ESC, also specified that there should be two main phases in the evaluation process. Phase 1 would start in the summer of 2012 and was to mainly address the implementation aspects of the reform, but it would also identify indicators of early (short-term) effects, so that relevant baseline data could be collected early on in the evaluation process. Phase 2 was to start in 2014 when those early effects were expected to show up.

The mandate also specified that regular meetings should be held between the evaluation project managers (who were part of the evaluation teams), the ESC and the HOD, in order to fulfill the formative aim of the evaluation. These meetings were designed to make it possible to detect needs for adjustments in the implementation of the reform instruments. During these meetings, the RCN accomplished its task of disseminating evaluation results to the HOD. I believe that these meetings also served to adjust information needs and expectations to the evaluation.

When looking back on these first months of the evaluation process, I found a shared understanding within the committee, and between the committee and HOD, that the evaluation mandate served as a solid point of departure for the formulation of the calls for tender for the evaluation projects. The main reason for this shared understanding, in my judgment, was the fact that the members of the committee were all committed to the idea of applied research and embraced the formative aim of the evaluation. But it also was due to the fact that the ESC had the opportunity to participate in the formulation of the evaluation mandate and thus could influence the mandate and hopefully obtain better evaluations in the end. In my opinion, the ESC/RCN as an intermediary committee contributed to making the evaluation more useful for the HOD.

Assessment and Selection of the Evaluation Projects

The calls for tender (announced in April 2012 and in April 2013, respectively) formulated by the ESC were very much in accordance with the evaluation mandate, but also provided leeway for creativity to the evaluators; e.g., applicants could add new evaluation questions, and could present justifications for selecting particular methods of data collection.

The ESC assessed and selected the evaluation offers: in total, 6 evaluation projects were selected out of 26 offers received. Most of the offers were submitted by research teams from university departments and research institutes. In a small country like Norway, where many of the researchers in public health know each other, it was especially important that the selection process was done by an independent committee which included non-Norwegian members as well.

The number of the submitted offers varied between the two calls. For tenders in the first call, there were 17 offers to choose from, but this was less the case in the second call, where only 9 offers were received. This was probably due to the fact that the second call focused on specific themes not covered in the first round, such as e-health and vulnerable groups. The assessment of each offer under both calls was done in two steps: first by each member of the ESC individually; and then second, collectively, at a meeting in the ESC. In some cases, the qualitative aspects of the offers were discussed within the ESC. Three projects were ultimately selected for financing under each call for tender, resulting in a total of about 34 million NOK being awarded for 6 evaluation projects.

Did the assessment and selection of evaluation projects influence demand and supply for evaluative information? In my opinion this was the case only in relation to the second call concerning the effects of the reform (the first call concerned the implementation and was the formative part). More evaluation proposals that better fulfilled the demand for "effects" evaluation had been expected. I believe this "gap" was partly due to the small number of offers to select among. Another reason was the "classic" one, i.e., that the time horizon of the evaluation (only four years from when the reform was launched) was too short for the effects of reform to develop. In retrospect, I believe that the ESC should have done more to reduce expectations – by modifying the evaluation mandate – about the likelihood of having solid evaluation information about effects after only four years.

Dialogue Between the Evaluators, the Evaluation Steering Committee, and the Ministry

The reform was defined as a so-called "retningsreform" (Helse- og Omsorgsdepartementet, 2011b) meaning that even if the reform entailed a number of policy instruments, they were not specified in advance but were to be specified and developed along the way.

For example, one of several policy instruments aimed at improving cooperation between hospitals and local healthcare services was the cooperation agreements between municipalities and the regional health authorities. The reform only states that such agreements should be implemented, but the content of each agreement was to be developed and specified as a result of dialogue between the municipalities and the regional health authorities.

With the aim of creating cohesion among the individual evaluations, and to inform the HOD of the evaluation process, the ESC held a series of five meetings with the evaluation project managers and with representatives from HOD. The purpose of these meetings was two-fold: to disseminate experience and preliminary results from the evaluations, and to provide opportunities for the ESC and HOD to ask for further elaborations and minor adjustments (not involving cost implications) in the future evaluation process. In addition, the different evaluation teams were informed about the status of each other's work and thus became aware of potential for cooperation among themselves.

In addition, a major conference on the preliminary results from the overall evaluation was organized by RCN and ESC in September 2015, and a final seminar was held in June 2016. In the conference and the seminar, a number of other relevant actors participated, such as the association of local governments and health professional associations as well as others. Direct communication between the ESC and the evaluators outside of planned meetings and conferences was very infrequent.

Alongside these meetings and conferences, each of the evaluation projects were obliged to deliver a progress report to the ESC every six months. These reports were subject to approval by the committee. It was no mere formality: in a few cases the evaluators were asked to rewrite or modify their reports before final approval. In that way expectations were clarified and adjusted.

In the meetings questions were asked and, in some cases, criticism was aired in an open and respectful way. To my knowledge suggestions made to the evaluators to expand or modify the focus of the evaluation were largely accepted by the evaluators. At the same time, evaluators could air difficulties they encountered, such as getting access to clinical registers or merging data from different registers. These concerns were passed on to the ministry and have, in my view, contributed to adjust expectations.

Evaluation Results to Date

In my view the expectations of HOD were made somewhat more realistic as to what the evaluators could deliver, and the evaluators got a better understanding of the HOD's expectations from the evaluation, as a result of this process. Without these conferences, meetings, and approval of progress reports in the context of a neutral and highly professional platform (the ESC) it is doubtful whether the evaluations would have fulfilled expectations to the degree they did.

Another aim of the evaluation process was to use the evaluation results to adjust the policy instruments of the reform if necessary. Were any policy instruments adjusted because of the information from the evaluations? I am not aware of any adjustment to policy instruments stemming from the evaluations before the end of the evaluation in June 2016. But the evaluation results have informed policy documents from the Norwegian parliament, the so-called *Stortingsmeldinger* (info on the seminar, June 2016). For example, possible future adjustments of policy instruments, based on the results of the evaluation, include: 1) cooperation agreements between municipalities and health trusts, 2) the role and place of general practitioners in the reform, including emphasis on specialist expertise in health issues in local governments, 3) consideration of patient/user participation to create more cohesive patient pathways and, finally 4) better use of digital technology in patient consultations.

Did the evaluations shed light on all the issues that HOD expected from the mandate? According to the ESC, all the major themes in the evaluation mandate were dealt with in a satisfactory way. However, a number of specific issues were not covered or were only weakly covered. These issues included the prioritization and focus of policy makers and top management in local governments on areas such as: how the resource allocation for healthcare in local government influences allocations to other policy sectors (e.g., childcare and schools); the degree to which interventions of the health reform have influenced inequalities in the health status in the population; and the extent to which appropriate indicators and strategies for raising healthcare competencies have been developed. According to the ESC's final report (Forskningsrådet, 2016) these "blind spots" were partly due to the fact that the evaluation applications (the response to calls for tender) did not fully cover all of the issues mentioned in the evaluation mandate. As mentioned above the evaluators had some leeway in choosing data collection methodologies and specifying evaluation questions.

Another reason was that the four-year timeframe for the evaluation, from the launching of the reform, was considered too short to be able to identify many of the expected short-term effects of the reform. The ESC should, in my view, have done more to highlight this obstacle. For instance, the effects of improving cohesive patient pathways could not be measured by health indicators, both because of the too-short time horizon and due to the lack of accessible clinical data registers. Thus, instead of pointing to hard data on effects, the evaluation pointed out that the clinical (diagnosis-based) patient pathways were inadequate for meeting the real needs of the municipalities, because of the large group of patients with multiple health problems. This would probably not have been any different without the intermediation of the ESC, but the ongoing dialogue in the organizational setup helped to adjust expectations along the way, so that "shocks" could be avoided when the evaluation was coming to an end.

An example of where the expectations of both commissioners and evaluators were met concerns financial policy instruments. The evaluation found that the municipalities' acceptance of financial responsibility for patients ready for discharge has had positive management effects: e.g., the number of hospital bed days has decreased, in accordance with a main goal of the Coordination Reform. Despite a huge and unexpected increase in the number of hospital admissions, no increases in the number of readmissions or in mortality rates were found.

It bears mentioning that – as always with large, complex reforms – a number of other initiatives and programs may run parallel to the reform process and potentially have influence on the same kind of effects. For example, the improvement of ICT in inter-professional communications was partly due to another government-supported program (*Meldingsløftet*). Also, local conditions may influence the effect of policy instruments in some areas. Although this was not clearly stated in the mandate, it is an aspect very much commented upon by evaluators during the evaluation process. For example, on the question of government subsidies for municipal emergency inpatient units (KAD – an instrument of the reform) the evaluation found that there was a reduction of emergency admissions to hospitals, but only in areas where a medical doctor was available in the KAD at all times.

Some of these constraints were well known to many of the actors beforehand; I believe, however, that the discussions between the evaluators and the HOD facilitated by the ESC, made these constraints more clearly understood and thus contributed to bridging the potential gap between the commissioner of the evaluation and the providers of the evaluation information throughout the evaluation period.

Conclusions

The main conclusion is that, in the case of the Norwegian Coordination Reform, an intermediary organization (the RCN), working with the commissioner of the evaluation (the HOD) on the one hand, and the evaluators on the other, in many ways fulfilled its role in mediating between the two sets of actors in such a way that the potential gap in expectations between the two was reduced. Two aspects that contributed to overcome or prevent this potential gap were: 1) the organizational setup, and 2) the experience and competence of the key actors involved.

The organizational setup was characterized by the formation of an ad hoc committee, the Evaluation Steering Committee (ESC), created specifically for the evaluation of the reform, as well as by formal institutional arrangements among the main actors in the evaluation process (the ministry (HOD), the Research Council (RCN), the steering committee, and the evaluators). These institutional arrangements made the expectations to the evaluation clearer, e.g., by facilitating ongoing dialogue between the main actors.

The experience and competence part can be characterized by at least three elements. One element was that the staff of the Research Council had long experience in running large evaluations. Another element was the professional background of the members of the ESC, as well as their common orientation towards formative evaluation and utilization-focused results. A third element was the existence of close and informal networks across university departments and research institutions in public health and evaluation that also involved staff of the Research Council. This might partly be attributable to the fact that this large evaluation was undertaken in a relatively small country (Norway has a population of about 5 million).

Thus, the case shows that the way the evaluation was organized – using an external intermediary organization (RCN/ESC), and the institutional context within which it was undertaken, were important factors in preventing and overcoming gaps between the demand and supply of information in the evaluation of the Norwegian health reform program. In my view, the intermediary also served as a useful platform for critical and constructive dialogue among the HOD, the ESC, and the evaluators, given the RCN's strong scientific reputation. I believe this dialogue contributed to raise the quality and relevance of the evaluation.

The formative aim of the evaluation was partly fulfilled: for example, the preliminary results from the evaluation were subsequently used by HOD in writing governmental policy documents about healthcare services. The main results of the evaluation, though, were not dramatic and did not initiate any huge political or public debate. In part, this may reflect a declining interest for the Coordination Reform in the face of other political priorities. Another reason may be the fact that one main policy instrument (the co-financing from local governments) was phased out.

Finally, it must be said that the hospitals did not show much interest in the reform. However, the steep increase in the elder population in Norway in the years to come will probably reactivate some of the issues brought to light by the evaluation.

References

Forskningsrådet. (2014, juli). *Oppmerksomhetspunkter ved evaluering av politiske reformer. Rapport fra metaevalueringen av evalueringen av NAV-reformen i Norge.* Metaevalueringens ekspertpanel.

Forskningsrådet. (2016). *Evaluering av samhandlingsreformen. Sluttrapport fra styrings-gruppen for forskningsbaseret følgeevaluering av samhandlingsreformen* (EVASAM). Division for samfunn og helse.

Grimsmo, A., & Magnussen, J. (2015). *Norsk samhandlingsreform i et internasjonalt perspektiv.* Institutt for samfunnsmedisin, NTNU, Forskningsrådet.

Hansen, M. B., Breidahl, K. N., Furubo, J. E., & Halvorsen, A. (2017). Eight attention points when evaluating large-scale public sector reforms. In B. Greve (Ed.), *Handbook of social policy evaluation* (pp. 460–472). London: Edward Elgar Publishing.

Helse- og Omsorgsdepartementet. (2011a). *Meld. St. nr. 16 (2010–2011) Nasjonal helse- og omsorgsplan.* Norges Forskningsråd 2012.

Helse- og Omsorgsdepartementet. (2011b). *Opdragsbrev til NFR: Følgeevaluering av Samhandlingsreformen. 8.07.2011.* Norges Forskningsråd 2011. Mål- og rammedokument for forskningsbaseret evaluering av Samhandlingsreformen, 10.02.2012.

7 Evaluation Plans in the EU Cohesion Policy

Redefining the Relation Between the Demand for and the Supply of Evaluation

Francesco Mazzeo Rinaldi

The evaluation of European Union Regional (i.e., Cohesion) Policy, became a substantial concern within the Member States and the European Commission (EC), as the volume of investment funds was increasing (Petropoulos, 2013). One of the main lessons drawn from past experiences in evaluating Cohesion Policy (since the 1994–1999 period) was the need for a radical shift from a conception of evaluations driven by regulatory imperatives towards a more flexible, local demand-driven approach (European Commission, 2007, p. 5). As compared with the previous programming period, the directives for the 2007–2013 period laid down a more flexible approach to evaluation. One of the key elements of the Cohesion Policy reform for 2007–2013 was, indeed, the introduction of the Evaluation Plan (EP) and Steering Groups for "guiding the evaluation process," in order to also reduce the gap between the demand for and supply of evaluation information. And it is this area which will be the main objective of this chapter.

The redefinition of the demand and supply for evaluation information in the 2007–2013 European Union Cohesion Policies is the main focus of the present chapter, which shows how and why it is crucial that a close relationship between the demanders for, and suppliers of, evaluation information should be built in already during the planning phase of the policies. More specifically, we shall examine the planning and implementing of a complex evaluation study on the effects of the policies of the Sardinia Region in support of research and development (R&D) during two EU programming periods: 1994–1999 and 2000–2006. The evaluation study was part of the EP of the 2007–2013 regional cohesion policy of the Sardinia Region. The study was chosen due to the fact that it presents several characteristics that allow us to analyze – from the selection of evaluation questions to the use of evaluation results – the challenges, difficulties, and opportunities inherent in bridging the gap between the demand for and supply of evaluation information.

The chapter is organized as follows: section one briefly introduces the European Union Cohesion Policy, its aims and, particularly, its evaluation during the 2007–2013 period; in the second section we describe the elaboration of the regional EP, analyzing the criteria used to identify the areas to be evaluated and the evaluation questions; in the third section, we examine one of the evaluation studies carried out in the context of the EP, which focused on the results of regional R&D policies implemented in the two previous programming cycles, specifying and detailing the questions and the areas of study chosen for the evaluation; in the fourth section, we discuss the problems that emerged during the study and the usefulness of its results; in the final section, we present a few final considerations.

Background on the EU Cohesion Policy and its Evaluation

The EU Cohesion Policy is an investment policy aimed at reducing regional disparities in economic development within its member countries. The policy is implemented by national and regional bodies in partnership with the EC. It involves the transfer of resources to regional and national authorities to support investments in areas such as education, the environment, the single market, employment, energy, and research and innovation (among others: Bachtler & Mendez, 2016; Molle, 2007). The EU Cohesion Policy framework is established for a period of seven years. Since its start, five programming periods have been implemented, the last two covering 2000–2006, and 2007–2013.[1] The EC required and strongly supported evaluation efforts to assess the success of these programs (among others: Bachtler & Mendez, 2016), especially after the 1998 reform of the Structural Funds[2] (Bachtler & Michie, 1995). The increase of Cohesion Policy expenditure over time (from 64 billion euro during the 1988–1993 programming period to about 345 billion euro during the 2007–2013 period), evidently highlighted the need for clear rules over their use, followed by a better understanding of its results (Petropoulos, 2013). This is also because the state of the empirical evidence on the performance of Cohesion Policy was very disappointing. The very limited information on effects underlined how important it was to make improvement in this direction. For instance, the rigid deadline leading to mid-term evaluation having been launched too early in many cases, or requirements and evaluation questions being too broad and complex, led, in many cases, to negative consequences (e.g., the impossibility of carrying out in-depth analysis of crucial evaluation questions, the incapacity to address the specific internal needs of the local administrations; European Commission, 2007, p. 5). Past experience and lessons learned highlighted the need to shift from a regulatory rules scheme towards a more flexible approach, driven by the needs of local decision-makers.

Hence, it was decided that in the 2007–2013 period it would not be practical to “evaluate everything” (i.e., all programs), and the EC recommended that the choice of which actions were to be evaluated should be left to regional authorities, based on their appreciation of which evaluation questions were the most significant. A second innovation under the 2007–2013 programming period was organizational: in response to a recommendation by the EC, two types of Evaluation Steering Groups (SGs) were established: 1) an overall Steering Group for the Evaluation Plan (EP) as a whole, whose role was largely consultative and aimed at coordinating the evaluation and review activities called for under the EP, and 2) a series of independent Steering Committees for each of the specific evaluations to be performed under the EP; the role of the latter was mainly technical and methodological in nature (European Commission, 2007), coordinating and overseeing implementation.

In Italy, the National Evaluation System – Sistema Nazionale di Valutazione (SNV) – attributed additional functions to the Steering Committee for the EP that were designed to ensure that the resulting individual evaluations would represent the interests of the different stakeholders involved in the evaluation, and, when necessary, to "culturally mediate" between the evaluator and the stakeholders (Sistema Nazionale di Valutazione della Politica Regionale [SNV], 2008).

What was the purpose of all this? Why such a complex organizational structure? Let us try to find some answers.

One reason was the effort to make the Regions, who were responsible for implementing their respective regional cohesion policies, more aware of the importance of evaluation choices; choices that for the first time were made with the full participation of stakeholders. The organizational structure was designed, therefore, to assure stakeholder participation not only in regard to the planning and implementation aspects of the program, but also in regard to evaluation. For the first time, functionaries of the different regional service Councillorships, and representatives of other institutional, economic, and social groups, would be involved with deciding which regional policies were most important to evaluate, and how to evaluate them, taking into account the different interests of the stakeholders affected by those policies (Zoppi, 2009).

Furthermore, the structure provided for engaging experts in specific fields and in evaluation methodology to bolster the capacity of regional administrative units to interact with evaluators. Since these experts followed each of the steps in the evaluation process, starting from the initial elaboration of the evaluation questions and possible reformulations, it was no longer a question of simply assigning someone to perform an evaluation and then waiting for the evaluator to hand in his or her completed report. The Steering Group for the EP, acting in its supervisory role, guaranteed the "quality of the process," that is, guaranteed that all of the required steps leading up to the presentation of the final evaluation report, had been carried out in a competent fashion.

The most immediate consequence should be the improved quality of the reports (Pacifico, 2009, p. 88). Organizing the evaluation planning and execution process in such a way meant, at least potentially, an opportunity to redefine the demand and supply for evaluation information in the 2007–2013 regional cohesion policies. This redefinition is the main focus of the present chapter, in line with the overall subject of the volume.

The Development of the Evaluation Plan – the Purpose of the Organizational Setup

One of the main principles was that evaluations listed in the EP were required to have clearly formulated evaluation questions aimed at acquiring specific information.

The content and form of these questions were consequently central to the entire process. Furthermore, it was intended that the questions should be elaborated as part of a cultural process among stakeholders, providing an opportunity for learning and improving the participants' knowledge of the dynamics and causes that had determined whether or not policy goals had been achieved.

The EP elaborated by the Public Investment Evaluation Unit of the Sardinian Region (NVVIP) consequently developed a methodology aimed at ensuring the active involvement of stakeholders in the identification and formulation of the evaluation questions and areas, as well as at facilitating the flow of demand for, and supply of, evaluation information and assuring transparency in the process.

The identification of evaluation questions and areas of study began with a series of bilateral meetings between NVVIP and the actors directly involved in the implementation of the programs – that is the management authorities of the various EU funds (ERDF, ESF, and EAFRD). These first meetings served to start a debate that helped identify the main problems, the topics of current interest, special requirements, and the evaluation questions to be asked, with the help of those who were directly responsible for implementing the programs and therefore could benefit from the knowledge and recommendations produced by the evaluation studies. This first series of meetings highlighted a number of evaluation problems and questions that provided the basis for the opening meeting of the Coordinating Group of the EP which included representatives of the various EU funds implementing programs and the above-mentioned NVVIP.

During those meetings, five areas to be evaluated were discussed and approved:

- Rural development: combined effect of policies and programs for rural development; effects of the LEADER program;
- Technological research and innovation: integration between the scientific-technological research system and the business system; low propensity of Sardinian firms towards investing in R&D;
- Local development: urban development interventions; policies for the restoration and promotion of the cultural heritage in relation to tourism development;
- Employment: effectiveness and validity of a number of instruments used for: young entrepreneurs and woman entrepreneurs, self-employment and employment services;
- School dropout rate: Causal relation with school commuting and public transportation.

At the end of the meeting, participants were asked to suggest experts for a number of Thematic Working Groups (Gruppi di Lavoro Tematici), which would serve as subgroups of the Coordinating Group. These subgroups were created to assist the Coordinating Group in dealing with a multitude of topics.

The Coordinating Group established five Thematic Working Groups, one for each evaluation area, and tasked them with summarizing the questions that had emerged from the meetings and establishing the evaluation questions. A total of around 40 people participated to the work of the five Thematic Working Groups, representing almost all the organizations involved, including the various institutional, economic, and social partners, ensuring their involvement in the identification and specification of the topics to be studied.

When the Thematic Working Groups had finished their work, their results were reported to the Coordinating Group, which then had the responsibility of approving a preliminary list of evaluation questions and areas of study, which would become the basis for discussions with the various social, economic, and institutional partners involved.

To ensure that the partners were actively involved, an effort was undertaken not only to make the various requirements and responsibilities that emerged from the debate explicit, but also to clarify that the representatives of the partners also had a say in the choices to be made, along with the Coordinating Group. It was crucial to ensure that, in this phase, the demand for evaluation results by the partners be elaborated in a manner that was clearly understood. Nevertheless, as the work proceeded, it became apparent that many demands for evaluation were impractical or had been formulated with little consideration of the potential use of evaluation results.

To manage the many, and often generic, evaluation questions proposed in the meetings, it was decided to adopt certain criteria to identify **priorities** and orient choices. Among these were:

- A clear risk of inefficiency or inefficacy of the investments, as evidenced by previous ex-post evaluations;
- The existence of controversies regarding the final effects, in terms of inequality, poverty, development gap, territorial balancing, etc.;
- The existence of similar interventions in previous cycles without any evident positive effects;
- The need to make urgent decisions in certain policy areas;
- Highly innovative interventions or "pilot" interventions.

Other criteria were used to establish the evaluability of the questions, namely:

- Clarity: clarity of the questions and of their goals;
- Sources: verification of the existence and accessibility of the information necessary to assess the goals of the study;
- Feasibility: evaluation of the questions on the basis of the resources necessary to carry out the required study (timing, cost of the study etc.);
- Utility of the results: that is, how they intended to use the results of selected evaluations.

Having identified the evaluations that would be undertaken through this shared process, the individual evaluation studies were begun. For each evaluation study, an Evaluation Leader was identified, who was responsible for the technical organization of the evaluation.

In the implementation phase, each Evaluation Leader was supported by the respective Steering Committee, not only in coordinating the various evaluations but also in ensuring the quality, credibility, and usefulness of the evaluations. The Steering Committee was conceived as a consulting panel with a variable composition, decided on a case by case basis by the NVVIP (depending on the needs of that particular evaluation area), with input from a group of experts, internal and external to the administration, and of individual stakeholders. The Steering Committee was assigned the following functions (SNV, 2008):

- Representative function: representing in the evaluation process the interests of all the parties involved;
- Cultural mediation: mediating between the evaluator or evaluation group, the stakeholders and the regional administration;
- Technical-methodological: ensuring the methodological rigor of evaluation activities and therefore the "usability" of the results by the regional administration and stakeholders.

The Case of R&D – Evaluation Questions and the Purpose of the Evaluation Process

As already mentioned, one of the five areas identified in the first meeting of the EP Coordinating Group was R&D. The Coordinating Group decided to focus on two aspects: 1) the integration of scientific research and technological innovation with the regional entrepreneurial system, and 2) the low propensity of Sardinian firms to invest in scientific research and technological innovation, compared with the rest of Italy.

As established in the EP, a thematic working group or R&D was constituted, and tasked with identifying evaluation questions for assessing the results in this area of the regional cohesion policy; these in turn were to be submitted to the Coordinating Group, which was ultimately responsible for deciding the priority areas of study and the relevant evaluation questions.

A number of meetings began, which were not easy to manage in the beginning, due to the novelty of the questions addressed. Nevertheless, the meetings were very interesting, thanks to the presence of actors who were directly involved in R&D policies (representatives of General Confederation of Italian Industry, banks, regional programmers, experts from R&D agencies, academics) and who had been for the first time encouraged to "redefine" their roles. It was no longer a traditional encounter, a negotiation aimed at defining the measures to be financed, protecting the interests of potential beneficiaries, ensuring the legal and technical feasibility of the measures, and so on. Rather, it was an occasion to reflect and discuss the results of over a decade of R&D investments, in which many of them had played a role, often in a position of responsibility. Nor was it simply a question of complying with yet another administrative directive requiring the presence of partners to legitimate an evaluation process defined by some exotic national or EU regulation. This time it was an occasion to stop, to think and reflect, to ask what had happened during those years, what should be avoided, what had gone well, and what could be usefully adopted in the new programming period that was about to begin. In short, it was a moment to look at what had been done so far and take informed decisions on what needed to be done in the future. The task of turning the demands of the participants into useful, realistic, and practical evaluation questions, was entrusted to experts of the NVVIP,[3] who participated in the meetings.

The elaboration of the final eight evaluation questions that resulted from this process was not easy. After a first phase, in which participants were made familiar with their role and the goals of the meetings, the participants began to advance a great number of evaluation questions, but these were often vague, confused, contradictory, or impractical. Sometimes, the way a question was framed influenced the answer. In the case of evaluation questions, generic or lengthy questions usually lead to results that are not relevant. Another problem was the explicit request by some of the participants to develop an impact evaluation using counterfactual techniques independently of the object of the evaluation.

A first selection among the questions was made according to the four criteria previously described. The debate was neither easy nor without misunderstandings, particularly in the initial phase. But the overall result was positive. For the first time, an analysis was being made of a policy that had always been considered fundamentally important for the region, not for the purpose of negotiating strategic choices in regards to upcoming investments, but rather to render more informed evaluation choices, independently of administrative requirements and aimed at avoiding, as far as possible, wasting the taxpayers' money.

In the little time available (two months), the process succeeded both in bringing to light the demand for evaluation and shaping that demand appropriately, by making participants appreciate the need to adapt demand to the above criteria. In that sense, the overall result was positive, although, as was to be expected, for some questions it proved more difficult to persuade participants to follow those criteria (despite warnings) that their questions were too generic in some cases, or too impractical in others.

In September 2008, the Coordinating Group approved eight evaluation questions proposed by the R&D thematic working group (Table 7.1). In February 2009, the Steering Committee was constituted. In the same month, the evaluation study officially began.

The eight evaluation questions selected as a result of the meetings of the thematic working group were still rather generic and had to be made more specific. Furthermore, in the light of findings that had emerged after a survey of the main programming documents it was decided to split the evaluation study into three components:

- Component 1: study of regional policy;
- Component 2: evaluation of policy results;

- Component 3: analysis of the "demand" for innovation and evaluation of the degree of satisfaction on the part of firms that benefited from the services and funding provided under the programs.

The scope of the **first component** was a study of the regional R&D policy, particularly in reference to its goals, strategies, organization, overall financial size, and actual destination of the resources. For this purpose, a number of interviews with prominent figures were carried out in the field[4] and a review of the main programming documents for the 1994–1999 and 2000–2006 periods was conducted. This study of the regional R&D policy allowed us to acquire information to contextualize the research effort, fine-tune our investigation tools, and provide answers to the more descriptive questions (Mazzeo Rinaldi & Spano, 2011), as for example, questions 2 and 3. However, the study also proved to be particularly difficult for a number of reasons (e.g., incomplete documentation, lack of data, need for reconstructing information ex-post, inadequately documented decision-making procedures) which negatively affected the possibility of effectively answering the evaluation questions.

Under the **second component** the results of regional policies were examined, especially those which came about due to the R&D infrastructure created in the period under examination, based on the operational efficiency and results achieved by firms that had benefited from services or funding. Five of the eight evaluation questions formulated by the Thematic Working Group (questions 1, 4, 5, 6, 7) were covered under this component. Each evaluation question was carefully examined in the light of the problems of misunderstanding and interpretation problems that had arisen during the implementation of the policy. Each question was consequently subdivided into sub-questions and an ad hoc analytical procedure was established which, based on information that was available or presumed to be available, was considered to be the best suited for structuring the response to the question. For example, question 1 (What have been the results in terms of attracting firms from the outside?) was made "operative" using the following sub-questions: Did the R&D policy attract external firms? If the

Table 7.1 Evaluation questions

1) What have been the results in terms of attracting firms from the outside?
2) What was the distribution of subsidized firms by sector and type?
3) How did the firms actually use the funding?
4) What were the actual results of the research and technological innovation projects?
5) What were the economic and financial outcomes (revenues from products, profits, etc.)?
6) What were the outcomes in terms of efficiency?
7) What were the effects on the creation of new companies and on the mortality rate of companies established with public funds thanks to the research and technological innovation projects?
8) Is there a demand for innovation on part of Sardinian firms and what are its characteristics?

Source: Adapted from Ljungman, Forti, and Mikkelsen (2005).

answer is yes, to what extent? What types of firms were attracted? Where did the entrepreneurs come from and what were the characteristics of the home or parent companies in terms of size, revenue, legal form, and area of specialization? What were the most effective policy instruments? Where were the local business units geographically located? In what sectors did they operate? In what measure did they benefit from public funding or from services provided by the public administration through the competent regional agencies?

Considering that no methods are absolutely superior to others when evaluating the results and effects of policies (among others: Stern et al., 2012) – although some of the participants to the Thematic Working Group believed the counterfactual method to be the only appropriate one for the evaluations of the R&D policy – the choice of evaluation methods was ultimately based on the questions and areas to be evaluated. For some questions, (e.g., question number 4 – What were the actual results of the research and technological innovation projects?), it was decided to perform benchmarking analyses both for the input indicators of the innovation process, and for the output indicators. In the case of other questions (e.g., question number 5 – What were the economic and financial outcomes?) the group developed a sectoral macroeconomic model based on information acquired under the first component of the study, to evaluate the impact of R&D policies, both in the short and in the long term. One should note that the capacity to provide answers to the questions under this second component was strongly affected by the availability and reliability of the data. For example, in the case of question number 6 (What were the outcomes in terms of efficiency?), the group had considered the interesting possibility of carrying out a Total Factor Productivity Analysis, but was greatly hampered by the scarcity of data when the study was carried out.

Question number 8 (Is there a demand for innovation on part of Sardinian firms and what are its characteristics?), in the **third component** of the evaluation, had the goal of ascertaining the "demand" for scientific research and technological innovation by Sardinian firms in order to provide policymakers with information that could orient their efforts to stimulate such activities. Due to the lack of data on specific firms that benefited from the program, it was decided to carry out a survey on a sample of 700 companies in Sardinia.

The Challenges of Making Evaluation Useful

One of the main challenges of the evaluation process was reconstructing what the actual policy for the two periods under consideration (1994–1999/2000–2006) had been. Since it was a particularly long period, it was necessary to examine many programming and implementing documents, from which it was not always possible to clearly grasp the strategic choices made, nor the guidelines governing the implementation processes. Successive versions of the programming documents included many substantial modifications that were not accompanied by explicit and detailed explanations. These modifications concerned the policy goals, the financial, indicators, target values, etc. The vagueness of the reasons behind these modifications was a serious obstacle to the evaluation process.

A second challenge, unfortunately common to many of the evaluation studies, was the lack or unreliability of information. For example, there was no complete list of the firms that benefited from the subsidies, nor of the financial resources set aside to support them. The difficulty of finding this information forced the group to significantly modify the study. It was also envisaged that the sample survey of 700 firms could be used to cross-check data with that of the companies that had received support under the program. This would have permitted a more accurate analysis of the effects of regional policies. However, the incompleteness and unreliability of data on the list of beneficiary firms made this cross-checking impossible, severely limiting the usefulness of the study.

These problems were largely due to the fact that when the regional R&D policies were established, the possibility of evaluating, and therefore the need for monitoring results had not been taken into account. Establishing evaluation strategies consistent with the nature of the program from the very start is the basis for developing monitoring systems that permit the gathering of data and information that will be useful to that evaluation. The more the evaluators, the program developers, and other involved actors jointly participate in identifying programming and organizational criteria, evaluation approaches and the information to be gathered, the more productive the monitoring will be, overcoming the limits that usually characterize it (Mazzeo Rinaldi, 2012, p. 114).

These difficulties highlight the importance of developing a common awareness of how crucial data is to any evaluation activity. As in the above case, the production of data is commonly neglected, whereas it is imperative that it be planned before the activities called for under the program begin, and then be monitored and supported during program implementation. Only in this way, is it possible to truly evaluate the effects of a program after it is over.

For each of the observed components, the study highlighted a number of challenges concerning the evaluation of the program's effects, but also brought to light certain opportunities for improving the possibility of evaluating the areas in question. For example, regarding consulting and advisory services, the ability to evaluate effects could be improved if it became possible to obtain exhaustive official data on the activities carried out by the responsible regional agencies, which instead proved to be highly lacking in this respect. Similarly, concerning the evaluation of the success of the program in attracting companies to Sardinia, the main difficulty encountered was the need to combine data from different sources to identify firms which, having benefited from the R&D regional policy, had opened a local subsidiary in Sardinia while maintaining their legal headquarters elsewhere. In this case, too, available databases, especially the ones maintained by regional agencies, provided only limited, inaccurate, or incomplete information on actions and projects financed under the program, which negatively affected the possibility of evaluating this policy.

Some of the problems which became evident under the study were analyzed in more detail, providing useful information on how to improve regional R&D strategies. Besides the above-mentioned difficulty of finding data, two other significant challenges emerged: 1) The lack of advisory initiatives aimed at developing R&D activities, which the firms indicated as being more important than the subsidies received, and 2) the limited coordination between the institutional actors involved and, in particular, between firms and universities (Mazzeo Rinaldi, Saba, & Spano, 2012).

These problems were carefully examined by regional policymakers, leading to significant decisions both in terms of choosing strategic priorities and of the implementing modalities of regional R&D policies. As regards data availability, the Sardinia Region decided to establish a database of the R&D support received by firms, to be used for future evaluation studies.

In regard to the second problem, it was decided to enact measures to encourage and support firms to invest in R&D. In particular, various programs were designed in close collaboration with universities to promote the birth of innovative start-ups and spin-offs, to further develop existing innovative firms and to fund the realization of R&D projects by recently established firms. Also interesting were the technological auditing programs, aimed at verifying the potential technological needs of the firms, to assist in establishing agreements for technology transfer, and to support internationalization of R&D results. Finally, investment incentives (direct subsidies) were created to improve relations between firms and universities, promoting collaborations and university spin-offs.

Clearly the modifications made to subsequent regional R&D programs were not exclusively the result of the above evaluation studies. The European Commission and other stakeholders had suggested modifying R&D support policies and strategies for firms. However, the observations and recommendations resulting from the Sardinia evaluation study certainly contributed to the redefinition of these policies, providing feedback on the effectiveness of the policy and the problems characterizing previously implemented strategies.

Conclusions

There are many questions raised by this difficult evaluation experience which I have briefly described. In light of the scope and goals of this book, I will focus on three interrelated aspects, which I believe to be of particular interest.

The EPs required participants not only to consider if, how, and what to evaluate, but also to ensure that the answers to evaluation questions ("supply-side") would actually benefit those in need of that information ("demand side"), by means of a group of third-party experts that interacted with the evaluators. The Thematic Working Groups first, and the Steering Committees later, had a mandate to ensure the "quality of the process," reducing the distance between the demand for and supply of evaluation information, thus qualitatively improving evaluations and making their results more useful for policymaking. The idea of looking for new forms and mechanisms of communication between demanders and suppliers of evaluation information described in the present chapter came from a desire to overcome a number of problems typically encountered when evaluating public policies and, in particular regional cohesion policies, which can be, perhaps simplistically summarized as: the **quality, usefulness, and practicality** of evaluation reports.

The EP had the objective – partly attained – of eliminating the "negative dynamics" created by the distance between "client" (demand) and evaluator (supply) for evaluation information. That is between, on the one hand, the factors that evaluators say hinder their work (vague, contradictory, or impractical evaluation questions, etc.), and on the other hand, the factors that limit (or in the worst case prevent) the use of evaluation reports by those who commission them (reports are too convoluted, long, boring, or interesting but not useful for the specific requirements of the administration). Having helped the actors who commission reports to define more accurately the questions and the information they need, to understand what they want to know, what would be useful to evaluate, what can be evaluated with available resources, and what can be expected from the evaluations, the EP certainly had a positive effect on reducing those negative dynamics, notwithstanding the limits we have described.

On the other hand – and here we move on to the second aspect I wish to highlight – what the Sardinia experience has demonstrated is that if an evaluation study is intended to understand and reflect on the results of given policies – which is an essential requirement in modern development of future policies – the evaluation cannot merely be an ex-post judgment prepared after the policy is concluded. Instead, proper care must be taken already in the policy planning phase to assure that needed information for the evaluation will be generated during the implementation of the policy. In other words, the experience we have described supports the notion that to improve the possibility of evaluating policies, and of using the results of the evaluation to guide future policies, it is necessary to have policies that are oriented in this direction, i.e.:

- Policies that clearly establish the role and responsibilities of the institutions involved in defining the strategies and the objectives, as well as the implementation of the policies;
- Policies that ensure constant attention to the implementation process and to dealing with possible obstacles, and that treat any divergence between "norm" and "practice" as a learning opportunity rather than simply a negative factor;
- Policies capable, as a consequence, of adjusting to changes in the situation, stakeholder interests, the opportunities, but also the difficulties, obstacles, and implementation delays;
- Policies, therefore, that define ex-ante the tools needed to obtain information on the processes, and which consider the evaluation of the actions undertaken as part of the policy as a crucial aspect of the entire policy itself.

The lack of reliable data makes it difficult to satisfy the growing (often implicit) demand for the application of "rigorous" analysis methodologies – usually involving counterfactuals – to evaluate the results of policies, and especially R&D policies, as in our case. The request the evaluation study had the most difficulty complying with was precisely the analysis of the effects of the policies, and here we are on to the third and last aspect I wanted to emphasize. Although the considerable length of the time period examined should have made it possible to examine medium-term results, the weakness of the databases, the many gaps, and the lack of structural information on causal relations, left many interpretive hypotheses open for discussion. There is, first of all, the problem of the availability and usefulness of data, common to all evaluation studies but especially in the case of R&D policies, which are characterized by temporal delays, causality that is difficult to demonstrate (at least explicitly), and the various types of support involved, which are not always susceptible to being monitored or collectively interpreted. This, despite the large number of programs and measures that have been funded over the years in an area where public investments have been quite consistent (the amount of R&D public investment in Sardinia was more than double that of the rest of Southern Italy) casts doubt on the "experimental" logic of the interventions to be evaluated. Second, one must take into account the difficulty of carrying out effective and credible counterfactual studies, given the limited number of beneficiary firms and the fact that public support policies can end up distorting the behavior and choices of actors – including actors who are not directly involved. Not to mention the "conditioning logic" that, in low competitive contexts, end up binding policymakers to the needs of potential beneficiaries. Nevertheless, evaluators are increasingly required to provide information and judgments to guide policymaking.

In conclusion, the lessons that can be derived from this evaluation study are mainly related to the importance of establishing a strong and timely relation between the demand for and the supply of evaluation. In other words, a close relationship between the demanders of, and suppliers of, evaluation information should be built in already during the planning phase of the policies. Only in this way is it possible to reduce structural problems that impede the collection of information and data necessary to evaluate the results of our actions. The difficulty of acquiring data and information has been a problem for much of the evaluation work done in the current study and demonstrates the crucial importance of establishing the connection between demand and supply of evaluation information already in the policy planning phase. Ex-post efforts can help but they certainly cannot solve the problem.

Notes

1 The current period covers the years 2014–2020.

2 The EU regional policy is delivered through three main funds: the European Regional Development Fund (ERDF), the Cohesion Fund (CF), and the European Social Fund (ESF). Together with the European Agricultural Fund for Rural Development (EAFRD) and the European Maritime and Fisheries Fund (EMFF), they make up the European Structural and Investment (ESI) Funds. For more information on EU regional policy see: http://ec.europa.eu/regional_policy/en/

3 Including the author of this article.

4 A semi-structured draft interview was prepared and used with 12 people who, in the 1994–2006 period, had held important posts in the political system, administration, university, or innovative companies operating in Sardinia. The interviews, carried out in the first three months of the study, dealt with the following topics: 1) Strategy, 2) The implementation of research or innovation policies, 3) The "demand" for innovation on part of Sardinian firms.

References

Bachtler, J., & Mendez, C. (2016). *EU cohesion policy and European integration: The dynamics of EU budget and regional policy reform*. London & New York: Routledge.

Bachtler, J., & Michie, R. (1995). A new era in EU regional policy evaluation? The appraisal of the Structural Funds. *Regional Studies, 29*, 745–751.

European Commission. (2007). *The new programming period 2007–2013 – Indicative guidelines on evaluation methods: Evaluation during the programming period.* Working Document no. 5, April 2007. Brussels: European Commission.

Mazzeo Rinaldi, F. (2012). *Il Monitoraggio per la Valutazione: Concetti, metodi e strumenti*. Milan, Italy: FrancoAngeli. Retrieved from http://ec.europa.eu/regional_policy/sources/docoffic/2007/working/wd5_ongoing_en.pdf

Mazzeo Rinaldi, F., Saba, A., & Spano, A. (Eds.). (2012). *L'impatto delle politiche regionali per la ricerca scientifica e l'innovazione tecnologica per le imprese*. Reggio Emilia, Italy: Kataconsulting.

Mazzeo Rinaldi, F., & Spano, A. (2011). I percorsi della ricerca e dell'innovazione: un'analisi sulla condizione delle imprese in Sardegna. *RIV Rassegna Italiana di Valutazione, XV*(51), 89–110.

Molle, W. (2007). *European cohesion policy*. Routledge.

Pacifico, M. (2009). Migliorare la qualità delle valutazioni attraverso Steering Group: è davvero una soluzione? *RIV Rassegna Italiana di Valutazione, XIII*(45), 84–92.

Petropoulos, S. (2013). *Evaluation of the European Structural Funds. A historical perspective*. The Jean Monnet Papers on Political Economy, 04/2013. Greece. Retrieved from www.uop.gr/images/files/petropoulos.pdf

Sistema Nazionale di Valutazione della Politica Regionale (SNV). (2008, February). Orientamenti per l'organizzazione della politica regionale: Il Piano di Valutazione. Rome, Italy: DPS Tesoro.

Stern, E., Stame, N., Mayne, J., Forss, K., Davies, R., & Befani, B. (2012). *Broadening the range of designs and methods for impact evaluations. DFID Working Paper 38.* London, UK: Department for International Development. Retrieved from www.oecd.org/derec/50399683.pdf

Zoppi, C. (2009). Alcune riflessioni sull'attuazione del Piano di Valutazione della politica regionale unitaria della Sardegna. *RIV Rassegna Italiana di Valutazione, XIII*(43–44), 135–159.

8 Assessing the Contribution of Research to Improved Policy and Practice

An Evaluation of CIFOR's Climate Change Research

Brian Belcher, John Young, and Daniel Suryadarma

In this chapter, the authors examine the increasing demands of results-based management in the context of research programs. Based on a review of programs undertaken for CGIAR (a global research partnership on agriculture and natural resources management), Belcher, Rasmussen, Kemshaw, and Zornes (2016) highlight the difficulty of evaluating the impact of research in quantitative terms, particularly with respect to expected long-term outcomes. Attempts to impose targets such as demonstrating value for money can lead to perverse results. But, they argue, by defining (and continuously refining) the Theory of Change underlying research proposals, it is possible to demonstrate the usefulness of research programs and improve their effectiveness. CIFOR, a forestry research center operating under the umbrella of CGIAR, consequently developed a theory-based evaluation approach which is gaining traction in CGIAR as a whole. CIFOR's model was then applied to three country-based research programs; of necessity the evaluation approach was highly participatory, and one of the principle benefits was a mutual understanding of the interrelationship of the roles of the different actors involved. Moreover, the ability to clearly demonstrate to outsiders how the research effort would lead to positive change was well-received by funding sources.

The Context: Trends and Challenges in Results-Based Management of Research for Development

There is a pronounced trend toward results-based management approaches in public administration (Behn, 2003; Meier, 2003; Sjöstedt, 2013), with four main drivers referred to by Morgan and Grant (2013) as the "4 As:" accountability, allocation, advocacy, and analysis. This trend is also manifest in the research world as increased demand from research funders and research managers to assess, evaluate, and demonstrate the quality and *impact* of research. Funding bodies are seeking ways to increase and improve accountability and to get better information to help allocate resources. Researchers feel the need to demonstrate the value of their research to justify continued funding. And there is a need for analysis, to understand whether and how research contributes to society.

The various agencies that administer public and private development budgets are looking for evidence of significant, large-scale improvements in health, welfare, economic progress, and environmental quality. A glance at any agency website will quickly reveal big ticket claims about the number of people whose lives have been (or will be) improved through health programs, improved governance, education, agricultural improvement, energy development, green technology, or other interventions.

The CGIAR, a global research partnership on agriculture and natural resources management, funded mainly by overseas development assistance budgets, is on a similar path to implementing results-based management (RBM). The CGIAR Strategy and Results Framework (The Consultative Group on International Agricultural Research [CGIAR], 2015) includes ambitious targets for poverty reduction, improvements in food security and nutrition, and in natural resources and ecosystem services. These are referred to as "System Level Outcomes (SLOs)."[1] Individual research programs are likewise expected to state their targets as so-called "Intermediate Development Outcomes (IDOs)" in quantitative terms and to demonstrate progress toward those IDOs. Such targets are helpful in providing direction. They reflect the kinds of changes to which donors want their investments to contribute, and there are efforts underway to develop appropriate indicators and measures of progress at the IDO level. However, there is still a substantial gap between changes at this scale and what can realistically be achieved with a research project or even a longer-term program. We need appropriate ways to define and assess impact at the project and program scale.

Such targets, or elements of these targets, regularly get imposed upon projects in the name of value for money, and often with perverse results (Martin, 2011). As one critic put it:

> Goals and targets have become more rigid, measurement has taken over from judgement, linear Newtonian thinking and action denies and obliterates non-linear realities, motivation has to be "incentivized" by carrots and now with PbR [Payment by Results] the sticks have no carrots at all, relationships have become distant, trust, discretion and flexibility have gone out of the window and reporting becomes more of a misleading nightmare.
>
> (Chambers, 2014, para. 4)

But, just as there are strong critiques of results-based approaches, there are also strong normative and instrumental arguments in favor of improved performance measurement. Whitty (2008, p. 13) notes that:

> If an organization takes a position in the public sphere and in the policy debate on the public assertion that it is working to further the interests of a

> group of people, we argue that the legitimacy of this claim, and the accountability of the organization requires justification publicly.

Clearly, it is fair and reasonable to ask that research done by publicly funded organizations demonstrate that their work is contributing to positive change.

The instrumental justification for improved attention to results is that stronger links and better communication to a wider range of stakeholders will make the research organization more effective (Whitty, 2008).

These tensions also apply in the broader development world where it is increasingly recognized that large-scale blueprint projects rarely achieve expected outcomes, especially if excessive attention is paid to measuring them. This has resulted in the emergence of a new approach sometimes called "Doing Development Differently (DDD)" (The DDD Manifesto Community, 2014) or "Problem-driven Iterative Approaches (PDIA)" (Andrews, Pritchett, & Woolcock, 2012). This approach focuses on solving locally identified problems, encourages experimentation, establishes rapid feedback loops to facilitate learning, and actively engages all stakeholders to ensure that reforms are viable, legitimate, relevant, and supportable.

Advancing this approach requires formative evaluation tools to learn, adapt, and improve based on experience. This has been driven partly by the same RBM-oriented reforms within the CGIAR. Since 2011, research centers and their programs have had an explicit shared responsibility for achieving development outcomes. This entails new ways of working, and better ways of planning, monitoring, and evaluating our work. Indeed, whereas accountability and allocation objectives get much attention in RBM discussions, the evolving interest in and use of research evaluation to support learning and improved design is less discussed. Arguably, this aspect is equally or more important as a means to advance and improve research practice and research effectiveness. In their review of current research impact evaluation methodologies, Morgan and Grant (2013) highlight analysis as an area that needs more attention to advance the impact agenda. Researchers and research managers, as well as research funders, need appropriate criteria and methods for evaluating research design and implementation. They need improved tools and methods to assess whether and how their work is contributing to its intended outcomes and impacts. As Carter (2013, p. 1) describes, the impact agenda "is about enabling, understanding, and describing the beneficial outcomes of research."

Current understanding about whether and how research contributes to social, economic, and environmental change is woefully inadequate. Research evaluation still relies primarily on publication and citation metrics, despite all the weaknesses inherent to bibliometric methods for assessing and demonstrating impact (Reinstein, Hasselback, Riley, & Sinason, 2011; Seglen, 1997; Tijssen, Visser, & van Leeuwen, 2002). Furthermore, there are multiple meanings of "impact," from "research impact" which focuses on the influence of research on other researchers, through to large-scale, long-term social and environmental changes (Belcher & Palenberg, 2016). There is increasing attention to the impact of research beyond the academic realm. For example, the UK's 2014 Research Excellence Framework (REF) allocated 20 percent of the total score to impact, defined as "an effect on, change or benefit to the economy, society, culture, public policy or services, health, the environment or quality of life, beyond academia" (Higher Education Funding Council for England [HEFCE], 2016, para. 1). In the REF, impact was assessed using qualitative indicators of knowledge sharing, uptake and use, but many of these are still largely anecdotal and do not reflect deliberate impact strategies. Moreover, as noted by Hinrichs and Grant (2015), the REF case studies tend to be positioned as advocacy tools within a summative evaluation context and would need to be repurposed with a more analytical focus. There is thus a need for more systematic approaches.

The learning objective of research evaluation is especially important as research approaches evolve, crossing disciplinary boundaries and engaging a broader range of actors in the quest to improve effectiveness (Belcher, Rasmussen, Kemshaw, & Zornes, 2016; Carter, 2013; Clark & Dickson, 2003; Gibbons et al., 1994; Wickson, Carew, & Russell, 2006). Contemporary social and environmental problems are complex and multi-dimensional, they often cross scales, and they involve many different stakeholders with differing and frequently conflicting interests and perspectives. Problems of climate change, natural resource over-exploitation, and environmental degradation converge with issues of poverty, social conflict, corruption, and inequality. Addressing such urgent and important issues requires combinations of knowledge and innovation, action, and engagement.

An analysis of the 2014 UK Research Excellence Framework found that many cases of societal impact resulted from multidisciplinary work (King's College London and Digital Science, 2015). This reflects the fact that university researchers have engaged with a range of public, private, and charitable organizations and local communities as part of the research process. They are deliberately aiming to produce knowledge and to promote and facilitate the use of that knowledge to enable change, solve problems, and support innovation (Clark & Dickson, 2003). Transdisciplinary approaches transcend disciplinary and institutional boundaries to contextualize research around the interests of stakeholders and actively involve the users of research, to foster more socially robust knowledge (Gibbons & Nowotny, 2001). A new discipline of Sustainability Science has emerged, with emphasis on the idea that knowledge needs to be co-produced through collaborations of scholars and practitioners (Berkes, 2009; Clark & Dickson, 2003; Holling, 1993). The literature on linking knowledge to action stresses the importance of non-linear, dialogical, and discursive approaches and acknowledges that knowledge is socially constructed (van Kerkhoff & Lebel, 2006). New approaches emphasize "boundary work," where knowledge is created in conjunction with action and policymaking (Clark et al., 2011; Kristjanson et al., 2009). Researchers and research organizations need to learn systematically from this experience to improve their effectiveness in achieving intended results in complex, policy-relevant research environments. Appropriate tools and methods to meet this research evaluation challenge are still lacking.

It is critically important to develop, test, and improve tools and methods for evaluating the impact of research, especially in inter- and transdisciplinary contexts where there are explicit goals to contribute to change and where approaches, methods, and epistemologies are in development and lack disciplinary guidance (Belcher et al., 2016). Researchers and research managers need tools and methods to learn from experience; what works, why, and how when research is employed in complex systems. In addition, as other chapters in this book have explained, funders as well as the taxpayers and private donors they represent have the right to demand evidence that their funds are being well used and are making a difference. Publicly funded research needs to be accountable to taxpayers, intermediary users, and the ultimate (intended) beneficiaries of research-based knowledge.

The Center for International Forestry Research (CIFOR), a research center under the umbrella of the CGIAR,[2] finds itself at the crest of these two waves. CIFOR's research funding comes mainly from overseas development assistance (ODA) budgets directly through project funding and indirectly through the CGIAR – all of which have increased demand for results information.

As a research-for-development organization using research on forests, landscapes, and natural resources management as a way to contribute to poverty alleviation, food security, and environmental benefits, CIFOR is increasingly employing inter- and transdisciplinary approaches. The rationale for this shift is that stronger links to the problem context and increased engagement and partnership in the research process are expected to improve the relevance, legitimacy and, ultimately, the effectiveness of the research (Belcher et al., 2016). Assessing the impact of such development-oriented research is inherently challenging because the results chain (or results web) is complex, with multiple actors, long time-lags, and numerous feedback loops. Research is seldom the main driving cause or even the main trigger for large-scale social, economic, and environmental change. Quantitative evaluation methods are therefore not appropriate for many of the kinds of projects and programs CIFOR undertakes. Stimulated by a reform process in the CGIAR, CIFOR has developed a theory-based evaluation approach and has begun to test it.

Evaluation of the GCS-REDD+ Program

The Program

The Global Comparison Study on REDD+[3] program was organized around four thematic modules focusing on: 1) understanding governance of national climate change policy, 2) learning from sub-national REDD+ projects, 3) improving emission measurement, reporting, and verification (MRV) systems, and 4) guiding carbon management at the landscape scale. A fifth cross-cutting module focuses on sharing and dissemination of knowledge. A new focus on benefit-sharing was added in Phase 2. Figure 8.1 shows the overall structure of GCS-REDD+ program.

Through the GCS-REDD+, CIFOR and its partner organizations investigate international, national, and sub-national REDD+ experiences through comparative studies of the implementation of REDD+ in 12 tropical forest countries to identify challenges and contribute to solutions that support effective, efficient, and equitable REDD+ policies and projects. Through guidelines, tools, and analyses derived from comparative research across these countries and elsewhere, GCS-REDD+ aims to support all countries in their efforts to reduce emissions in an effective, efficient, and equitable way.

The first phase of GCS-REDD+ was completed in 2013, and the second phase was completed in December 2015.

Demand for Results Information

There were several sources of demand for the current evaluation. Most immediately, funders of the current GCS-REDD+ program wanted analysis of the work to help satisfy accountability needs. The program proponents and prospective donors for additional phases of research work also wanted the evaluation results for advocacy and allocation purposes – evidence of successful implementation and positive contributions from past work support efforts to provide further investment and support. There was and is also strong demand from the larger CGIAR to demonstrate results as part of the RBM approach discussed above. There has been a fundamental shift that began a reform process in 2011. Previously centers, their programs, projects, and scientists were primarily accountable for producing high quality scientific outputs. It was always intended that science and the knowledge produced would be relevant to priority development and conservation issues. However, the focus was on the science products. The emphasis has shifted, and centers and their programs now have an explicit shared responsibility for achieving development outcomes. This requires new ways of working, and better ways of planning, monitoring, and evaluating our work. There is a strong demand from research managers at CIFOR, and more broadly for analysis, to learn lessons about what works and how, in research-for-development contexts.

CIFOR has been developing theory-based approaches for monitoring and evaluating outcomes and impacts, and the approach has gained considerable traction in the CGIAR as a whole, with all programs required to develop Theories of Change (ToC) as part of the reform process. There has also been a groundswell of interest in theory-based evaluation in the evaluation community more broadly (Stern et al., 2012; White, 2009). In essence, we are developing and promoting a system in which the intended contributions of research are deliberate, explicit and testable, which improves our ability to gather evidence, assess, and communicate our outcomes and impacts for enhanced accountability, and our ability to learn from our experience. But the theory has been ahead of the practice (Mayne, Stern, & Douthwaite, 2013; Mayne & Stern, 2013; White, 2009; White & Phillips, 2012). There is a need for well-tested methods to assess the outcomes and the impacts of research for development. It is challenging. The interventions themselves involve many different aspects and relationships. CIFOR has deliberately developed a strategy around three pillars of knowledge creation (the research), capacity building, and engagement. Hence, there are multiple points of intervention and multiple actors involved in complex systems. With the evaluation reported here, and some other related activities, we have begun to test theory-based evaluation approaches.

Evaluation Design

The main evaluation question was: How well has the GCS-REDD+ achieved its goals, and how could it be improved?

The evaluation was based on testing an overall ToC and three country-level ToCs. It sought evidence to assess whether or not individual stages in the ToCs were achieved and whether the overall program goals were achieved (ToC development is discussed below).

The evaluation was led by John Young from the Overseas Development Institute (ODI) with a large team that included four ODI staff, three members of CIFOR's Monitoring, Evaluation and Impact Assessment (MEIA) team, a team of three from Royal Roads University, and three independent researchers. The work was done in a participatory mode with regular engagement of GCS-REDD+ scientists.

We used a mixed methods approach to collect data to test the ToCs in the country studies and other sub-studies, investigating different impact pathways to help answer a series of seven evaluation questions:

- How has GCS activity contributed to its end-of-program outcomes?
- Are the target audiences using the GCS work?
- Are the target audiences aware of GCS work?
- Have GCS engagement and communication channels been effective?
- Have GCS projects produced relevant science to achieve its goals?
- Have the GCS program and its projects been effectively integrated across scales (sub-national, national, and global)?
- Has the GCS utilized coherent strategies to achieve its outcomes?

The overall process is illustrated in Figure 8.1.

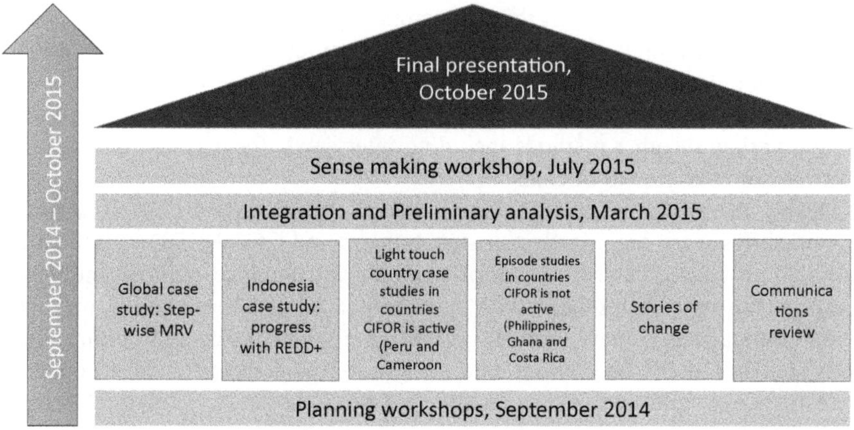

Figure 8.1 GCS-REDD+ Outcome Evaluation Process (copied from Young & Bird, 2015).

Implementation

The evaluation was implemented in four stages, with GCS-REDD+ program scientists engaged in each stage of the evaluation.

During the initial preparation and planning phase (August–September 2014), there was a two-day inception workshop in CIFOR headquarters involving all component leaders and senior management and a one-day workshop for CIFOR staff who would be undertaking the CIFOR country case studies, as well as a series of individual consultations. These meetings were used to familiarize scientists with the overall objectives and approach, to co-develop the evaluation questions, to identify individual studies and, importantly, to articulate and document the ToCs (discussed below).

The main data collection work was done during the research phase (October 2014–February 2015) with six individual studies.[4] A wide range of approaches and methods was used across these components including clarification of the program's ToC; literature review and interviews to assess whether the expected outputs were delivered and had the expected effect; episode studies (Young, Kajume, & Wanyama, 2003) to describe the evolution of REDD+ policies over time; stories of change to illustrate and explore specific cases where CIFOR work seemed to have had an impact; audience surveys to assess the reach and uptake of CIFOR's publications; and workshops and focus group discussions. The challenge with approaches to assess the impact of research on policy is that the classical case study approach – tracing forward from project activities – tends to overemphasize the impact of the project, while historical analysis – tracing back from observed policy changes – tends to emphasize wider political processes. The RAPID Outcome Assessment Approach (Leksmono, Young, Hooton, Muriuki, & Romney, 2006) is a participatory workshop-based approach in which key stakeholders in a policy process construct a historical narrative of the key behavioral changes in the key actors in a policy process, tracking back from an agreed policy change. They then construct a project or intervention timeline and identify specific contributions that project activities may have made to these changes. The validity of these contributions can then be triangulated using a variety of other methods including interviews, focus group discussions, questionnaires, or stories of change.

During the analysis and reporting phase (February–March 2015), a series of workshops were organized with stakeholders and GCS-REDD+ researchers and staff to share, verify, and improve data and analyses. These included: country case study workshops with stakeholders in Indonesia and Cameroon; a communications review workshop with component leads and communications staff at CIFOR HQ; and a data integration workshop for the evaluation team to review and synthesize results to date, finalize the analytical framework, and identify additional data needs. Data were systematically extracted from the various studies against the overall ToC and against key evaluation questions in two separate results charts (with considerable overlap between the two). Each results chart presents summaries of results corresponding to ToC nodes and key evaluation questions respectively, with evidence reported as bullet points of relevant data by source, and the source for each piece of data. A companion evidence table collated references for all the source material.

Finally, a learning and sharing phase (July–October 2015) included a sense-making workshop involving research module leaders and CIFOR research managers to discuss and further develop emerging findings, conclusions, and recommendations. A presentation and discussion of the final results were given at the CIFOR Annual Meeting in October 2015. The final report including recommendations was prepared by ODI (Young & Bird, 2015).

Theory of Change Development and Use

The evaluation was based on an overall GCS-REDD+ ToC and country-level ToCs for Indonesia, Peru, and Cameroon. While elements of these ToCs were explicit in some of the original project documents and in CIFOR's larger strategy, there was no fully articulated program ToC from which to work. A major component of the preparation and planning phase was to collaboratively develop and document the overall and country-level ToCs. This was done iteratively. We developed draft ToCs in the form of diagrams during the inception workshop and in subsequent working group meetings, and revised them through subsequent review and discussion, remotely and in-person.

Evaluation Results

A summary of the results against the key evaluation questions is provided in Box 8.1.

Box 8.1 Summary of the results against the key evaluation questions[5]

- **How well has the GCS-REDD+ achieved its goals, and how could it be improved?** The main goal of the GCS-REDD+ program is hugely ambitious for a research organization like CIFOR, especially in such a highly contested policy arena, and clearly remains out of reach in the absence of a global agreement on REDD+. There is evidence, however, that the GCS-REDD+ program is influencing the development of systems that are effective, efficient, and equitable for when a global agreement is reached. CIFOR has influenced the United Nations Framework Convention on Climate Change (UNFCCC) to adopt a stepwise approach to setting reference levels internationally. The approach has also been adopted in several countries and CIFOR has demonstrably increased the capacity and influenced the behavior of national policymakers and other relevant actors.
- **How has GCS-REDD+ activity contributed to its end-of-program outcomes?** CIFOR has achieved these outcomes in five main ways: 1) production of high quality independent research and publications and extended outreach, 2) development of approaches and tools such as the stepwise approach, 3) provision of expert support at the international and national level, 4) hosting of international events and training, and 5) collaboration with and capacity development of national partners.
- **Are target audiences using the GCS-REDD+ work?** The GCS-REDD+ ToC identifies six categories of actor expected to use CIFOR research: 1) national research partners, 2) proponents (national organizations involved in pilot projects), 3) national practitioners (operational agencies and practitioners, including communities, the private sector and the media), 4) national policymakers, 5) international research partners, and 6) international policy actors (e.g., Intergovernmental Panel on Climate Change (IPCC), bilateral and multilateral donors). The assessment found strong evidence that all these stakeholders are using CIFOR research in their work.
- **Are the target audiences aware of GCS-REDD+ work?** There is widespread awareness of CIFOR's work among the people contacted as part of this assessment. This is not surprising, however, since the assessment used CIFOR mailing lists for the surveys and interacted largely with those working with CIFOR staff for the country studies. However, the fact that many people are using the work indicates that they must be aware of the work.
- **Have GCS-REDD+ engagement and communication channels been effective?** GCS-REDD+ uses a very wide range of channels for communication and engagement including digital (web and social media), publications, events and conferences, research collaboration, personal engagement, formal engagement with national governments, and practical engagement with practitioners. The assessment found strong evidence that all these channels are being used effectively. CIFOR has a particularly strong digital strategy to reach global audiences, CIFOR publications are well regarded and frequently consulted, international events and conferences are well known, well attended and attract high-level participants. Respondents in the national case studies and the Indonesia Country Study workshop asked, however, for more national events. Research collaboration is clearly a very effective element of CIFOR's

engagement work. CIFOR also engages effectively with a wide range of practitioners at the national level, including proponents (organisations testing REDD+ approaches at the field level).

- **Have GCS-REDD+ projects produced relevant science to achieve its goals?** The GCS-REDD+ program has produced a vast range of relevant and useful science including 5 books and 84 book chapters, 157 journal articles, 48 working and occasional papers, 48 policy and information briefs, and 5 doctoral theses.
- **Has the GCS-REDD+ program and its projects been effectively integrated across scales (sub-national, national, and global)?** The GCS-REDD+ was designed from the start as an integrated program with interlocking components. Management and coordination mechanisms have been flexible and responsive and have evolved appropriately, as the program has developed, but this seems to work best at international level among staff based in Indonesia, whereas some country-level staff have described not being fully aware of what other components are doing.
- **Has the GCS-REDD+ used coherent strategies to achieve its outcomes?** The original project design has been strengthened by the development of a global ToC identifying specific boundary partners and uptake pathways, but there remains some confusion among lower-level staff about the theory and practice of ToC.

Source: Young and Bird (2015, pp. 7–8)

Feedback from Key Constituents

The GCS-REDD+ evaluation has been well-received by various key constituencies. The program team appreciated being involved as active participants. This was a novelty for most, having previously been subjected to independent summative evaluations that have high time costs preparing inputs but little genuine engagement, and that often yield results that are seriously compromised because the evaluators did not fully understand important aspects of the project. The process itself was highly reflective, with a great deal of mutual discovery and learning. This benefit may be especially pronounced in the context of a research organization where people are inherently analytical and self-critical.

Key donors to the program have expressed a high appreciation for the evaluation and one donor included it in their project completion report. Another donor representative is using the evaluation presentation PowerPoint to help communicate the project and its accomplishments to colleagues. An international knowledge organization with a similar model to CIFOR decided to adopt the method in one of its evaluations.

Lessons Learned

Participatory Evaluation

The GCS-REDD+ evaluation made a deliberate choice to use a participatory approach with a high level of engagement by the scientists and managers whose program was being evaluated. Although the participatory nature carries a risk of being perceived as biased, especially in an era where professed need for independence permeates the evaluation community, this was motivated by two main considerations. First, we felt that the learning objective would be best served by involving the scientists and managers in the process. This is consistent with contemporary knowledge theory (Cash et al., 2002; van Kerkhoff & Lebel, 2006) and indeed with CIFOR's and the GCS-REDD+ ToCs that highlight the role of engagement and co-generation of knowledge results in supporting knowledge uptake and use. Staff were initially wary of making a major contribution because they are already very busy, and many had recently been involved in other evaluations and felt their views had not been adequately reflected in the final reports. However, the structure and approach to facilitation of the workshops, with obvious learning through shared information, processes of explanation and negotiation during the design phase, exposure to raw data, collaborative analysis and interpretation of those data, and immediate awareness and appreciation of results and recommendations overcame this reticence. By the end of the exercise, staff were enthusiastic to participate and found that the process provided a valuable platform for self-reflection within the research team, also increasing their willingness to participate in any further evaluation-type activities.

Second, from a practical perspective, it would be difficult or impossible to do an evaluation of this kind without a high level of participation. The intervention logic is complex, with multiple relationships and processes. Staff needed to be fully engaged to facilitate understanding by the evaluation team of the purpose and the approach, and to be able to provide necessary information on contacts, networks, and events. A less participatory evaluation would run a high risk of missing and misunderstanding the full range and the subtleties of the program.

The country studies also included highly participatory workshops, bringing together key informants and other stakeholders to review emerging results. A simplified version of ODI's RAPID Outcome Assessment (Leksmono et al., 2006) was used for this purpose, and provided an opportunity to assess the specific contribution that CIFOR's work had made to observed changes in REDD+ policies and programs.

Theory of Change Development and Use

The ToC is the backbone of this kind of evaluation (Figure 8.2). It enables us to construct hypotheses that we need to test in the assessment. It defines what kind of evidence is needed and where to seek that evidence. It provides the basis for assembling data into evidence, and extrapolating beyond the end-of-program (EOP) stage to make at least plausible arguments about how the intervention – in this case, a research program – can contribute to higher-level outcomes and overall impacts.

It was a challenge to develop the ToC retrospectively. Inevitably, there was some revisionism; the ToC developed as part of the evaluation includes recent insights and additions and is not a completely accurate representation of an

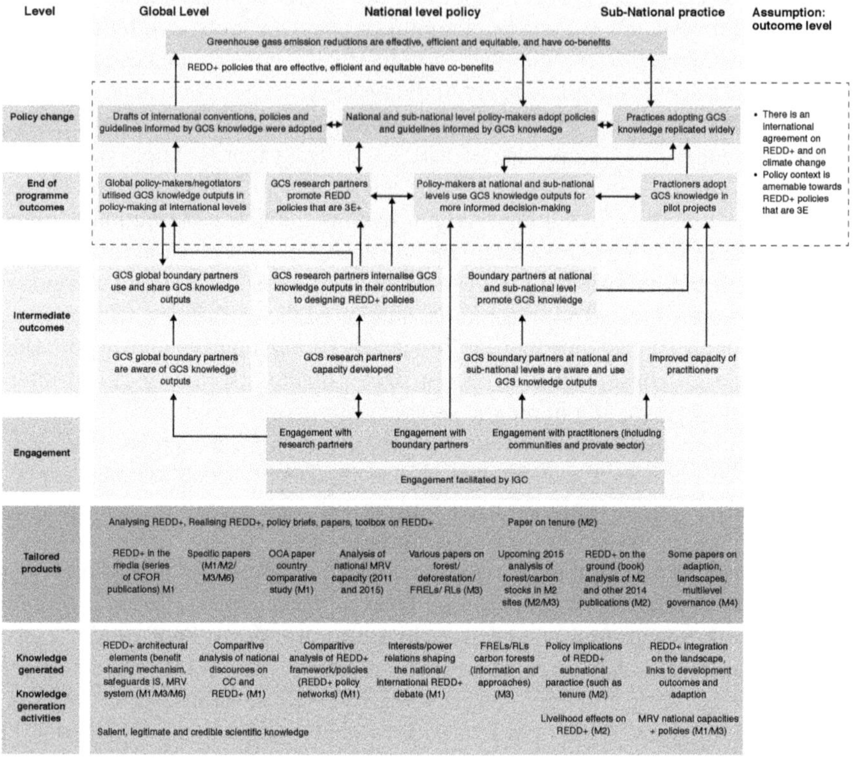

Figure 8.2 GCS Theory of Change (copied from Young & Bird, 2015).

original ToC. We do not feel that this undermines the evaluation in any way. We are interested to know whether and how the research and related activities contribute to change processes, and we need to test the most current understanding. Even if there had been a well-documented original ToC, it would be reasonable to expect that it would have been revised and improved with experience and that a revised and improved ToC would be the appropriate basis for evaluation.

The process of ToC development was valuable. It provided a platform for scientists and managers to discuss underlying assumptions, strategies, and tactics, and to discover that their ideas and perspectives were not always aligned, even within the same module. However, it is clear that these kinds of discussions would be much more helpful if they started at the design stage and can be used to guide implementation. CIFOR has made a policy decision that all new projects over US$500,000 must develop a ToC and identify key partners, pathways, and intervention strategies. This does not obviate the need for ongoing reflection, discussion, and adaptation, but will provide a stronger starting point.

More challenging, perhaps, is to improve the quality of ToCs. The current GCS-REDD+ ToC is still highly schematic, with limited supporting theory. As discussed above, the program is multifaceted, with numerous research activities and support activities, a wide range of research and other partners, in multiple sites, and it is intervening in complex systems. On face value, it assumes a knowledge deficit, and implies that by providing knowledge and information, and also by motivating and facilitating other actors, the program can stimulate more beneficial outcomes. The analysis in the evaluation was constrained by the incomplete identification of key intended audiences and theory about how they would respond to the program outputs. For example, the third level in the ToC concerning "tailored products" suggests that the audiences and their needs are known, and the products were specifically designed to meet those needs. In practice, the program made a strong effort to produce and disseminate information in formats accessible to non-technical audiences, but it is not clear that there was strategic and targeted tailoring. It is highly likely that more could be done to identify and engage strategically at various points in the ToC.

In addition, the discussions and joint analysis during the evaluation revealed theories and strategies that were employed but were not reflected in the overall or national-level ToCs. As one small example, scientists discussed a practice of inviting influential individuals to act as peer reviewers for research or popular articles as a way to both increase the likelihood that those individuals would read that material and to engage them in subsequent dialogue. The Indonesia country case study revealed that a major contributor to the impact of CIFOR's work in that country was through the employment of a senior Indonesian policymaker/researcher, who had personal contacts and the ability to convey the results of CIFOR's research directly and personally to senior Indonesian policymakers.

Generally speaking, scientific understanding of knowledge translation, particularly in policy processes, is still not well-developed. Moreover, scientists working on climate change (or other areas of CIFOR) research are not necessarily experts in knowledge translation and policy influence. Further research is needed, including ongoing ToC testing, to improve our understanding about how research contributes to change. More support is needed to help develop better-informed and more theoretically sophisticated ToCs. For example, managers in research organizations might consider recruiting senior staff not only on the basis of their research skills, but also for their knowledge of policy processes and ability to relate directly to policymakers.

Tools and Methods

While many of the methods and tools, including episode studies, stories of change and RAPID Outcome Assessment workshops, have been used widely by ODI and other organizations with a specific interest in the impact of research on policy, this is the first time that they have been brought together with collaborative outcomes reporting to develop a performance story (Dart & Roberts, 2014).

Sub-evaluation questions used in the evaluation were derived from previous ODI work on assessing the impact of research on policy. They provided a useful framework, but in practice it was difficult to distinguish between Question 3 ("Are the target audiences aware of GCS work?") and Question 2 ("Are the target audiences using GCS work?"). In retrospect, sub-questions mapped closely to the ToC and could have been derived directly from the ToC (Young & Bird, 2015).

The results tables proved to be a very effective way to assemble a wide range of data. Much of these data might, in isolation, be considered anecdotal with limited value. By structuring a large amount of qualitative data within a theoretical structure, it becomes much more convincing and possible to employ this data as evidence in a defensible argument.

Quality of Evidence

There were problems with quality and relevance of some data for multiple reasons, including:

- Insufficiently articulated ToC (discussed above);
- Considerable difficulties in formulating interview questions and workshop techniques to explore possible alternative scenarios (i.e., what would have happened without the program);
- Insufficient skills in interviewing by some enumerators;
- Incomplete understanding of the underlying principles of the evaluation, and therefore the data requirements, by contracted authors of sub-studies;
- The focus in the communications review on aggregate numbers instead of on disaggregated assessment of tailoring and targeting of outputs;
- Operational delays with some of the components such that some data were not available in time for the integration and sense-making workshops.

There is also an important weakness in the overall argument. Any assessment of change due to an intervention must consider what would have happened without the intervention. In classical impact evaluation, this is called the counterfactual. The strength of randomized control trials is that they deal with counterfactuals experimentally. Constructing the counterfactual is much more complicated in qualitative evaluations. Contribution analysis (Mayne, 2012) tries to construct an alternative hypothesis which considers the change that has happened and asks if there are plausible explanations other than the intervention being investigated. If there is a convincing theoretical and empirical case that the intervention has had a causal role, and if there is no plausible alternative hypothesis, then there is a strong case to claim a contribution. If there is a plausible alternative hypothesis, then more work is needed to try to determine if one or both mechanisms were at work and, if possible, their relative contributions. This depends on the systematic collection of information about other actors and political factors shaping policy processes, for example, in order to assess the program's contribution.

The RAPID Outcome Assessment Approach attempts to do this through a participatory process where a wide range of stakeholders map the policy process over a long period, assessing the whole range of influences from both the project and that which otherwise contributed to key events in the policy process. However, this was only possible in the Indonesia country case study, and only to a limited extent.

Another attempt was made to assess the counterfactual using the Redstone Strategy approach (Redstone Strategy Group, 2013) during the sense-making workshop. The method assumes that six "conditions" are essential for the effective implementation of policy change: 1) functioning institutions, 2) responsive and accessible supporting research, 3) a feasible, specific, and flexible solution, 4) powerful champions in the key institutions, 5) a well-planned, led, and supported campaign, and 6) a clear implementation path (Redstone Strategy Group, 2013). Informants familiar with the situation assess the status of each condition (as a percentage "sufficient") before and after an intervention and estimate what proportion of the increase could be attributed to the intervention, and what other actors also contributed. The outcome depends on the representativeness, knowledge, and expertise of the participants, and is highly subjective. The GCS-REDD+ evaluation tried this method, but the participants were mainly from the research team, which was not adequately representative. Repeating the same exercise with other stakeholders, such that a sufficient sample size is acquired, might be a way to improve the validity of the exercise. Nevertheless, the process effectively stimulated deep consideration and discussion about the various processes and the roles of key actors.

Conclusions

The GCS-REDD+ evaluation reported here helps bridge the substantial attribution gap between a multifaceted research program and the conservation and development impacts the research seeks to contribute to by articulating and testing a ToC. A key element in this approach is the clear definition of EOP outcomes; in this case, changes in the discourse and in actions in both practice and policy realms that are logically linked to knowledge production, capacity development and engagement by the GCS-REDD+ program. These EOP outcomes are well outside the sphere of control of the program yet remain within its sphere of influence. The ToC also illustrates the anticipated/hypothesized pathways by which those changes may lead to development impacts beyond the EOP outcomes. This produces a plausible story of change and a means of testing that is useful to researchers, research managers, and funders.

The approach generates a well-organized evidence base in the results chart and evidence table. In combination with the ToC, these tables help to transform what would otherwise be weak circumstantial evidence – individual instances of research utilization and even opinion by users on the utility and value of the research program – into structured evidence to help confirm or disconfirm the ToC.

The experience with the GCS-REDD+ evaluation suggests several areas for improvement that would make the evidence and theory testing stronger. First, the data collection could be strengthened. The evaluation involved a large number of individual component studies, each with its own design and different teams. Inevitably, some of the component studies were stronger than others, but all could be improved with better interview guides used in key informant interviews and with more training for enumerators and especially for external consultants to ensure a more complete and coherent understanding of the overall purpose and approach. We have refined the instruments based on this experience.

Second, we need to strengthen the assessment of causality. Assessing evidence against the ToC allows us to determine if the hypothesized outcomes have been realized. If they have not, we need to consider that the program has failed in some way, that the ToC is incorrect, or that something in the context has been misjudged or has changed. Investigating these possibilities further will help build our understanding of the change process and how to intervene more successfully. However, even if outcomes have been realized, we still do not know if the change was caused by the intervention, other factors, or a combination of both. As discussed earlier, constructing a counterfactual in complex environments is exceedingly difficult. The RAPID Outcome Assessment Approach and the Redstone Strategy approach both seek to facilitate a thorough and honest exploration of causality based on expert judgment from a wide range of perspectives. Applying these approaches more effectively, or some variant of them, would be worth exploring in future evaluations.

Third, the ToC used in the evaluation is rather simplistic. It essentially assumes that the research, the capacity building, and the engagement will inject valuable and useful knowledge into processes where it will be used to improve policy and practice with positive results. The thematic work in the modules had a more sophisticated understanding of the political economy, policy processes at national and international levels, and the practical realities on the ground than is reflected in Figure 8.2. Indeed, part of the research focus was to improve understanding of those aspects. Still, there is substantial scope to draw on social scientific theories of knowledge translation and policy processes to develop more sophisticated ToCs. The challenge of articulating the ToC retrospectively, and the high value realized in the process, makes a strong argument for developing an explicit ToC as part of project planning. Doing so would help anticipate and plan for change processes, develop a shared vision among the team, provide an improved basis for discussion/negotiation with donors, encourage reasonable expectations about what can be achieved and provide a good foundation for monitoring and evaluating the work. CIFOR has taken a policy decision that all new projects and programs should have an explicit ToC and have invested in training staff and facilitating project inception workshops to build capacity and improve implementation in this area.

It is difficult to accurately estimate the cost of the evaluation because it involved many different people who contributed their time. We estimate that the cost of the evaluation was approximately 1 percent of the resources invested in the program. The GCS-REDD+ program is large and complex, so it required a relatively large evaluation. Again, with the experience of this round, we will be able to refine the approach in the future.

This evaluation generated a substantial and credible body of evidence of the outcomes and effectiveness of the CIFOR GCS-REDD+ program, and provided space for a wide range of stakeholders from inside and outside the program to reflect on progress and learn how to do it better. A key test of the method is whether or not it is acceptable to the main audiences; does it satisfy demand? In this case, main donors have expressed their appreciation for the evaluation and have used the results in their own presentations. They found evaluation to be sufficiently rigorous and informative to use to promote the program further. Current and new funders have invested in the next phase of work. For the researchers, the systematic hypothesis testing used in this method provided a familiar and credible analytical framework. The participatory approach that involved project scientists in the design of the evaluation, the ToC articulation, data collection, and rounds of analysis obviously supported team learning about past work and about possible adaptations for the future. It also gave additional opportunities for sharing across the components of the GCS-REDD+ project, an element that the evaluation found had been suboptimal during program implementation. The evaluation also provided exposure to feedback from various partners and representatives of intended research users, who were not all entirely satisfied with their relationships. It is safe to say that this learning has been substantially stronger and deeper than would have been achieved with an independent external evaluation. Furthermore, the value to research managers at CIFOR is clearly indicated by the policy decision to use ToC in new project- and program design, planning, monitoring, and evaluation as a systematic way to improve accountability, decision-making, and learning. With the improvements described above, we strongly recommend the approach for the evaluation of projects and programs in complex environments, especially for projects where the gap between their end-of-project outputs and intended impacts is large and requires a long time to realize.

Notes

1 Most widely-used definitions would call them impacts rather than outcomes (Belcher & Palenberg, 2016).
2 www.cgiar.org/
3 REDD+ stands for countries' efforts to reduce emissions from deforestation and forest degradation, and foster conservation, sustainable management of forests, and enhancement of forest carbon stocks.
4 The case studies were:

> A case study on the contribution of GCS-REDD+ work to the adoption of the stepwise approach in setting reference emission levels and reference levels (REL/RL) in international processes, and the degree to which that has been reflected in national-level plans.
>
> A case study on the contribution GCS-REDD+ work to REDD+ readiness (REDD+ policy development, procedures, and capacity) in Indonesia.
>
> Light-touch country case studies in Peru and Cameroon, countries where CIFOR has undertaken GCS-REDD+ research at country level, to assess the contribution to REDD+ readiness both through international channels – focusing on the MRV story – and through direct engagement in the country.

Episode studies in countries where CIFOR has not been active to assess the influence of the GCS-REDD+ program in countries where there was no active country-level research program (these studies were commissioned from independent researchers).

Ten "stories of change" to document events/changes identified by CIFOR staff and other stakeholders where CIFOR work seems to have been influential.

Communications review, including two surveys to assess the reach and uptake of GCS-REDD+ information.

5 For general results statements: Strong evidence implies four or more citations from several assessment types (e.g., global study, country studies, episode studies); Moderate evidence implies two to four citations; Poor evidence implies single or implicit citations only. Cited evidence does not include all the evidence gathered, only examples of evidence that clearly link to the expected results.

References

Andrews, M., Pritchett, L., & Woolcock, M. (2012). *Escaping capability traps through Problem-Driven Iterative Adaptation (PDIA). CGD Working Paper 299.* Washington, DC: Center for Global Development.

Behn, R. D. (2003). Why measure performance? Different purposes require different measures. *Public Administration Review, 63,* 586–606.

Belcher, B., & Palenberg, M. (2016). *Outcomes and impact terminology: Towards conceptual clarity.* Expert Lecture to the American Evaluation Association, Atlanta, GA, USA. October 26–29, 2016.

Belcher, B. M., Rasmussen, K. E., Kemshaw, M. R., & Zornes, D. A. (2016). Defining and assessing research quality in a transdisciplinary context. *Research Evaluation, 25,* 1–17.

Belcher, B., Suryadarma, D., & Halimanjaya, A. (2017). Evaluating policy-relevant research: Lessons from a series of theory-based outcomes assessments. *Palgrave Communications, 3,* 1–16.

Berkes, F. (2009). Evolution of co-management: Role of knowledge generation, bridging organizations and social learning. *Journal of Environmental Management, 90,* 1692–1702.

Carter, I. M. (2013). The impact of impact on universities: Skills, resources and organizational structures. In A. Dean, M. Wykes, & H. Stevens (Eds.), *7 essays on impact* (pp. 14–24). DESCRIBE Project Report. University of Exeter. Retrieved from www.exeter.ac.uk/media/universityofexeter/research/ourresearchexcellence/describeproject/pdfs/2013_06_04_7_Essays_on_Impact_FINAL.pdf

Cash, D., Clark, W. C., Alcock, F., Dickson, N. M., Eckley, N., & Jäger, J. (2002). *Salience, credibility, legitimacy and boundaries: Linking research, assessment and decision-making.* KSG Faculty Research Working Papers Series, 2003. John F. Kennedy School of Government, Harvard University.

CGIAR. (2015). CGIAR strategy and results framework 2015–2030. Montpellier, France: CGIAR Consortium Office.

Chambers, R. (2014). Perverse payment by results: Frogs in a pot and straitjackets for obstacle courses. Participation, power and social change research at IDS. *An Institute of Development Studies Blog.* Retrieved from https://participationpower.wordpress.com/2014/09/03/perverse-payment-by-results-frogs-in-a-pot-and-straitjackets-for-obstacle-courses/

Clark, W. C., & Dickson, N. M. (2003). Sustainability science: The emerging research program. *Proceedings of the National Academy of Sciences of the United States of America, 100*, 8059–8061.

Clark, W. C., Tomich, T. P., van Noordwijk, M., Guston, D., Catacutan, D., Dickson, N. M., McNie, E. (2011). Boundary work for sustainable development: Natural resource management at the Consultative Group on International Agricultural Research (CGIAR). *Proceedings of the National Academy of Sciences of the United States of America, 113*(17), 4615–4622.

Dart, J., & Roberts, M. (2014). Collaborative outcomes reporting. *Better Evaluation – Sharing information to improve evaluation.* Retrieved from http://betterevaluation.org/plan/approach/cort

The DDD Manifesto Community. (2014). Doing Development Differently. A statement from the October 2014 "Doing Development Differently" workshop. *The DDD Manifesto Community.*

Gibbons, M., Limoges, C., Nowotny, H., Schwartzman, S., Scott, P., & Trow, M. (1994). *The new production of knowledge: The dynamics of science and research in contemporary studies*. London, UK: SAGE Publications.

Gibbons, M., & Nowotny, H. (2001). The potential of transdisciplinarity. In J. Thompson Klein, W. Grossenbacher-Mansuy, R. Häberli, A. Bill, R. W. Scholz, & M. Welti (Eds.), *Transdisciplinarity: Joint problem solving among science, technology, and society: An effective way of managing complexity* (pp. 67–80). Basel, Switzerland: Birkhäuser Basel.

Higher Education Funding Council for England [HEFCE]. (2016). REF impact. *HEFCE.*

Hinrichs, S., & Grant, J. (2015). A new resource for identifying and assessing the impacts of research. *BMC Medicine, 13*, 148–150.

Holling, C. S. (1993). Investing in research for sustainability. *Ecological Applications, 3*, 552–555.

King's College London and Digital Science. (2015). *The nature, scale and beneficiaries of research impact: An initial analysis of Research Excellence Framework (REF) 2014 impact case studies*. King's College London.

Kristjanson, P., Reid, R. S., Dickson, N., Clark, W. C., Romney, D., Puskur, R., MacMillan, S., & Grace, D. (2009). Linking international agricultural research knowledge with action for sustainable development. *Proceedings of the National Academy of Sciences of the United States of America, 106*, 5047–5052.

Leksmono, C., Young, J., Hooton, N., Muriuki, H., & Romney, D. (2006). *Informal traders lock horns with the formal milk industry: The role of research in pro-poor dairy policy shift in Kenya*. London, UK: Overseas Development Institute. Retrieved from www.odi.org.uk/resources/download/135.pdf

Martin, B. R. (2011). The research excellence framework and the "impact agenda:" Are we creating a Frankenstein monster? *Research Evaluation, 20*, 247–254.

Mayne, J. (2012). Contribution analysis: Coming of age? *Evaluation, 18*, 270–280.

Mayne, J., & Stern, E. (2013). *Impact evaluation of natural resource management research programs: A broader view. ACIAR Impact Assessment Series Report No. 84.* Canberra: Australian Centre for International Agricultural Research.

Mayne, J., Stern, E., & Douthwaite, B. (2013). *AAS practice brief: Evaluating natural resource management programs*. Penang, Malaysia: CGIAR Research Program on Aquatic Agricultural Systems.

Meier, W. (2003). *Results-based management: Towards a common understanding among development cooperation agencies.* Managing for Development Results.

Morgan, M., & Grant, J. (2013). Making the grade: Methodologies for assessing and evidencing research impact. In A. Dean, M. Wykes, & H. Stevens (Eds.), *7 essays on impact* (pp. 25–43). DESCRIBE Project Report. University of Exeter. Retrieved from www.exeter.ac.uk/media/universityofexeter/research/ourresearchexcellence/describe-project/pdfs/2013_06_04_7_Essays_on_Impact_FINAL.pdf

Redstone Strategy Group. (2013). *Helping think tanks measure impact.* Boulder, CO: Redstone Strategy Group. Retrieved from www.redstonestrategy.com/wp-content/uploads/2013/09/2013-09-30-IDRC-Helping-think-tanks-measure-impact.pdf

Reinstein, A., Hasselback, J. R., Riley, M. E., & Sinason, D. H. (2011). Pitfalls of using citation indices for making academic accounting promotion, tenure, teaching load, and merit pay decisions. *Issues in Accounting Education, 26*, 99–131.

Seglen, P. O. (1997). Citations and journal impact factors: Questionable indicators of research quality. *Allergy, 52*, 1050–1056.

Sjöstedt, M. (2013). Aid effectiveness and the Paris Declaration: A mismatch between ownership and results-based management? *Public Administration and Development, 33*, 143–155.

Stern, E., Stame, N., Mayne, J., Forss, K., Davies, R., & Befani, B. (2012). *Broadening the range of designs and methods for impact evaluations. DFID Working Paper 38.* London, UK: Department for International Development. Retrieved from www.gov.uk/government/uploads/system/uploads/attachment_data/file/67427/design-method-impact-eval.pdf

Tijssen, R. J., Visser, M. S., & van Leeuwen, T. N. (2002). Benchmarking international scientific excellence: Are highly cited research papers an appropriate frame of reference? *Scientometrics, 54*, 381–397.

van Kerkhoff, L., & Lebel, L. (2006). Linking knowledge and action for sustainable development. *Annual Review of Environment and Resources, 31*, 445–477.

White, H. (2009). *Theory-based impact evaluation: Principles and practice. International Initiative for Impact Evaluation Working Paper 3.* International Initiative for Impact Evaluation.

White, H., & Phillips, D. (2012). *Addressing attribution of cause and effect in small n impact evaluations: Towards an integrated framework. International Initiative for Impact Evaluation Working Paper 15.* International Initiative for Impact Evaluation.

Whitty, B. (2008). *Accountability principles for research organizations.* London, UK: One World Trust.

Wickson, F., Carew, A. L., & Russell, A. W. (2006). Transdisciplinary research: Characteristics, quandaries and quality. *Futures, 38*, 1046–1059.

Young, J., & Bird, N. (2015). *Informing REDD+: An assessment of CIFOR's Global Comparative Study.* London, UK: Overseas Development Institute. The full report can be downloaded at: www.odi.org/sites/odi.org.uk/files/odi-assets/publications-opinion-files/10024.pdf and was published under a Creative Commons Attribution-Non Commercial Licence (CC BY-NC 3.0).

Young, J., Kajume, J., & Wanyama, J. (2003). *Animal health care in Kenya: The road to community-based animal health service delivery. ODI Working Paper 214.* Overseas Development Institute.

9 Mind the Gaps

Integrating Human Rights and Sustainable Development Goals into Evaluation Practice

Pearl Eliadis

The gap between the supply and demand of results information – the central topic of this book – can pose problems for those who are required to integrate and reflect human rights standards in policy and programming. International human rights laws, for example, require evaluators to demonstrate that public policies and programs have operated in a manner that respects, protects, and fulfills human rights. Governments are required (or should be required) to report these results to legislators, international human rights oversight bodies and, of course, to their own people. The ambitious goals of the 2030 Agenda for Sustainable Development (2030 Agenda) have increased this pressure because the 17 Sustainable Development Goals (SDGs) now integrate human rights into most of these global goals and associated targets (United Nations, 2015).

A human rights-based approach (HRBA) is a key strategy to achieving these objectives and goals. It is used within the United Nations system across a wide range of substantive areas, including labor, migration, the rights of children, education, health, science, demographics, and women's rights, to name but a few. HRBA requires the development of policies and programs with human rights in mind and the 2030 Agenda commits the world's nations to "leaving no one behind." These are lofty ideals, but they are not easy to systematically implement. Municipal planning, for example, through which transit, community, and other local infrastructure programs are delivered, rarely includes a regular assessment of the needs of those who are marginalized and vulnerable and most likely to need such services.

HRBA offers technical approaches that support evaluators to "get at" human rights standards, for example, through techniques like participatory approaches and the systematic disaggregation of data to identify impacts of municipal services on marginalized and excluded groups. Failure to identify these techniques and use them consistently can result in the perpetuation of inequality and discrimination (Balan, 2015). On the other hand, closing the gap between human rights standards and evaluation results can be achieved by techniques that are commonly used to integrate human rights principles into project planning, consultation, and results. First, the evaluators needed to move beyond "checking the boxes" of human rights categories when faced with evaluation frameworks and use evaluation as a tool to integrate human rights standards into program design.

Thinking in terms of whole systems can help, where those systems are inherently complex, but also reflect stakeholder engagement and international human rights standards and their iterations in regional and national laws as starting points. Second, HRBA can be used as a lens though which policies and evaluation frameworks are reoriented to align with human rights standards. For example, gender-integrative dimensions (gender mainstreaming) is a well-established technique for assessing programs and reorienting them towards women's rights, which also helps to achieve SDG 5 (Gender Equality). Third, using applicable legal standards offers a starting point for HRBA and consciously reorienting policies and programs, means that a shift takes place from needs-based to rights-based approaches. A concrete example is offered to show how that shift can occur.

Human Rights and Evaluators: Beyond "Checking the Boxes"

Evaluators in national and multilateral organizations are sometimes reduced to "checking the boxes" to make sure that some dimension of, say, gender equality or minority rights, has been addressed. If the program was not designed with human rights standards in mind, this is necessarily an artificial exercise. I have worked with many evaluators in multilateral organizations who simply have no idea where to begin when they are required to "supply" results information to policy developers to support the development of human rights-compliant public policy. Does the policy achieve gender equality? Does it meet the needs of indigenous peoples? When policies and programs (again, typically outside rule of law, justice, and human rights sectors) are not designed to comply with human rights standards from the outset, evaluators can be forced to retrofit data to standards that the program was not originally designed to meet. In some cases, evaluators may sense that simply ticking off boxes will suffice for the powers that be, provided there is minimal evidence of some human rights-oriented outcome. Worse, they may sense that the organization has no real desire or will to overhaul programs to meet human rights standards or to make substantive recommendations to reorient projects.

HRBA, on the other hand, reflects an authentic process of using systems-based thinking and applying it using human rights laws and standards, understanding that human rights involve both process and outcome. Systems-based thinking understands that many policies and programs are nested in other interconnected policy objectives and broader frameworks. Michael Patton argues that systems-based thinking requires reflection on how human rights are applied, both as cross-cutting themes and specific objectives:

> Systems-thinking shifts the focus from categorical separations and siloed distinctions to interconnections and interrelationships … Generating credible, meaningful and relevant information is the function of the evaluation. Without evaluation capacity, […] informed decision-making is not possible, which undercuts democracy and threatens the commitment to human rights.

> This web of interconnections cannot be reduced to distinct processes and outcomes. These are system, and systemic, interrelationships, each element of which must function for the whole to function.
>
> (Patton, 2016, p. 6)

Realigning policy development and evaluation frameworks in this way is not an obvious task. There are multiple international human rights standards to consider (see Table 9.1), as well as regional and national standards, and a much larger group of "soft" principles. Human rights standards also exist at the sub-national level (for example, provincial or state laws). These standards typically include legal rights, gender equality laws, the rights of persons with disabilities, the rights of religious and ethnic minorities, migrant rights, and the rights of indigenous peoples. Social, economic, and cultural rights, such as rights education, health, and decent work, have to be integrated across entire programs. All of this "systems-thinking" can seem overwhelming.

For example, how do evaluators consider the needs of persons with disabilities when deciding whether general policies and programs comply with the UN Convention on the Rights of Persons with Disabilities? How should evaluators integrate gender equality into all aspects of public policy planning? Or is it preferable to have stand-alone, specific projects that support women's rights? How does one integrate legal norms into policy development or build an evaluation framework with a theory of change capable of supporting the translation of those standards in practice? The key point here is that although the number of legal standards may seem daunting, each level (international, regional, national, etc.) contains similar rules, and the standards form a set of interlocking norms, beginning at the international level, which are reiterated at the regional, national and, often, local levels where they are enforced.

Adding to the complexity are stakeholders, who have become increasingly active and engaged in shaping policy (Jacob, 2011). A HRBA is seen as a way of

Table 9.1 Sample core international human rights instruments/treaties

CAT	Convention against Torture and Other Cruel, Inhuman or Degrading Treatment or Punishment
CEDAW	Convention on the Elimination of All Forms of Discrimination against Women
CPED	International Convention for the Protection of All Persons from Enforced Disappearance
CRC	Convention on the Rights of the Child
CRPD	Convention on the Rights of Persons with Disabilities
ICCPR	International Covenant on Civil and Political Rights
ICERD	International Convention on the Elimination of All Forms of Racial Discrimination
ICESCR	International Covenant on Economic, Social and Cultural Rights
ICMW	International Convention on the Protection of the Rights of All Migrant Workers and Members of Their Families

ensuring broad participation in public policy development, access to information and data, and democratic accountability. Stakeholders demand a "voice" in policy design and in the consideration of human rights norms. The UN system's guidance on the HRBA and data collection as they relate to participation, self-identification, transparency, and privacy, provide support for conceptualizing public policy and programming in a way that is aimed at putting people first. (United Nations Human Rights Office of the High Commissioner [OHCHR], 2016).

Reorienting Policy Design and Evaluation Frameworks to Human Rights-Based Approaches

A HRBA offers a critical path for integrating human rights into evaluation practice (United Nations Evaluation Group [UNEG], 2014). Using a HRBA in human rights projects is a relatively straightforward exercise, but a rights-based approach is especially important for other projects too, especially because they do not explicitly include human rights components. The design, delivery, data collection, monitoring, and reporting of all programs have to use a conceptual framework that puts people first and gives priority to human rights. Starting with the applicable human rights standards, as noted earlier, programs should be normatively based on international human rights standards (see Appendix 1 for a sample of core international human rights instruments), as well as ensuring that regional, constitutional, and sub-national are respected.

Reorienting policy frameworks based on a rights-based approach requires that they be operationally directed to promoting and protecting human rights (UNEG, 2014). HRBAs have important features that are reflected in both their practical articulation and their results. HRBAs are:

- **Equality-focused**: Policies and programs should "leave no one behind" and should therefore focus their outcomes to consider and even prioritize groups experiencing discrimination and marginalization. A rights-based approach meets people's needs at the planning, development, and implementation phases;
- **People-centered**: States and (sometimes) third parties owe duties to people, not programs or policies;
- **Based on a progressive realization of** certain social, economic, and cultural rights that include key sectors like education, health, and access to public services such as transit, social assistance, etc. Progressive realization means long-term planning is essential for States to achieve outcomes respecting basic human rights in these areas, since few States can meet targets in the short term that require significant investments in infrastructure and programs;
- **Process-oriented**: Equal importance is given to the outcome and process of policy development, which in turn emphasizes the importance of stakeholder participation (as noted in the previous section) as a key strategy to ensuring the input of those most affected, as well as ensuring results

information is later disaggregated, so that impacts can be determined and fed back into the policy cycle.

Equality assumes particular importance in both the process and the substance of generating effective results information. Equality-focused programs and policies are more likely to promote social inclusion of women, men, children, people with disabilities, racialized minorities, and other groups who experience marginalization and discrimination. At the very least, policies and projects should not perpetuate inequality gaps and should actively seek to diminish them by eliminating system barriers.

The target of the results information is not derived from formal equality (treating everyone the same) but from substantive equality, so that programs and policies are developed and delivered in a way that is fully accessible to diverse clients or user groups. It is necessary to treat people differently in order to achieve equality. That means the policy designer must mitigate inequality by using the techniques noted earlier, such as ensuring the participation of marginalized and disadvantaged groups in consultation processes, and by desegregating results information to identify and address impacts on marginalized or socially excluded groups.

Rather than focusing on the needs of programs or policies in the abstract, people-first programming requires a mental shift to reorient programs so the rights and perspectives of those most likely to need the policy or program in question, or who are the most likely to be affected, are taken into consideration from the outset. Participatory approaches establish and strengthen choices and opportunities for self-development and self-fulfillment within a sustainable development framework.

From Needs-Based to Human Rights-Based Approaches

Table 9.2 highlights important differences between needs-based and human rights-based approaches, and the implications for results information. As noted in the previous section, a rights-based approach requires *substantive* equality and that vulnerable or marginalized users participate in program development (see, e.g., Ljungman, Forti, & Mikkelsen, 2005). Without suggesting that rights-based and needs-based approaches are mutually exclusive, the following table highlights important differences for the purposes of understanding why a HRBA reorients how programs are conceived and developed. A HRBA does not accept unanticipated (let alone planned) results favoring the wealthy or privileged as an acceptable outcome of policy design.

Needs-based approaches tend to focus on effectiveness, efficiency, and equity and outputs, without necessarily concentrating on human impacts. Needs-based approaches do not always generate disaggregated results information to determine impacts on the most vulnerable and marginalized populations. The results of needs-based approaches can operate to mask unequal, discriminatory outcomes.

Table 9.2 Needs-based versus human rights-based approaches

Needs-based approach	*Human rights-based approach*
Policies and programs emerge from an assessment grounded in broad socio-economic indicators without a normative foundation. Generic needs of the population are identified.	Programs and policies are clearly and explicitly based on human rights norms, including international human rights standards. While human needs are central to HRBA, the filter used to determine the policy approach includes an assessment of the extent to which the approach responds to human rights norms.
Needs-based approaches are grounded in the goodwill of the donor or funder and are seen as privileges or optional programs that government can take up or dispense with at will.	Rights-based approaches recognize that States have a legal obligation to respect, protect, and fulfill human rights, and that public policy is a critical means of fulfilling those obligations.
Users ask for services but are not necessarily empowered in the process.	Rights holders participate in democratic processes and hold the duty bearer (State) to account. The development of policies and programs involves rights holders themselves and obtains their input through participatory and consultative processes.

In short, needs-based approaches are not consciously connected to human rights norms and are indifferent to the achievement of rights and freedoms or to the particular outcomes experienced by those who are protected by human rights law (unless, again, the project framework is itself rights-based).

A HRBA on the other hand, pays attention to people and explicitly uses human rights as normative principles from the outset, drawing from the identified gaps in program delivery as identified through consultation. A rights-based approach focuses on equality, non-discrimination, accountability, transparency, and participation. As an approach, a HRBA consciously connects policy and program outputs to impacts on people, and especially those who are voiceless and marginalized. A HRBA actively seeks compliance or at least consistency with international human rights law, national constitutional laws, and local standards. As a practical matter, then, a rights-based approach reorients programmatic and strategic objectives, starting with an overview of the relevant human rights standards.

Baseline information can provide a foundation for understanding the starting point of the project, but it needs disaggregated data to analyze differential impacts across particular populations and geographic or regional areas, especially rural areas that may be underserved. Once marginalized and vulnerable communities are identified, and the impacts of a particular policy or program are determined, it becomes much easier to redesign programs to prioritize those who are least well off. A HRBA leads to specific and targeted performance indicators that genuinely reflect human rights standards. As noted earlier, consultation of key groups is essential, as is the monitoring of impacts using evaluation frameworks to permit adjustments to programs.

Guidelines from both the UN and World Bank show how the gap between "supply" and "demand" of the results information could be reduced by observing the following general principles in the process of consultation and participation exercises designed to elicit information from participants:

- **Obligations to participants**: Evaluations should respect and protect the rights and welfare of women and men, and the communities of which they are members;
- **Participation and inclusion**: Evaluations should always consult people in evaluated organizations and project beneficiaries, especially those who are voiceless, marginalized, and most in need of the services;
- **Respect for dignity and diversity**: Evaluations should respect differences in culture, local customs, religious beliefs and practices, personal interaction, sex and gender roles, disability, age, and ethnicity. Evaluators should be mindful of the potential implications of these differences when planning, carrying out, and reporting on evaluations, while using evaluation instruments appropriate to the cultural setting;
- **Right to self-determination**: Evaluations should treat prospective participants as autonomous agents, allowing adequate time and information to decide whether subjects wish to participate, without pressure or fear of penalty for not participating. From human rights and gender equality perspectives, this implies carefully considering the particular issues and challenges faced by women and men who are at high risk of having their rights violated, and the constraints and potential risks of their participation;
- **Fair representation**: Evaluators should select participants fairly in relation to the aims of the evaluation, not simply because of their availability, or because it is relatively easy to secure their participation. Care should be taken to ensure the participation of women and men who are relatively powerless, "hidden," or otherwise excluded;
- **Compliance with codes of behavior and ethics**: Evaluators must be aware of and comply with international and/or national legal provisions and principles governing, for example, interviewing children, young people, and people who are traumatized. In addition, evaluators must acknowledge and understand the cultural norms that may favor or undermine the participation of community members involved in the evaluation, particularly those most vulnerable (e.g., victims of sexual violence). Individual agencies may also impose additional ethical guidelines specific to their mandate, which evaluators should consult when applicable (e.g., ethics of research involving young children or vulnerable groups);
- **Redress**: Stakeholders should receive sufficient information on:
    - How to seek redress for any perceived disadvantage suffered from the evaluation or any projects it covers; and

    - How to register a complaint concerning the conduct of an implementing or executing agency. In human rights and gender equality-responsive evaluation, specific mechanisms to cater for the need for redress by women and individuals/groups who are marginalized and/or discriminated against must be in place;
- **Confidentiality**: Evaluators must respect the right to provide information in confidence and should make participants aware of the scope and limits of confidentiality. Evaluators must ensure that sensitive information cannot be traced to its source, thus ensuring that individuals, particularly women and individuals/groups who are most discriminated against, are protected from reprisals;
- **Avoidance of harm**: Evaluators should seek to minimize risks to, and burdens on, those participating in the evaluation; and to maximize the benefits and reduce any unnecessary harm that might occur from negative or critical evaluation, without compromising the integrity of the evaluation. Evaluators must be aware of the risks faced by those women and individuals/groups most discriminated against in speaking freely about rights violations;
- **Respect for the rule of law**: Evaluators should always ensure that all interventions and evaluation activities are in compliance with national and local human rights law and norms, and must ensure that evaluation goals, outputs and outcomes are consistent with these laws and norms (Adapted from UNEG, 2014; World Bank, 2013).

The following section explores two examples. The first example shows the failure of these principles in the context of public transit in Canada. The second is a successful public works program in Sweden.

Connecting Normative Standards to Results Information: Accessible Transit

At the time of writing, 167 countries had ratified the Convention on the Rights of Persons with Disabilities, which contains specific obligations imposed on states regarding the development of accessible public facilities, including transportation facilities. Article 9 of the Convention on the Rights of Disabilities provides, in part, that:

> 1. To enable persons with disabilities to live independently and participate fully in all aspects of life, States Parties shall take appropriate measures to ensure that persons with disabilities [have] access, on an equal basis with others, to the physical environment, to transportation … and to other facilities and services open or provided to the public, both in urban and in rural areas. […]

SDG 11 sets a goal for sustainable cities and communities, including target 11.2 which provides that states should:

> By 2030, provide access to safe, affordable, accessible and sustainable transport systems for all, improving road safety, notably by expanding public transport, with special attention to the needs of those in vulnerable situations, women, children, persons with disabilities and older persons.

In Montreal, Canada, public transit policies and programs are the responsibility of the Société de Transport de Montréal (STM), a municipal authority that operates under provincial law. STM policies and plans support sustainability, as well as overall user service and accessibility, but beyond the rhetorical emphasis on sustainability and citizens, the STM does not offer accessible services to persons with disabilities.

Persons with disabilities tend to be underemployed and undereducated in relation to the general population and experience health issues that are more significant than the general population. The combination of economic disadvantage and social isolation means that accessible public transit is critical to ensuring that people can get to work and school and participate in public and social life. Lack of accessible transit therefore disproportionately affects people with mobility restrictions, people with visual limitations, people who are deaf or hard of hearing, and people with cardiovascular disease, and arthritis, to name a few. A HRBA for one group will often improve the service's accessibility for many other groups as well. Improving accessibility for persons with disabilities using more universal and integrative principles of design also benefits parents with small children, frail or elderly persons, people who are injured, poor people, recent immigrants and refugees, and people travelling with packages, bags, or baby strollers for whom staircases can be awkward or even dangerous.

Traditional development approaches to accessible public transit typically focus on general infrastructure metrics and effectiveness indicators. For example, common standard metrics include bus route distances and the percentage of geographic areas within a specific range of accessible transit facilities. The demand for results information in a needs-based approach might therefore include the number of subway lines or bus routes, or the percentage of a metropolitan population covered by the service. Traditional metrics will also include the program's efficiency (usually the cost per ride).

A HRBA, on the other hand, operates to change the orientation of the program and the results information. By being people-centered, rather than infrastructure-centered, a rights-based approach asks who is accessing the transit system, how, and from where. It involves determining the particular needs of disadvantaged and marginalized communities, including people with disabilities, and looking at the relevant standards in law. A HRBA requires the policy developer to determine the number of persons with disabilities in the relevant geographic area, and the extent to which persons with disabilities can access public transit using both conventional and adapted facilities. As noted in the previous section, consultation with the most affected groups, undertaken in an appropriate manner, will reinforce the dignity and inclusion of transit system users, and identify the quality of their experiences, as well as the extent to which the existing system meets accessibility standards.

In Montreal at the time of writing, 11 of the 68 metro (subway) stations were accessible to persons with disabilities (Commission des droits de la personne et des droits de la jeunesse [CDPDJ], 2017). Only one of six regional trains was accessible. Based on STM statistics, it will not be until the 23rd century that the metro system will reach full accessibility. Very little user information from people with disabilities is available on the official municipal websites and the information that does exist points to significant problems in accessibility for this group (Eliadis, 2014). Following several human rights complaints and advocacy for improved infrastructure, the STM says it has and will make significant investments in public infrastructure to improve accessibility and sustainability for transit systems but there is little in the way of concrete solutions for the thousands of people who cannot use the system.

STM users with disabilities have complained for years about the inaccessibility of the overall system. Human rights complaints to the provincial human rights body have not been successful because the municipal authority argues that it cannot afford the improvements and the human rights commission took that at face value (CDPDJ, 2017). It may be that the human rights commission in Quebec, as a state-appointed body, is intimidated by the idea of forcing a public authority to invest in a significant and particular program. Whatever the reason, disability groups have now been forced to turn to the courts and file representative claims (similar to class actions) before the courts, to force the STM to adapt the transit system. The views and perspectives of these users and their public protests have generated crucial information and awareness about the inaccessibility of the system's usability. The STM responded with a needs-based and service-provider-oriented approach, rather than a people-first approach, arguing historical factors, technical difficulties, and lack of political will. In short, the system was designed to be inaccessible and the current plans for the future are merely sustaining the cycle of inadequate accessibility. The failure to accommodate people with disabilities has led to a contentious public discourse. Fixing the transit system will require hundreds of millions of dollars, simply because no one bothered to build in accessibility at the outset or to plan for it until two decades after accessibility standards were developed. The cost is borne mainly by people with disabilities and older people. In the absence of political will to change the transit system for the 10 to 15 percent of the population who need it most, the sad reality is that the status quo will continue.

Putting HRBA to Work: Sustainable Gender Equality and Snow-Clearing in Sweden

Gender equality and non-discrimination are key norms in the Convention on the Elimination of All Forms of Discrimination against Women. Articles 10, 11, and 13, respectively, of the Convention affirm women's rights to non-discrimination in education, employment, and economic and social activities. As well, SDG 5 aims to achieve gender equality and empower all women and girls, while its first goal target is to eliminate discrimination.

A HRBA does not need to be expensive or complex. A rights-based approach can be remarkably simple. Gender mainstreaming is an excellent example. One strategy that has recently attracted attention is the analysis of differences based on gender, and an attempt to find ways to integrate or mainstream that information into project planning. Planners must therefore assess the disadvantages that may be specific to different groups by mapping the consequences and impacts on women and men.

Sweden is a Nordic country with among the highest levels of gender equality in the world. Its "Gender Mainstreaming in Government Agencies" program has been in effect since 2013, and now extends to the majority of government agencies. Snow removal is not an area where one might expect to hear discussions about gender mainstreaming, but the severe winters and high amounts of snowfall affect the mobility of entire populations in affected areas. Officials from the Swedish municipality of Karlskoga knew they possessed little information on the impact of their snow removal services on women, even though regional and national policy targets demanded results information on gender equality for all programs. By undertaking an assessment of the gendered impact of snow removal services, officials discovered surprising information.

A gender-based analysis of the municipality's snow removal system revealed that the snow removal service began with highways and beltway/ring roads, followed by principal roads that tended to lead to male-dominated workplaces. Men benefited because they were more likely to use private cars and benefit from cleared beltway and circle roads, as well as main roads leading to facilities and places of business. The last priorities in terms of snow clearance were bus stops, pedestrian walkways, and bike paths. Because a gendered analysis showed that more women than men used public transit, bike paths, and had to take children to school and/or bus stops, women were more likely to have to walk on snow-covered paths and roads, sometimes with small children, in order to get to bus stops and bus stations (Balan, 2015, Swedish Association of Local Authorities and Regions [SALAR], 2014).

Karlskoga municipal authorities realized they had to reorient their approach to focus on the people who needed the services most, rather than on "system needs" linked to metrics of snow clearance and road distances in generic terms. They changed the priorities of municipal snow removal services to start with sidewalks and walkways that led to main streets, kindergartens, and primary schools. Parents (usually women) more likely to drop children off before going to work in the morning benefited. Next, the municipality cleared roads to workplaces dominated by female workforces – health care and social assistance institutions, for example – and the third priority was roads to other schools.

The reorganization of municipal snow removal services required a new snow-clearing schedule based on disaggregated information. The new schedule did not generate new costs beyond the time it took to reallocate the priorities. As a result, the new schedule was more equitable and non-discriminatory for women and children, and engendered economic benefits connected to improving work productivity of these groups. Additional benefits were reduced injuries caused by slippage and motor vehicle accidents involving pedestrians (SALAR, 2014). The disaggregated results information then fed into the next policy cycle. It is important to acknowledge that these targeted outcomes may not reflect a generalized improvement of costs and benefits (because operating costs are largely the same and benefits are more targeted to specific groups), but they do reflect a conscious choice to give priority to certain groups based on a HRBA and human rights standards.

Conclusion

A rights-based approach ensures that people, rather than the needs of a system, are the focus of program design. It includes the input of vulnerable and marginalized populations, based on human rights standards in national legislation and policy, as well as international human rights law. Using a HRBA narrows the "gap" between the supply and demand of results information by ensuring that the original design of programs is more likely to generate human rights-sensitive information and results in both the development and evaluation of public policy.

A HRBA offers an alternative that moves beyond generic needs, effectiveness, and efficiency to determine whether a policy or program is actually making a difference for those who are most likely to need it. A rights-based approach reorients policy and programming, and serves as an entry point for both policy developers and evaluators, resulting in improved capacity to show human rights impacts across all program areas, not just those designated explicitly for human rights outcomes.

References

Balan, V. (2015, May 30). *Human rights based approach to local development: Sweden, Moldova, Canada.* Working Paper, Annual Graduate Conference, McGill University, Faculty of Law.

Commission des droits de la personne et des droits de la jeunesse [CDPDJ]. (2017, January 19). *Regroupement des activistes pour l'inclusion au Québec (RAPLIQ) v. Société de transport de Montréal.* C2221_11.

Eliadis, P. (2014). *Speaking out on human rights: Debating Canada's human rights system.* Montreal & Kingston: McGill-Queen's University Press.

Jacob, S. (2011). Sharing power among evaluation players: Mission possible? In E. Pearl, J. E. Furubo, & S. Jacob (Eds.), *Evaluation: Seeking truth or power? Comparative Policy Evaluation, 17.* New Brunswick, NJ: Transaction.

Ljungman, C. M., Forti, S., & Mikkelsen, B. (2005). A rights-based approach to development. In B. Mikkelsen (Ed.), *Methods for development work and research: A new guide for practitioners* (2nd ed., pp. 199–216). Newbury Park, CA: Sage Publications.

Patton, M. Q. (2016, April). *Reflections on the systemic interconnections that weave together democracy, human rights, and evaluation capacity.* OECD: Evaluation Capacity Development News: ECD Newsletter, 3.

Swedish Association of Local Authorities and Regions (SALAR). (2014). SALAR starter kit for gender equality. *European Charter for Equality of Women and Men in Local Life.* Retrieved from www.charter-equality.eu/multimedia/videos/swedish-starter-kit-for-sustainable-gender-equality.html

United Nations. (2015, September 25). *Transforming our world: The 2030 Agenda for sustainable development (2030 Agenda)*. UNGA Resolution A/RES/70/1.

United Nations Evaluation Group (UNEG). (2014). Guidance document: Integrating human rights and gender equality in evaluations. *UNEVAL.* Retrieved from www.uneval.org/document/detail/980

United Nations Human Rights Office of the High Commissioner (OHCHR). (2016). *Guidance note: Human rights-based approaches to data: Leaving no one behind in the 2030 Sustainable Development Agenda.*

World Bank. (2013). *A study of gender and human rights-based approaches in development.* World Bank.

10 Mending the Theory Gap in Evaluation

Moving Towards Theory Knitting

Sebastian Lemire, Christina Christie, and Steffen Bohni Nielsen

Exploring the gap between demand and supply of results information is an important topic in evaluation. As Palenberg and Paulson remind us in the introductory chapter of this book, "demand is driven by accountability requirements, the requirement to better understand how interventions are working so they can be better managed, and by the need for evidence-based learning to support rational decision-making in future operations." Stated differently, the demand for results information is both for accountability and learning, for rigorous and actionable evidence. This is admittedly a tall order. However, if policymakers are to better understand how policies and programs work, then they must come to understand their programmatic cogs and wheels – their inner workings. This places program theory at the heart and center of providing adequate results information.

In this chapter, we propose that a central part of attending to the gap between supply and demand for results information involves a stronger awareness – and perhaps more importantly a stronger integration – of social science theory and program theory in evaluation practice. More specifically, we argue that social science theories may serve to inform our program theories in ways that will support the validity and use of results information. Inspired by Riemer and Bickman (2011), we pursue and operationalize the notion of "theory knitting," whereby stronger theory integration may emerge. The position we hold is that theory knitting enhances the specificity, testability, and generalizability of our program theories and in effect promotes actionable evidence. As such, theory knitting provides a potential bridge across the gap between the supply and demand of results information.

The chapter is structured according to four sections. In section one we define and consider three different types of theories in evaluation: evaluation theory, social science theory, and program theory. We also reflect on the "theory gap" in evaluation, that is, the compelling yet all-too-often limited use of social science theory in theory-based evaluation. In the second section, and towards better understanding this gap, we examine the existing literature on the role of social science theory in relation to theory-based evaluation, awarding particular attention to the intended role of social science theory in developing program theories. To conclude the section, we present a theory knitting model – a heuristic and operational framework to examine and promote theory knitting in theory-based evaluation. We intentionally situate our promotion of theory knitting in the theory-based evaluation tradition because it both provides fertile grounds for this type of theory integration and also represents a common context for results information in evaluation. In the third section, and with the aim of systematically examining how social science theories are used in evaluation practice, we apply the theory knitting model in a review of 57 published theory-based evaluations. The findings of the review are presented and discussed. In the fourth section, we share what we consider to be the major benefits and implications of stronger theory knitting in evaluation, emphasizing the ways in which theory knitting may build a bridge across the gap between the supply and demand of results information. Finally, a brief set of concluding thoughts brings the chapter to a close.

Revisiting the Old Adage: "Nothing as Practical as Good Theory"[1]

Theories are here, there, and everywhere in evaluation. Evaluators develop and test theories, use theories to describe and understand social programs, to explain how programs bring about change, to build causal claims, and to make predictions about outcomes yet to come. We build theories to describe programs, and theories to prescribe how to evaluate same said programs. Painting in broad strokes, theories serve to bridge the conceptual and empirical aspects of our evaluation practice.

Given this wide variety of theories used in our practice, it is important to define what we mean when we use the word "theory" in evaluation. In this regard, we propose that at least three types of theories are discernible: evaluation theories, social science theories, and program theories. Each of these deserves a few words.

First, there are evaluation theories, that is, evaluation approaches and models for how to best conduct an evaluation. These prescriptive theories are informed by what the theorist believes to be the primary purpose of evaluation. Thus, we have evaluation theories that are intended to promote the utilization of evaluation results (Patton, 1978), encourage stakeholder empowerment (Fetterman, 1994), or bring attention to context-mechanism-outcome configurations (Pawson & Tilley, 1997), to name but a few. These theories, referred to by some as evaluation models or evaluation approaches, are based on both the experience and viewpoints of those who advance these approaches to evaluation. In this way, evaluation theories can be viewed as theory-laden in the sense of being founded upon specific ontological and epistemological convictions (Pawson & Tilley, 1997).

Another strand of theory is in the form of social science theories, which are developed in and reflective of the accumulated knowledge in disciplinary fields (e.g., psychology, sociology, among others). Icek Ajzen's theory of planned behavior (1988), Albert Bandura's (1977) model of self-efficacy, and the diffusion of innovations theory by Everett Rogers (1962) are but a few examples of social science theories. These theories can be viewed as coherent sets of propositions and concepts that collectively serve to describe, explain, and model specific phenomena.

A central, shared characteristic of these theories is that of generality (or broad applicability). Thus, social science theories are by their nature abstract.

Lastly, there is program theory, which can be viewed as an articulation of the way in which a program is intended to bring about a desired set of outcomes (Weiss, 1997, among others).[2] In the words of Bickman (1987), a program theory is "a plausible and sensible model of how a program is supposed to work" (p. 5). These program theories are explanatory in purpose. By explicating salient program mechanisms and their relationship to the intended outcomes, these program theories allow us to examine and better understand how and in what way programs work (or fail to work). As such, and as noted by Funnell and Rogers (2011), the development of program theories supports better program design, management, and evaluation by identifying key program features (and contextual conditions) and outcomes, which may serve as foci for the data collection and analysis and thus provide for a more focused evaluation. In contradistinction with social science theories, program theories are local and context-bound, aiming to explain how a program functions in a specific setting and time.

Given the sustained interest in and importance of theory in evaluation, it is somewhat surprising how little attention we tend to award social science theories in our practice. In the authors' experience, policymakers rarely consult social science theories in commissioning new programs and policies; program staff and managers tend to pay little attention to existing social science theories when designing and implementing those programs and policies; and evaluators rarely engage with social science theory when evaluating same said programs and policies. Social science theory is perhaps more talked about than acted on in evaluation practice.

There are likely several reasons for this "theory gap" in evaluation. For one thing, evaluators are, in the context of commissioned evaluations, often focused on evaluating social programs deeply embedded in local contexts, while the application of more abstract social science theories might be considered irrelevant. For another, the very purpose of many and likely most evaluations is to generate local knowledge for local decision-making, again suggesting a lesser role for social science theories. From this perspective, theorizing beyond the local program theory is likely considered beyond the scope of many a commissioned evaluation.

The potential for social science theory in evaluation, however, has not gone unnoticed among evaluators. Over the years, repeated calls have been made for a stronger integration between evaluation and social science theory in general (Chen & Rossi, 1980; Donaldson, 2007; Rog, 2015; Schwandt, 2014; Vaessen & Leeuw, 2010), and more specifically in relation to social psychology (Mark, Donaldson, & Campbell, 2011), cognitive science (Patton, 2013), economics (Speer, 2010), public management (Schwartz, 2010), and criminology (Tilley, 2010), to name but a few. In our view, these repeated calls speak to a sustained interest in a stronger – yet as of now unfulfilled – interplay between social science theory and evaluation.

Attending to this theory gap only becomes all the more compelling when considering the supply and demand gap in relation to results information. In responding to the demand for results information, evaluators may, with different degrees of confidence, demonstrate if a program works (or fails to work). In the best of cases, which rarely occur, evaluators are furthermore able to identify key drivers in a program (i.e., critical ingredients), and key mediators connecting program activities with outcomes (i.e., mechanisms), and perhaps even contextual conditions (i.e., influencing factors) that moderate the desired outcomes. Indeed, results information that identifies the program's underlying mechanisms, triggered in particular contexts, for a particular participant group, leading to certain outcomes, is increasingly pursued and prized by policymakers and program funders.

The underlying need for this type of information, for understanding how and why programs work, is two-fold. First and foremost, understanding how and why a program works serves to substantiate the causal connection between a program and a set of desired outcomes (internal validity). Second, the ability to explain how and why programs work also facilitates claims about how the program would work in different settings and times, perhaps even with different target groups (external validity). Taken collectively, then, understanding why programs work is increasingly what evaluations are asked to provide because it allows for a deeper and more robust understanding of program performance, which can in turn support future program refinements and designs.

More than that, stronger theory integration even supports the accumulation of knowledge across evaluations. All these benefits speak directly to the closing, or at the very least to a narrowing, of the gap between supply and demand for results information. Before advancing this argument any further, however, we will first turn our attention to the current role of social science theory in evaluation, in both theory and practice.

The Theory Fabric of Theory-Based Evaluation

Theory-Based Evaluation

The role of theory is perhaps most compelling in relation to the aptly named theory-based evaluation (Vaessen & Leeuw, 2010). Theory-based evaluation holds a prominent position in evaluation. The volume of books, journal articles, special issues, and conference presentations dedicated to the theory and practice of theory-based evaluation is significant, and it continues to grow. As noted by Vaessen and Leeuw (2010), the theory-based tradition is perhaps best viewed as a systematization of a sustained focus and interest among many evaluators on the underlying assumptions of programs. We agree. Reaffirming this sustained interest in the theory-based evaluation tradition, new variants of theory-based approaches, including realist evaluation (Pawson & Tilley, 1997) and more recently contribution analysis (Mayne, 2001), continue to emerge, gain traction, and push our evaluation practice in new directions.

This is not the place to review the distinct features of the broad array of approaches comprising the theory-based evaluation tradition. For the present purposes, it suffices to say that the shared modus operandi of these distinct – yet related – theory-based approaches revolves around the development and empirical examination of a program theory reflecting how and in what way the program is intended to bring about change.[3] A central aspect of this program theorizing is the explication – conceptually and empirically – of the underlying processes, also known as mechanisms, driving the desired outcomes (see Astbury & Leeuw, 2010, for an exemplary conceptual examination of the term mechanism).

Another central aspect of theory-based evaluation is the anchoring of program theories in social science theory. Echoing Chen and Rossi's (1980, 1983) earlier work on theory-based evaluation, Chen (1990) proposes that "program theory based upon knowledge of both how the program is operated and social science theory may provide a better opportunity to understand program structure, processes, and consequences" (pp. 67–68).

This anchoring of program theories in social science theory is also resurfaced across other notable contributions on theory-based evaluation (see Donaldson, 2007; Mark, Donaldson, & Campbell, 2011; Pawson & Tilley, 1997; Weiss, 1997). As such, theory-based evaluation provides fertile grounds for bringing together social science theory and program evaluation. Here, the notion of theory knitting is pertinent.

The Idea of Theory Knitting

The idea of theory knitting is nothing new in the social sciences and can be traced back to work on theory development in psychology by Kalmar and Sternberg (1988). In their words, theory knitting is an approach to "integrate the best aspects of a set of given theories with one's own ideas regarding the domain under investigation" (1988, p. 153). In evaluation circles, and decades later, theory knitting emerges with Riemer and Bickman (2011), who, referencing Kalmar and Sternberg (1988), propose theory knitting as a way for social psychology to advance evaluation, and vice versa. Short of providing a definition of theory knitting, the stated purpose of Riemer and Bickman is to develop a "process that translates several basic theories and combines them into one coherent applied model of change" (2011, p. 108). And thus, the connection between social science theory and program theory is made. More recently, Leeuw and Donaldson (2015) have further promoted this linking of domain theories, theories on policymaking processes, and behavioral theories, offering a compelling example on theory knitting in relation to producing "public goods."[4]

To be sure, the case for theory knitting is easily made. As noted by Mark et al. (2011), among others, the active and explicit use of social science theory promotes the specificity of key program theory components, including purported mechanisms, whereby the testability of the program theories is enhanced. On a similar note, Vaessen and Leeuw (2010) compellingly argue that using specific behavioral theories to substantiate and explain causal mechanisms can serve to enhance internal validity of causal claims. Equally important, and in relation to external validity, the use of social science theory also supports the generalizability of these conclusions. As argued by Donaldson and Lipsey (2006), the integration of social science theory and program theory "constitutes a (if not the) major way that evaluation contributes to social betterment by way of knowledge development" (cited in Donaldson & Crano, 2011, p. 145).

Yet, despite these promising aspects of pursuing a stronger theoretical grounding, knowledge about the ways in which evaluators use theory in theory-based evaluation is scant. In a landmark review by Coryn, Noakes, Westine, and Schröter (2011), it was reported that 91 percent of the identified theory-based evaluations formulated their program theory on "the basis of existing research and theory" (p. 212). Unfortunately, this finding fails to distinguish between "research" and "theory," which in fundamental ways are different. Whereas "research" may refer to the findings or conclusions of one or more empirical studies, the term "theory" is usually, at least in the experience of the authors, reserved for a coherent system of propositions that serves to describe, explain, or model a phenomenon (recall description of social science theory above). Accordingly, a distinction as to whether the program theories identified in the Coryn et al. (2011) review were grounded on research, social science theory, or a combination of both, is surely worth further consideration.

Moreover, the Coryn et al. (2011) review offered no analysis of how and in what way the theories were used in the theory-based evaluations. This is unfortunate because social science theory can be used in many different ways, some of which are likely to be more beneficial than others. Painting in broad strokes, we hold that theories can be used in at least three distinct ways:

- Theory labeling defined as a general reference to one or more social science theories as the motivator or grounding for the underlying logic of the program theory. While the reference may specify one or more specific social science theories, there is no specification as to how or in what way these theories informed the program theory;
- Theory (retro)fitting defined as the retroactive use of one or more social science theories to inform and make sense of the analysis and evaluation of the program theory;
- Theory knitting is where one or more social science theories are used as the conceptual grounding for both the design of the program and the program theory.

Taken collectively, these are three main approaches for using social science theories in theory-based evaluations. Our position is that theory knitting, as compared with theory labeling and retrofitting, represents a stronger integration of social science theory and program theory, and why further pursuit of theory knitting is called for.

Towards this end, we developed a framework to support the systematic and transparent integration and examination of social science theory in program theories. The framework was inspired by a coding scheme developed by Michie and

Prestwich (2010), originally developed for the purpose of coding experimental and quasi-experimental studies in health psychology. Grounded on their work, we developed a theory knitting model structured around the core program theory components that may be informed by social science theory. The model is presented in Figure 10.1.

As the figure indicates, the anchoring of social science theory can be made in regard to many different aspects of a program and program theory. For instance, theory might inform the program participant selection, the delivery mode of the program services, the selection and definition of primary outcomes, the hypothesized mechanisms generating the desired outcomes (i.e., how program activities are intended to contribute to specific outcomes), the influencing factors enhancing or depressing the program performance, and even the plausible rival explanations for the observed outcomes. In all these ways, social science theory may inform program theory.

Conversely, the evaluation of the program theory may also inform the social science theories on which the program theory was grounded. In this way, the evaluation may potentially serve as a feedback loop to the social science theories, whereby the results of individual evaluation are used to connect back with and refine the social science theories.

The proposed theory knitting model can be applied in several different ways. First and foremost, it can support evaluators in determining which aspects of their program theory can be informed by social science theories. In this way, the framework may serve as a structure for the mapping of existing evidence in support of specific program theory components. Second, and in the context of the present chapter, the framework may also serve as a heuristic tool for better understanding the ways in which social science theory is used in relation to different components of a program theory. Towards this aim, we now turn to an application of the framework in a review of 57 theory-based evaluations.

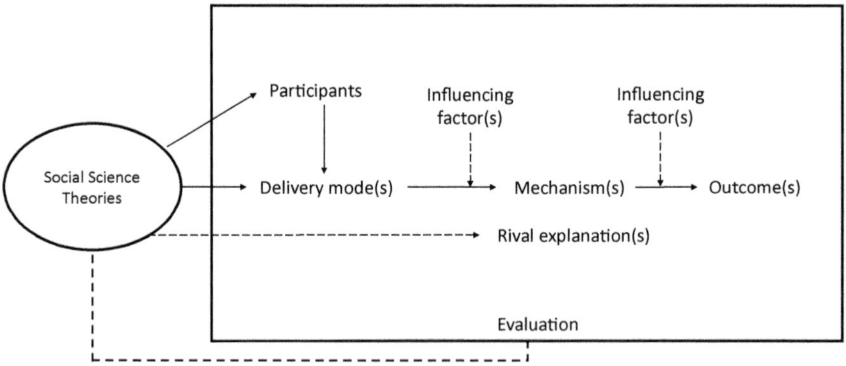

Figure 10.1 The Theory Knitting Model (adapted from Michie & Prestwich, 2010).

Unpacking the Use of Theory in Theory-Based Evaluation

In order to promote theory knitting in theory-based evaluation, we need an understanding of how and in what way social science theory is currently used in the development and testing of program theories. In other words, we need an empirical review of current theory use in theory-based evaluation. Toward this aim, we applied the theory knitting model in a review of 57 theory-based evaluations identified through the oft-cited Coryn et al. (2011) and Marchal, van Belle, van Olmen, Hoerêe, and Kegel (2012) reviews of theory-based and realist evaluations, respectively. Considered collectively, these reviews cover a broad array of published evaluations in the time period from 1992–2011 (see Coryn et al., 2011; Marchal et al., 2012, for more detailed descriptions of the reviews).

For the purposes of the present chapter, the published studies were printed in full and carefully reviewed, then coded, by the first author of the present chapter. The coding was structured around a coding tree, covering background and design features of the study (e.g., publication year and sector), program theory construction (e.g., by evaluator or by stakeholder participation), program theory content (e.g., output, outcomes, and mechanisms), and the use of social science theory in the design of the program and its corresponding program theory (i.e., theory labeling, retrofitting, or knitting), among other things. For studies engaging in theory knitting, a subset of codes captured the specific aspects of the program theory informed by social science theory (following the structure of the theory knitting framework presented in Figure 10.1). These included the use of social science theory to define the primary program outcomes, to specify the postulated mechanisms generating these outcomes, and to identify influencing factors.

The 57 studies included in the present review identified as either theory-based evaluations (41 studies) or realist evaluations (16 studies). The studies primarily covered programs in the health sector (30 studies) and education (12 studies). Most studies were based on observational designs (35 studies), followed by quasi-experimental designs (13 studies), and a few experimental designs (5 studies).[5] In terms of methodological orientation, the studies were for the most part mixed methods (26 studies) or quantitative-oriented (20), and to a lesser extent exclusively qualitative (10 studies).[6]

In relation to the use of social science theory, many theory-based evaluations offered no indication of theory use. Of the 57 studies, a total of 33 studies offered no mention of social science theory in either program or evaluation design. Another 13 studies gave mention to social science theory, though, without providing specific information about how and in what way the referenced theory informed the program or the evaluation – what we term theory labeling. Finally, only 1 study indicated theory retrofitting – the retroactive use of social science theory to make sense of evaluation findings.

In terms of theory knitting, the main subject of the present inquiry, a total of 10 studies, specified social science theories as the conceptual grounding for both

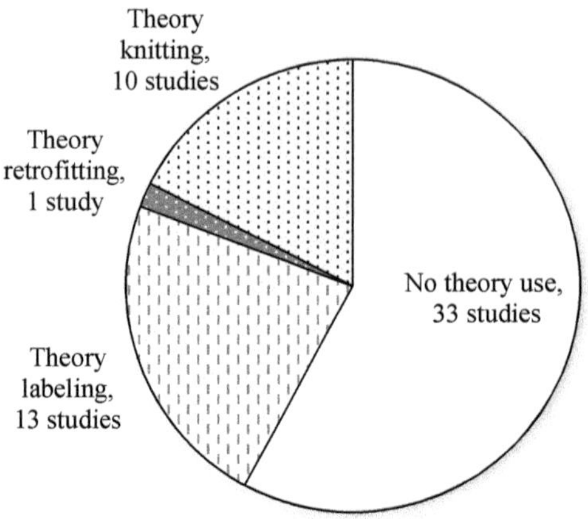

Figure 10.2 Theory use in theory-based evaluation.

program design and program theory. (Eight of these evaluations identified as theory-based evaluations, while two identified as realist evaluations.) Towards advancing our analyses of these studies, their specific use of social science theory was coded and mapped onto the theory knitting model. The results are presented in Figure 10.3. As the figure shows, the use of social science theory was primarily to select and define the primary program outcomes (9 studies), to specify the postulated mechanisms generating the outcomes (8 studies), and to identify the influencing factors that may affect the program's ability to generate the desired outcomes (7 studies). In 3 studies, theory knitting informed the delivery mode of the program.

Using social science theory to inform delivery modes tailored to specific subsets of program participants (1 study) or to identify rival explanations (1 study) was noticeably less common. Finally, there was one instance of social science theory being refined on the basis of findings from an evaluation.

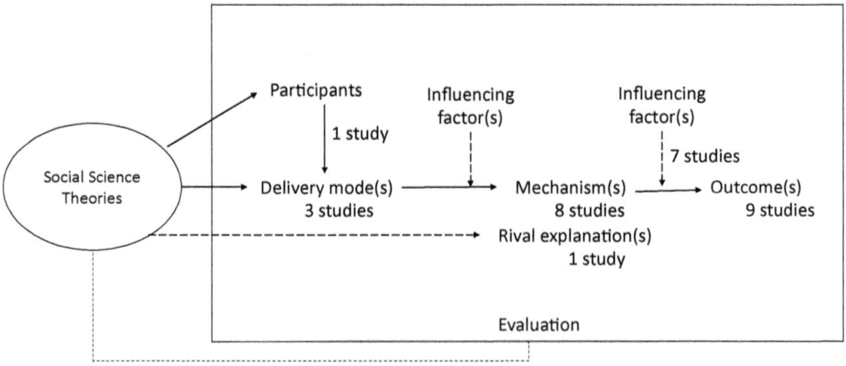

Figure 10.3 Theory Knitting in published theory-based evaluations ($n = 10$).

A preliminary conclusion is that theory knitting, at least in published theory-based evaluations, serves primarily to define primary program outcomes, underlying program mechanisms, and influencing factors that may affect the program's ability to generate the desired outcomes.

Examining the theory knitting studies in more detail also reveals a number of inspiring ways in which social science theory may serve an active role in program planning and evaluation. To illustrate, Farber and Sabatino (2007) describe how two competing theories – gestalt and cognitive behavior therapy, respectively – guided the program staff's decision on how to design and implement specific program activities in a therapeutic summer program for grieving children. Whereas the program clinicians, citing gestalt therapy, "wished to retain the 'drumming aspects' of an activity because drumming rituals are commonly used to honor the departed loved ones in many cultures," they also, informed by cognitive behavior therapy, considered "how sound may impact the meaning children derive from the activity" (Farber & Sabatino, 2007, p. 395). Accordingly, the activity was restructured (reduced loudness) and re-evaluated with an eye towards children's engagement and sense of meaning with the activity.

Another inspiring example is that of Heflinger, Bickman, Northrup, and Sonnichsen (1997), who report on the use of Bandura's (1977) model of self-efficacy as the conceptual grounding for a family empowerment intervention. More specifically, the model of self-efficacy served to inform the intervention methods (e.g., enactive attainment and verbal persuasion) as well as define the predicted outcomes. Citing Bandura (1977), the authors posit that "enactive attainment, or practice, provides the most influential source of efficacy information because it is based on authentic mastery experiences" (1997, p. 185). Accordingly, enactive attainment was embedded in the training methods and reflected in the program theory.

Taken collectively, the present review suggests that published theory-based evaluations are largely a-theoretical in the sense that they rarely rely on social science theory (at least not explicitly) or fail to induce new theories on the basis of evaluation results and the program theory tested. That being said, the few theory-based evaluations that do engage social science theory inspire and motivate evaluation practice in this direction. Informed by these findings, we will now turn our attention to the question framing this chapter: How does theory knitting serve to bridge the gap between the supply and demand sides of results information?

Theory Knitting Across the Supply and Demand Gap

The motivation for this chapter is to propose theory knitting as a worthwhile avenue for bridging the gap between demand and supply of results information. Use of results information is highly complex. It is messy and unpredictable. As argued by Weiss (1997), information is likely to be used in an actionable way when it reduces uncertainty or clarifies a situation. It is critical then, that our evaluation studies be well-conducted and well-communicated, which means that studies should be highly rigorous so to stand the test of time and in effect be accessible and relevant to decision-makers (and other stakeholders) who may be conducting studies later. The position we hold is that social science theories may serve to inform our program theories in ways that will support the validity and use of results information. By theory knitting social science theories into the fabric of our program theories, we enhance the validity and use of our results information for both accountability and learning purposes.

From this perspective, theory knitting bridges the gap between supply and demand in at least two related – yet distinct – ways. First and foremost, and as suggested by Lipsey (1993), among others, theory knitting enhances the construct, and the internal and external validity of the results information produced by individual evaluations. This provides for more rigorous and actionable evaluations. Second, theory knitting also supports the development of an accumulated body of knowledge about how programs work across a larger set of individual evaluations. This provides for a body of knowledge that may stand the test of time and inform decision-makers conducting future evaluation studies. Let us consider these in turn.

Theory knitting serves well to enhance the construct validity of evaluations. By using social science theory to define and formulate key constructs in the evaluation, theory knitting strengthens the connection between the operationalizations in your study and the theoretical constructs on which those operationalizations are based, whereby the construct validity is enhanced (Trochim, 2000). In this way, theory knitting bridges what Trochim (2000) terms "land of theory" and the "land of observation." As evidenced in the review above, theory knitting often requires the definition and formulation of key outcomes. This role for theory knitting is particularly compelling in evaluations involving complex and difficult-to-discern concepts, such as "happiness," "self-efficacy," or "empowerment," to name but a few. By sharpening the definition of key outcomes, their construct validity is enhanced.

Theory knitting also supports internal validity. Theory knitting may inform the articulation of how program activities are expected to generate desired (and undesired) outcomes, the identification of mechanisms underlying these expectations, and the specification of salient influencing factors that might enhance or impede these generative strands, as well as the formulation of salient rival explanations (Vaessen & Leeuw, 2010). As indicated in our review, theory knitting is commonly directed at identifying and specifying salient mechanisms and influential factors. Using social science theory in this way allows for the development of more specific and in effect more testable propositions in our theory-based evaluations, which in turn serves to enhance the internal validity of the conclusions drawn.

Extending beyond internal validity, the anchoring of program theories in social science theory may furthermore enhance the generalizability of the results information (external validity). By unpacking how and why a program brings about change, by detailing the programmatic cogs and wheels of how it works, we are better able to project how the program may fare in other settings, times, and with other participants. This type of generalizability – perhaps better termed transferability – is particularly useful for later roll-out or scale up of the program in other settings, times, and contexts.

Moreover, and in addition to these benefits at the level of individual evaluations, there are also cumulative benefits to theory knitting. The use of theory knitting may actively contribute to a larger body of theory within which to situate the findings and conclusions of theory-based evaluations. Patterns of how, why, for whom, and under what circumstances a program worked, or failed to work, can be cross-examined, compared, and contrasted with programs reflecting manifestations of the same social science theories. This not only serves the validity of the individual evaluation, but also promotes the accumulation of knowledge across the field of evaluation more broadly.

From this perspective, each individual evaluation comes to serve as one of many "real world" instantiations of the overarching social science theory. By viewing individual evaluations in this way, as testing grounds for social science theories, the resultant findings and conclusions are more readily situated within a broader knowledge base.

This type of local theorizing may hold practical benefits for both the supply and demand side of results information. On the supply side, if program theories build upon accepted causal mechanisms drawn from social science theories, it may be sufficient to report on early results that are easier to assess and understand, without having to argue about how these results will ultimately lead to outcomes and impact.[7] Likewise, on the demand side, reliance on widely accepted social science theories can diminish the demand for detailed information in terms of outcomes or impacts (which are costlier to collect and involve a longer time frame) and still give policymakers and budgetary authorities "something solid" to use for accountability and learning purposes.

Taken collectively, then, all these benefits serve to bridge the gap between supply and demand for results information. The potential for theory knitting to enhance the construct and internal validity of individual evaluations provides for more rigorous and in effect credible results information. By enhancing the generalizability (or transferability) of findings from individual studies, theory knitting also supports more actionable results information. Finally, and in moving beyond the benefits tied to individual evaluations, theory knitting also allows for the accumulation of results information across multiple evaluations. As such, theory knitting serves well to narrow the gap between supply and demand for results information. This is an important potential worth pursuing in practice.

Concluding Thoughts

The explicit use of social science theory is a central yet unfulfilled promise in theory-based evaluation. This paradox is what motivates the present chapter. The position we promote is that we need to move more firmly towards theory knitting – the transparent and systematic weaving of social science theory into the fabric of evaluation practice. By doing so we enhance the specificity, testability, and generalizability of our program theories and in effect promote credible and actionable evidence. Towards this aim, we hope the present chapter – and the theory knitting model presented – will serve to motivate further development and integration of social science theories in program planning and evaluation.

Notes

1 The statement "nothing as practical as good theory" is perhaps needless to say inspired by the title of a seminal plenary address on theory, evidence, and learning in evaluation given by the esteemed evaluator Ray Pawson (2003). As some readers may be aware, it can be traced back to its originator Kurt Lewin (1952), who made the statement in the context of social psychology.
2 In practical applications, these program theories are known by a broad range of labels, including logic models, policy theories, intervention theories, theories of change, results chains, or Context-Mechanism-Outcome Configuration theories (Tilley, 2010).
3 We use the term program theory as a generic term for the broad array of labels used in theory-based evaluation literature, including policy theories, intervention theories, and theories of change. We find that the term program theory appears to be the most widely applied label.
4 See also Olson's Logic of Collective Action (1965) and Bennet and Segerberg's Logic of Connective Action (2012) from which Leeuw and Donaldson find their inspiration.
5 Two studies were in the form of reviews, one study was ex-ante, and one study did not disclose a study design.
6 One study did not disclose the data collection methods employed.
7 For example, in nutrition programs food intake can be taken as a "lead indicator" of improved nutrition without having to prove the link to subsequent outcomes in terms of improved health status. Similarly, in health programs, vaccination rates can be accepted as a lead indicator of disease reduction since many previous clinical studies have documented the link between cause and effect.

References

Ajzen, I. (1988). *Attitudes, personality, and behaviour*. Chicago, IL: Dorsey.

Astbury, B., & Leeuw, F. L. (2010). Unpacking black boxes: Mechanisms and theory building in evaluation. *American Journal of Evaluation, 31*, 363–381.

Bandura, A. (1977). Self-efficacy: Toward a unifying theory of behavioral change. *Psychological Review, 84*, 191–215.

Bennett, W. L., & Segerberg, A. (2012). The logic of connective action. *Information, Communication & Society, 15*, 739–768.

Bickman, L. (1987). Using program theory in evaluation. *New Directions for Program Evaluation, 33*. San Francisco, CA: Jossey-Bass.

Chen, H. T. (1990). *Theory-driven evaluations*. Newbury Park, CA: Sage Publications.

Chen, H. T., & Rossi, P. H. (1980). The multi-goal, theory-driven approach to evaluation: A model linking basic and applied social science. *Social Forces, 59*, 106–122.

Chen, H. T., & Rossi, P. H. (1983). Evaluating with sense: The theory-driven approach. *Evaluation Review, 7*, 283–302.

Coryn, C. L. S., Noakes, L. A., Westine, C. D., & Schröter, D. C. (2011). A systematic review of theory-driven evaluation practice from 1990 to 2009. *American Journal of Evaluation, 32*, 199–226.

Donaldson, S. I. (2007). *Program theory-driven evaluation science: Strategies and applications*. Mahwah, NJ: Erlbaum.

Donaldson S. I., & Crano, W. D. (2011). Theory-driven evaluation science and applied social psychology: Exploring the intersection. In M. M. Mark, S. I. Donaldson, & B. Campbell (Eds.), *Social psychology and evaluation* (pp. 141–160). New York, NY: Guilford Press.

Farber, M. L. Z., & Sabatino, C. A. (2007). A therapeutic summer weekend camp for grieving children: Supporting clinical practice through empirical evaluation. *Children Adolescent Social Work Journal, 24*, 385–402.

Fetterman, D. M. (1994). Steps of empowerment evaluation: From California to Cape Town. *Evaluation and Program Planning, 17*, 305–313.

Funnell, S. C., & Rogers, P. J. (2011). *Purposeful program theory – Effective use of theories of change and logic models.* San Francisco, CA: Jossey-Bass.

Heflinger, C. A., Bickman, L., Northrup, D., & Sonnichsen, S. (1997). A theory-driven intervention and evaluation to explore family caregiver empowerment. *Journal of Emotional and Behavioral Disorders, 5*, 184–191.

Kalmar, D. A., & Sternberg, R. J. (1988). Theory knitting: An integrative approach to theory development. *Philosophical Psychology, 1*, 153–170.

Leeuw, F. L., & Donaldson, S. I. (2015). Theory in evaluation: Reducing confusion and encouraging debate. *Evaluation, 21*, 467–480.

Lewin, K. (1952). *Field theory in social science: Selected theoretical papers by Kurt Lewin.* London, UK: Tavistock.

Lipsey, M. W. (1993). *Theory as method: Small theories of treatments. Special Issue: Understanding causes and generalizing about them.* New Directions for Evaluation, 57. 5–38. Hoboken, NJ: Wiley.

Marchal, B., van Belle, S., van Olmen, J., Hoerêe, T., & Kegel, G. (2012). Is realist evaluation keeping its promise? A review of published empirical studies in the field of health systems research. *Evaluation, 18*, 192–212.

Mark, M. M., Donaldson, S. I., & Campbell, B. (2011). The past, the present, and possible futures of social psychology and evaluation. In M. M. Mark, S. I. Donaldson, & B. Campbell (Eds.), *Social psychology and evaluation* (pp. 4–27). New York, NY: Guilford Press.

Mayne, J. (2001). Addressing attribution through contribution analysis: Using performance measures sensibly. *The Canadian Journal of Program Evaluation, 18*, 1–24.

Michie, S., & Prestwich, A. (2010). Are interventions theory-based? Development of a theory-coding scheme. *Health Psychology, 29*, 1–8.

Olson, M. (1965). *The logic of collective action.* Cambridge, MA: Harvard University Press.

Patton, M. Q. (1978). *Utilization-focused evaluation.* Beverly Hills, CA: Sage Publications.

Patton, M. Q. (2013). What brain sciences reveal about integrating theory and practice. *American Journal of Evaluation, 3*, 237–244.

Pawson, R. (2003). Nothing as practical as good theory. *Evaluation, 9*, 471–490.

Pawson, R., & Tilley, N. (1997). *Realistic evaluation.* London, UK: Sage Publications.

Riemer, M., & Bickman, L. (2011). Using program theory to link social psychology and program evaluation. In M. M. Mark, S. I. Donaldson, & B. Campbell (Eds.), *Social psychology and evaluation* (pp. 104–138). New York, NY: Guilford Press.

Rog, D. J. (2015). Infusing theory into practice, practice into theory: Small wins and big gains for evaluation. *American Journal of Evaluation, 36*, 223–238.

Rogers, E. M. (1962). *Diffusion of innovations*. New York, NY: Free Press.

Schwandt, T. (2014). On the mutually informing relationship between practice and theory in evaluation. *American Journal of Evaluation*, *35*, 231–236.

Schwartz, R. (2010). Public management theory, evaluation, and evidence-based policy. In J. Vaessen, & F. L. Leeuw (Eds.), *Mind the gap – Perspectives on policy evaluation and the social sciences* (pp. 121–140). New Brunswick, NJ: Transaction Publishers.

Speer, S. (2010). Economics and evaluation. In J. Vaessen & F. L. Leeuw (Eds.), *Mind the gap – Perspectives on policy evaluation and the social sciences* (pp. 69–90). New Brunswick, NJ: Transaction Publishers.

Tilley, N. (2010). Realistic evaluation and disciplinary knowledge: Applications from the field of criminology. In J. Vaessen, & F. L. Leeuw (Eds.), *Mind the gap – Perspectives on policy evaluation and the social sciences* (pp. 203–236). New Brunswick, NJ: Transaction Publishers.

Trochim, W. (2000). *The research methods knowledge base* (2nd ed.). Cincinnati, OH: Atomic Dog Publishing.

Vaessen, J., & Leeuw, F. L. (2010). Interventions as theories: Closing the gap between evaluation and the disciplines. In J. Vaessen, & F. L. Leeuw (Eds.), *Mind the gap – Perspectives on policy evaluation and the social sciences* (pp. 141–170). New Brunswick, NJ: Transaction Publishers.

Weiss, C. H. (1997). *Evaluation* (2nd ed.). Upper Saddle River, NJ: Prentice-Hall.

11 Realistic Commissioning of Impact Evaluations

Getting What You Ask For?

John Mayne

Interventions to improve the wellbeing of citizens are becoming more complex as their goals have become increasingly ambitious, aimed at such ends as reducing poverty, empowering women, enhancing democracy, or strengthening innovation (Ramalingam, 2013). To address such aims, these interventions are often quite multifaceted, involving multiple players and sectors, are focused on several target groups over a long timeframe, involve a number of varied activities, and the results aimed for are influenced by a number of factors other than the activities of the intervention and its partners.

Evaluating the impact of such complex interventions is challenging, especially addressing the causality issue of what the intervention "caused," since there are many factors involved in bringing about observed impacts. Nevertheless, managers and staff, as well as funders of such interventions, want to know if the intervention efforts have made (or will likely make) a difference. They likely also want to know why or why not the intervention has made a difference, or if it has met its objectives. But the causal relationships between the activities of the intervention and any observed impacts are not at all straightforward; indeed, they are often very complicated. What does "make a difference" or "meeting objectives" mean in these complex settings? Asking unrealistic or misunderstood questions about impact can only lead to unrealistic expectations for impact evaluation, and ultimately weak evaluations.

This chapter explores the gap between impact questions that can be asked, and the answers that can be realistically provided. Just by posing an impact question in a term of reference does not mean it can be credibly and usefully answered.

Evaluation questions on impact have been around as long as the practice of evaluation. But many evaluation questions were formulated when interventions were often conceived of in simpler terms and in simpler settings, including experimental settings, and, I will argue, are misleading, not that meaningful, and often unrealistic in the case of today's complex interventions. This chapter looks critically at these more traditional evaluation impact questions and identifies and discusses more meaningful and realistic impact questions for the context of complex multifaceted interventions. It discusses the kinds of evaluation findings that can realistically be arrived at in these settings and argues that commissioners of impact evaluations need to better understand the complexities involved and what can be realistically expected.

After defining a few terms, the chapter first discusses the characteristics of interventions in complex settings and discusses the kinds of perspectives on causality that are needed to address the thorny causality issues involved. It then assesses more traditional impact questions in light of this complexity. The article sets out the kinds of evaluation questions that can be credibly addressed in these more complex settings from both an accountability and a learning perspective, and the kinds of findings that can realistically be expected.

Some Terms

I use the term **results** to denote the sequence of effects emanating from an intervention: outputs, outcomes, and impacts are specific types of results. In particular, **impacts** are the longer-term effects on beneficiaries that result from an intervention.

Theories of change and impact pathways set out how an intervention is expected to work, showing the causal links between the outputs produced and the subsequent chain of results leading to the desired final outcome or impact. **Impact pathways** describe these result chains, showing the linkages between the sequence of steps in getting to impact. A **theory of change** adds to an impact pathway by describing the causal assumptions behind the links in the pathway – what has to happen for the causal linkages to be realized.

The term **intervention** is used here to describe specific activities undertaken to make a positive difference in outcomes and impacts of interest. It covers policies, programs, and projects.

Complex and Multifaceted Interventions

Complex multifaceted interventions are becoming more the norm than the exception, especially in development settings (Byrne, 2013; Copestake, 2014; Garcia & Zazueta, 2015; Gerrits & Verweij, 2015; Ramalingam, 2013; Ramalingam & Jones, 2008). Interventions in the developing world are expected to involve a variety of types of partners, aim at several target groups, and are intended to contribute to the high-level global Sustainable Development Goals (SDGs) (United Nations, 2015). These interventions can be characterized by some or all of:

- A mix of intervention strategies and components. Employing a mix of often participatory intervention activities to change the behavior of individuals, households, institutions, markets, and policies;
- A number of partners. Engaging a possibly large number of partners and stakeholders in governments, NGOs, and the private sector in collaboration needed to bring about change;
- Extended and possibly emergent pathways to impact. Involving pathways from actions to impact that have many cause-effect relationships, are multiple,

can involve long timeframes and long causal sequences of outcomes, may involve complex systems, and are not always completely known;
- External influences. Events and conditions outside those of the intervention can influence the extent to which the impacts are brought about;
- Interventions expected to evolve over time. In response to increased understanding of context and results to date, complex interventions evolve as they unfold (Rist, Felton, Samuelsson, Sandström, & Rosvall, 2013; Wild, Booth, Cumming, Foresti, & Wales, 2015; Woolcock, 2009);
- Multi-leveled, multi-place operations. Operating at local, regional, national, and perhaps global levels;
- Impact can take time. It can take more than a few years to bring about significant change in societies that complex interventions often aim at, such as reducing poverty, enhancing the role of women, and enhancing the environment.

Within this complexity, a number of types of interventions can be identified:

Core interventions with supporting engagement efforts. Examples of these are agriculture research for development interventions where it is realized that quite a bit more is needed if the benefits from agriculture research are going to reach the rural poor, such as fair markets, supporting regulation, and/or changes in culture norms. Examples of these types of interventions are discussed by Mayne and Johnson (2015).

Here the core intervention is clearly not the sole cause of any observed impact. The intervention plus efforts of perhaps many others are together needed to bring about intended changes. In what sense then has the core intervention made a difference, if indeed it has? What does success mean?

Multi-component interventions. In these settings, an overall intervention is composed of a number of quite different components often aimed at different target groups, all of which are undertaken to achieve some overall goal, perhaps by a coalition of partners and/or different delivery agents. An example is the DFID intervention to reform police services in a country, with components directed at the police, police institutions, the judiciary, levels of governments, the media and civil society, all aimed at improving police services and enhancing safety and perceptions of safety in society (Palladium, 2015).

In these cases, it is the collected efforts of the various components that are needed to bring about change. What effect does each component cause? What is success for the intervention?

Several things are clear with these multifaceted or integrated interventions:

- There are many causal factors at work;
- Any specific set of activities in the intervention is likely not the sole cause of an observed change;
- These are not experimental settings; indeed the interventions may be expected to evolve over time to be successful. See, for example, Andrews, Pritchett, and Woolcock (2013).

To discuss realistic impact questions, we need to first understand causality in these settings.

Causality in Complex Settings

In simpler settings and perhaps simpler times, the evaluation of interventions saw causality from a counterfactual perspective based on experimental settings. In these cases, one could literally test the counterfactual question: what would have happened without the intervention? And this question tended to define causality.

I (and others) have argued that several key concepts from the causality literature, in particular, generative causality, causal packages, and contributory causes, are often more relevant and more useful for the complex interventions being discussed here (Befani, 2013; Cartwright & Hardie, 2012; Mayne, 2012, 2015; Scriven, 2015; Shaffer, 2014; Stern et al., 2012). Each of these concepts will be briefly introduced.

There are a number of ways other than through the counterfactual lens to view and interpret causality, with a large and long literature to support them (Stern et al., 2012). In particular, there is considerable interest in many evaluation quarters with generative causality that sees causality as a sequence of linked steps from cause to effect. And indeed, this is the perspective that we normally take in our daily lives when addressing causality. You know the cause of the broken window because you saw the boy throw the ball at the window. Theories of change are clearly models of generative causality. To show causality, the relevant chain of events needs to be confirmed, along with evidence on why each link in the chain worked.

For the multifaceted complex interventions of interest here, there are clearly a number of types of causal factors at work:

- Components of the intervention. Each component – which in essence is a mini-intervention – would typically support a causal factor and would be aimed at bringing about or supporting the bringing about of the intended results. It is likely to have its own pathway to results, setting out just how it is expected that the component activities undertaken will contribute to the observed results. Component causal factors are typically the direct proximate result of the component activities.
- Causal factors along a pathway. The activities of a component on their own are not likely to contribute to the results. Rather, the outputs of the intervention activity together with other supporting factors – the causal link assumptions along the component pathway theory of change – will make a contribution to bringing about the results.[1] And some of the factors in the causal packages may indeed be other intervention components. Key to note is that all the factors in a causal package are necessary to bring about the specific change.
- External causal factors. These are the factors outside the intervention such as socio-economic trends or other interventions that could have played a role in bringing about the results and hence made a contribution.

In a well-designed intervention, the expectation is that the collection of intervention components and their causal packages will together be able to bring about the desired results. That is, the intervention causal package is sufficient to realize the expected benefits. The causal package would typically include the actions of the various partners involved in the collective effort.

If we are able to show that a pathway causal package for an intervention component worked, then we can make a causal claim that the causal package indeed did make a positive contribution to the observed results – that it did make a difference. That conclusion would stand no matter what else might have been affecting the observed results, such as the contributions of other intervention components. Further, there may indeed have been other causal packages associated with other external influences at work, unrelated to the intervention causal package, such as quite separate interventions or socio-economic trends.

The answer then to the question about what caused the observed results would be the combination of all the above. Each intervention component and each external factor could have contributed in some way. But often the relevant question is less about explaining an observed result, and more about determining if the intervention made a positive contribution to the observed results. If, on the other hand, it could be shown that there were no significant other external causal packages at play, then we could make the stronger causal claim that the intervention – the collection of intervention component causal packages – caused the observed results. In these more complex settings, causality is indeed more complex and nuanced!

And more difficult. Some circumstances may allow forms of quasi-experimental designs to be undertaken and with them some sorting-out of the relative quantitative contribution of some of the causal factors at play. So much the better. In many complex settings however, this will not be possible and only more general contribution claims can be made.

Showing that an intervention component has been a contributory cause is showing that the component made a difference, and that it was a necessary part of the causal package in bringing about a positive contribution to the observed results. It is often the case that one cannot sort out quantitatively the relative size of the contributions being made by the various causal factors.

But we may want to say more than an intervention component was one of a number of causal factors. One thing that might be done is to explore the relative importance of each contributing causal factor, such as by assessing the perceived importance by key actors of the causal factors at work (Mayne, 2019). Another possibility is to explore the role played by the intervention components, such as:

- As a **trigger** – the sparks that start the fire. One can explore the extent to which it was the intervention that completed the causal package to bring about the intended results; it started the chain reaction that led to impact. This might have happened through the provision of essential funds, by clearing a blockage in a process by providing the right motivation for others to get involved;

- As a **supporting role**. Providing, perhaps, essential skills and knowledge or other forms of support as the intervention proceeded to ensure overall success;
- As a **facilitator**, bringing key actors together to form the essential causal package of activities;
- Changing behavior requires changes in capabilities, opportunities, and motivation (Michie, 2013). An intervention's role may be aimed at changing one or more of these attributes of capacity, a specific **change role**;
- As an **accelerator**, so that through its support, the timeline when the expected results are realized is shortened.

This discussion was aimed at setting out the various key concepts needed to understand and talk about causality in the multifaceted complex settings being examined. These concepts and ideas need to be kept in mind when we next talk about meaningful evaluation impact questions.

Realistic Evaluation Impact Questions

A defining characteristic of impact evaluation is the need to address causality, to explore causal links between the intervention activities and observed impacts. But typically, the same causal questions can be raised about the links with observed outcomes. I have argued (Mayne, 2015, 2018) that the terms "impacts" and "outcomes" are often not that helpful for distinguishing different types of "results." I will continue to use the terms "impact evaluation" and "impacts," but for the most part the arguments apply equally well to outcomes.

With this understanding and a more nuanced perspective on causality, let us look at the kinds of evaluation questions that have traditionally been set out as impact questions (Table 11.1).[2]

If we look at these issues in the context of complex multifaceted interventions, we can see that without further explanation they are not that meaningful. In particular:

- *To what extent has the intervention met its objectives and/or expected impacts?* The question could be interpreted simply as whether or not the stated objectives (results) were realized, ignoring the causality issue, but typically the implication is that there is some sort of a causal link with the intervention.

Table 11.1 Traditional impact evaluation questions

1.	To what extent has the intervention met its objectives and/or expected impacts?
2.	Has the intervention been effective?
3.	What has happened as a result of the intervention?
4.	What would have happened without the intervention?

In the setting being considered, it is not really clear what "met (or achieved) its objectives" means. It depends somewhat on how the objectives have been set out. Set out as specific results, it is the causal packages involved, not the intervention per se, that may have brought about the objectives, although more realistically, contributed to the objectives. We can expect that the intervention was a contributory cause to the objectives. Does that mean it met its objectives?

- *Has the intervention been effective?*
  Effectiveness is usually meant to relate to the extent to which objectives have been met, and hence has the same weaknesses as the first question. In anything but a very simple intervention, what does it really mean?
- *What has happened as a result of the intervention?*
  Again, without more discussion, it is not clear what this question is asking. It is the causal package that brings about or contributes to any observed impacts. The intervention on its own would have caused little to happen. One can explore the role played by the intervention as part of the causal package. The question needs to be reinterpreted in light of the concept of contributory causes.
- *What would have happened without the intervention?*
  This is the counterfactual question. It is unlikely that an actual counterfactual can be set out, although perhaps some hypothetical counterfactuals might be explored. In terms of contributory causes, the question could be interpreted as if the intervention (or perhaps an intervention component) was a necessary part of the (sufficient) causal package, but that is not what is usually meant by the question. To get an answer, an experimental design is needed, which usually in these settings is not feasible.

  Of course, the question of real interest is rather what happened with the intervention in place.

Without further specific explanation as to what exactly is being asked, these questions are open to interpretation – they are not, I would argue, useful impact questions. I think they persist in being used because they sound sensible and the complexity of causality in most interventions is not understood or appreciated.

Meaningful Impact Evaluation Issues for Complex Interventions

The introductory chapter set out the general evaluation issues the book is exploring.

These are recast from a contribution perspective in Table 11.2 in summary form and elaborated on below[3]:

1 **Impacts**. Without considering causality, what changes in the impacts of interest have been observed?
   - This is the basic measurement question (not implying that the measuring will necessarily be straightforward!).

Table 11.2 Meaningful impact evaluation questions

1. Impacts. What have been the observed impacts?
2. Contribution to impacts. Did the intervention make a contribution to impacts? How and why has the intervention made a contribution? What role did the intervention play?
3. Other influences. What other influencing causal factors were at play?
4. Relative importance. What is the relative importance of the various causal factors at work?
5. Sustainability. Are the results achieved sustainable?
6. Generalizability. Will the intervention work elsewhere? Can it be scaled up?
7. Lessons. What lessons on bringing about long-term impact can be learned for future programming?
8. Likely future impact. Is it likely the intervention will make a contribution to impacts in the future?

2 **Contribution to impacts**. Did the intervention contribute to observed impacts; how and why did it make a difference, i.e.:
   - What have been the observed impacts?
   - Was the intervention a contributory cause to those impacts?
   - Did the intervention contribute to outcomes along the pathway(s) to impact?
   - How and why have the observed impacts come about (or not)? What causal factors or mechanisms in what combination have resulted in the observed impacts? Why have the impacts not been realized?
   - How has the intervention contributed to the various outcomes along the pathway(s) to impact?
   - For whom does the intervention work and not work, and why?[4]
   - Where relevant, were the impacts not realized because of program design failure or implementation failure?
   - What matters about how the intervention is implemented for it to work?
   - What matters about the contexts into which it is introduced in order for it to work?
   - Has the intervention resulted in any unintended impacts, and if so, how?
   - What roles did the intervention play in bringing about the observed outcomes and impacts? Did it act as a trigger to start change? As a support factor in bringing about change with others?

3 **Other influences**. What other influencing causal factors outside the intervention contributed to bringing about the impacts?
   - To what extent did other influences play a role in bringing about the impacts?

4 **Relative importance.** We can show that different causal factors involved in an intervention made a contribution, but what about their relative importance?
   - What was the relative importance of the different causal factors that made a contribution, in terms of such perspectives as perceived influence, roles played, funds expended and/or the degree of difficulty in bringing about the causal factor?

5 **Sustainability**. Are the results associated with the intervention sustainable?
   - If the intervention has ended, are the impacts still being realized? Why or why not? Will they continue to be realized?
   - If the intervention ends, will the conditions needed for impact likely continue?

6 **Generalizability**. Will the intervention work elsewhere?
   - In what contexts and circumstances will this intervention's theory of change work and not work, and why? Can this intervention be transferred elsewhere and scaled up?
   - What generalizable lessons have we learned about how the intervention led to impact?

7 **Lessons**. What lessons on bringing about long-term impact can be learned for future programming?
   - What generalizable lessons have been learned about how the intervention contributed to impact?

And there is another set of questions that are of interest. We tend to talk about evaluating impact after the impacts have been realized, which of course may be many years off. Frequently though, an evaluation is commissioned well before the longer-terms impacts are expected, such as at project or program termination. This I call the in-between case – in between implementation and when final impacts can be expected. In this case, there are somewhat different impact questions:

8 **Likely future impact**. Given current understanding about results to date, is it likely that the intervention will contribute to future, longer-term impacts?
   - What are the apparent results to date?
   - Was the intervention a contributory cause for those results?
   - Is the theory of change still robust? That is, given the knowledge to date, is it likely that the future part of the theory of change will be realized?
   - What can be done to enhance the likelihood of achieving future impacts?

Theory-based approaches using theories of change for addressing these issues have been discussed extensively (Copestake, 2014; Institute of Development Studies, 2013; Ling, 2012, 2014; Mayne, Stern, & Douthwaite, 2013; Stern et al., 2012; United Nations Evaluation Group [UNEG], 2013).

The use of these types of evaluation questions exploring impact issues in a research setting is discussed in Mayne (2017), along with examples.

Accountability and Learning

Impact evaluations are commissioned for both learning and accountability ends. Sometimes they try to meet both these aims, but I have argued this often results in weak evaluations (Mayne, 2007). Certainly, accountability often pushes out learning by dominating the focus of an evaluation (Guijt, 2010; Hutchings, 2014; Regeer, Wildt-Liesveld, Mierlo, & Bunders, 2016). But consider this accountability versus learning dilemma for complex multifaceted interventions and in light of the above discussion on meaningful impact evaluation questions.

The learning focus of the impact questions in Table 11.2 are obvious, especially from questions 3, 5, 6, and 7. The accountability focus is perhaps not so clear.

First, the questions in Table 11.1 are often seen as the key accountability questions, asking if the intervention has delivered as intended and what results can be attributed to the intervention itself. I have argued that these are probably less than useful impact questions, indeed questions that likely cannot be credibly answered as posed. If so, where does this leave accountability? Funders have a legitimate interest in knowing if their investment has been a good one.

The answer, I suggest, is that: a) there is a need to rethink what meaningful accountability in these contexts means, and b) the second set of impact questions discussed above do indeed address good accountability questions.

In the face of complicated and complex interventions, with ambitious goals yet uncertain pathway(s) to impact and multiple partners, simplistic accountability that merely calls for reporting against milestones and targets runs counter to good management practices, and indeed common sense. It leads to a "managing to indicators" mentality, the opposite of what managing for results ought to foster. It focuses management's attention on meeting somewhat arbitrary preset targets at the expense of pushing management to adapt to current conditions and increased understanding so as to better maximize the chance that the intervention will be successful in contributing to the ambitious goals and aims. It also tends to focus on the short term. A much more useful form of accountability is needed.

I would suggest that in this context, a useful form of accountability would ask the intervention management to demonstrate the questions in Table 11.3:[5]

This interpretation of accountability is very consistent with a results-based organization expecting its managers to be innovative and adapt their activities as they learn more about how to best bring about development change. Answers to these questions, I argue, would show that the funds invested in the intervention are being well spent.

If we then review the set of "meaningful" impact questions discussed above (Table 11.2), the second question about making a difference directly addresses the first two accountability questions in Table 11.3, as would the eighth impact question about future success. The third accountability question in Table 11.3 is one the intervention would be expected to demonstrate; that the implementers are learning. The second impact question in Table 11.2 on how and why a difference was made would be mainly addressed at learning, and of course be based on evidence found in the first question. The sustainability issue is included in both tables.

Thus, I would argue, the impact evaluation questions in Table 11.2 do address both accountability and learning concerns, as well as, with the sixth and seventh questions, policy concerns.

Table 11.3 Meaningful accountability questions

1. Is the intervention making progress on results? • Demonstrating the intervention is measuring the extent to which the results of interest along the pathways in the theory of change, including targets and relevant milestones, are being realized.
2. Is the intervention contributing to results? • Demonstrating the intervention is assessing the nature and extent of their contribution to the results, i.e., if they are making a difference, and in what manner.
3. Is learning from the results of the intervention occurring? • Demonstrating the intervention implementers have learned and adjusted their activities and the theories of change as results become known.
4. Is the intervention sustainable? • Demonstrating that attention has been paid to issues of sustainability – whether the benefits realized will last once the intervention ends.

In the complex multifaceted interventions being discussed, there is an increased appreciation of the need for adaptive management, for adjusting the intervention and its delivery as time goes on (Andrews et al., 2013; Barder & Ramalingam, 2012; Ramalingam, 2013; Rogers, 2017). But too often, commissioners are still looking for traditional accountability, the antithesis of adaptive managing (Douthwaite & Hoffecker, 2017).

Realistic Commissioning of Impact Evaluations

I am arguing the need to understand the causal complexities involved in complex multifaceted integrated interventions and hence the need for thoughtful articulation of impact questions when commissioning evaluations. Pushing interventions to partner with others in governments, civil society, and the private sector is good practice, but realize that this complicates issues of causality – you likely will not be able to sort out in any detail who caused what, and hence who gets credit for the results. Accepting longer time frames when aiming for fundamental change is realistic, but likely increases the factors involved in bringing about and explaining change. Asking impact questions that could only be answered with an experimental design, when such is not possible, will result in weak or misleading answers. Expecting robust answers to impact questions in complex settings, but providing limited resources will, of course, result in limited answers.

Evaluators are required to follow the terms of reference of evaluations and will do so, even if the impact questions posed are "meaningless," i.e., cannot really be credibly answered in the way they are posed. They will do their best, but the answers will likely be less than useful and probably represent a significant waste of evaluation resources.

Commissioners do not need to give up on getting robust information, including for accountability. They do need to think a little differently about what kinds of information on accountability they should ask for and expect to get.

The accountability issues in Table 11.3 are quite demanding and would provide good information on whether the intervention is making a difference and managing funds wisely.

Commissioners will get the information they ask for, and if they are asking inappropriate impact questions, they will get less than useful answers. If they ask meaningful impact questions, they should expect to get good robust answers from the evaluation profession. You tend to get what you ask for, and of course, what you pay for.

On the other hand, evaluators have a responsibility, I suggest, to be upfront on the kinds of causal claims they can deliver on. They should lay out early on the kinds of answers they will likely be able to arrive at, given the impact questions being addressed and the setting. They may have to argue the need to reformulate original impact questions into more meaningful and useful evaluation questions. Speaking truth to commissioners is not easy – and may cost evaluators contracts – but should be what is expected of professional evaluators.

Notes

1 In these causal packages we are looking for *salient* factors, factors that are relevant to the situation and context (Mayne, 2015, p. 124).
2 See for example Organisation for Economic Co-operation and Development [OECD] (1991).
3 Here, when the term intervention is used, it is taken to mean the set of components making up the intervention. Thus, for example, "the intervention making a contribution" means one or more of its components made a contribution.
4 These are the realist evaluation questions (Westhorp, 2014).
5 These are the issues related to impact. Other aspects of accountability might call for evidence that the intervention plans for results and is efficient.

References

Andrews, M., Pritchett, L., & Woolcock, M. (2013). Escaping capability traps through problem-driven iterative adaptation (PDIA). *World Development, 51*, 234–244. Retrieved from https://dash.harvard.edu/bitstream/handle/1/9403175/RWP12-036_Andrews_Pritchett.pdf

Barder, O., & Ramalingam, B. (2012). *Complexity, adaptation, and results. Global Development: Views from the Center.* Washington, DC: Center for Global Development.

Befani, B. (2013). *Methodological challenges for impact evaluations of development interventions*. UK: Institute of Development Studies.

Byrne, D. (2013). Evaluating complex social interventions in a complex world. *Evaluation, 19*, 217–228.

Cartwright, N., & Hardie, J. (2012). *Evidence-based policy: Doing it better. A practical guide to predicting if a policy will work for you.* Oxford: Oxford University Press.

Copestake, J. (2014). Credible impact evaluation in complex contexts: Confirmatory and exploratory approaches. *Evaluation, 20*, 412–427.

Douthwaite, B., & Hoffecker. E. (2017). Towards a complexity-aware theory of change for participatory research programs working within agricultural innovation systems. *Agricultural Systems, 155*, 88–102.

Garcia, J. R., & Zazueta, A. (2015). Going beyond mixed methods to mixed approaches: A systems perspective for asking the right questions. *IDS Bulletin, 46*, 30–43. Retrieved from https://opendocs.ids.ac.uk/opendocs/bitstream/handle/20.500.12413/7266/IDSB_46_1_10.1111-1759-5436.12119.pdf?sequence=1

Gerrits, L., & Verweij, S. (2015). Taking stock of complexity in evaluation: A discussion of three recent publications. *Evaluation, 2*, 481–491.

Guijt, I. (2010). Accountability and learning: Exploding the myth of incompatibility between accountability and learning. In A. Fowler & J. Ubels (Eds.), *Capacity development in practice*. Oxford: Routledge.

Hutchings, C. (2014). Balancing accountability and learning: A review of Oxfam GB's global performance framework. *Journal of Development Effectiveness, 6*, 425–435. Retrieved from https://oxfamilibrary.openrepository.com/bitstream/handle/10546/337230/jo-balancing-accountability-learning-171114-en.pdf?sequence=1

Institute of Development Studies (2013). *Impact innovation and learning: Towards a research and practice agenda for the future. Report of an international workshop, Brighton, 26–27 March 2013*. Institute for Development Studies. Retrieved from www.ids.ac.uk/files/dmfile/WebsiteReport.pdf

Ling, T. (2012). Evaluating complex and unfolding interventions in real time. *Evaluation, 18*, 79–91.

Ling, T. (2014). *Putting impact evaluation in its place. RAND Europe*. Norwich: University of East Anglia. Retrieved from www.uea.ac.uk/documents/6347571/7859678/Documents UEA+Impact+Evaluation.pdf/4b33bbce-65ed-4c58-b77e-e38f155b16d5

Mayne, J. (2007). Evaluation for accountability: Reality or myth? In M.-L. Bemelmans-Videc, J. Lonsdale, & B. Perrin (Eds.), *Making accountability work: Dilemmas for evaluation and for audit* (pp. 63–84). New Brunswick, NJ: Transaction Publishers.

Mayne, J. (2012). Contribution analysis: Coming of age? *Evaluation, 18*, 270–280.

Mayne, J. (2015). Useful theory of change models. *Canadian Journal of Program Evaluation, 30*, 119–142.

Mayne, J. (2017). *Developing a framework and approach for IDRC targeted impact evaluations*. Ottawa: IDRC.

Mayne, J. (2018). The COM-B theory of change model: Working paper. ResearchGate. Retrieved from www.researchgate.net/publication/323868561_The_COMB_ToC_Model4.

Mayne, J. (2019). *Assessing the relative importance of causal factors*. CDI practice paper 21. Brighton: IDS.

Mayne, J., & Johnson, N. (2015). Using theories of change in the agriculture for nutrition and health CGIAR research program. *Evaluation, 2*, 407–428.

Mayne, J., Stern, E., & Douthwaite, B. (2013). *Evaluating natural resource management programs, practice brief, AAS-2013–23*. Penang, Malaysia: CGIAR Research Program on Aquatic Agricultural Systems. CGIAR.

Michie, S. (2013). *The behaviour change wheel: A cross-disciplinary model*. UCL Grand Challenges Town meeting, May 2013.

Organisation for Economic Co-operation and Development (OECD) (1991). *Principles for the evaluation of development assistance*. Paris: Development Assistance Committee. OECD. Retrieved from www.oecd.org/dataoecd/31/12/2755284.pdf

Palladium. (2015). *Independent evaluation of the security sector accountability and police reform programme: Final evaluation report: DFID*. Department for International Development. Retrieved from http://r4d.dfid.gov.uk/pdf/outputs/SSAPRP-DRC/SSAPR_Complete_Impact_Evaluation_Rep_Final-Eng.pdf

Ramalingam, B. (2013). *Aid on the edge of chaos: Rethinking international cooperation in a complex world.* Oxford: Oxford University Press.

Ramalingam, B., & Jones, H. (2008). *Exploring the science of complexity: Ideas and implications for development and humanitarian efforts, Working Paper 285.* London, UK: The Overseas Development Institute.

Regeer, B. J., Wildt-Liesveld, R. d., Mierlo, B. v., & Bunders, J. F. G. (2016). Exploring ways to reconcile accountability and learning in the evaluation of niche experiments. *Evaluation, 22*, 6–28.

Rist, L., Felton, A., Samuelsson, L., Sandström, C., & Rosvall, O. (2013). A new paradigm for adaptive management. *Ecology and Society, 18*, 63. http://dx.doi.org/10.5751/ES-06183-180463

Rogers, P. (2017). Does evaluation need to be done differently to support adaptive management? *Better evaluation – Sharing information to improve evaluation.* Retrieved from www.betterevaluation.org/en/blog/evaluation_for_adaptive_management

Scriven, M. (2015). Demythologizing causation and evidence. In S. Donaldson, C. Christie, & M. Mark (Eds.), *Credible and actionable evidence: The foundations of rigorous and influential evaluations* (2nd ed.). Newbury Park, CA: Sage.

Shaffer, P. (2014). Two concepts of causation: Implications for poverty. *Development and Change, 46*, 148–166. Retrieved from http://onlinelibrary.wiley.com/doi/10.1111/dech.12140/epdf

Stern, E., Stame, N., Mayne, J., Forss, K., Davies, R., & Befani, B. (2012). *Broadening the range of designs and methods for impact evaluations. Working Paper, 38.* Department for International Development. London: DFID. Retrieved from http://r4d.dfid.gov.uk/Output/189575/

United Nations. (2015). Sustainable development goals. *United Nations.*

United Nations Evaluation Group (UNEG). (2013). *Impact evaluation in UN agency evaluation systems: Guidance on selection, planning and management, guidance document.* New York: UNEG. Retrieved from www.uneval.org/papersandpubs/documentdetail.jsp?doc_id=1433

Westhorp, G. (2014). *Realist impact evaluation: An introduction: Methods lab.* London: ODI. Retrieved from www.odi.org/sites/odi.org.uk/files/odi-assets/publications-opinion-files/9138.pdf

Wild, L., Booth, D., Cumming, C., Foresti, M., & Wales, J. (2015). *Adapting development: Improving services to the poor.* London: ODI. Retrieved from www.odi.org/sites/odi.org.uk/files/odi-assets/publications-opinion-files/9437.pdf

Woolcock, M. (2009). *Towards a plurality of methods in project evaluation: A contextualised approach to understanding impact trajectories and efficacy.* Working Paper 73: University of Manchester. Manchester: Brooks World Poverty Institute.

12 Realpolitik of Demand and Supply Regarding Results Information

R. Pablo Guerrero

This book has examined a basic question about evaluation, that is, whether the demand for evaluation of public policies, programs, and projects generates robust information about results achieved, and how evaluation practice – the supply side – may be improved to ensure it meets demand. The subject is addressed from three angles: the enabling environment and market that define the nature of the demand for evaluation results; the robustness and comprehensiveness of various evaluation methods used; and, the gaps that arise between the nature of the demand and supply of evaluation results. Demand and supply of evaluation results are two sides of the same coin. As such they are intertwined and symbiotic and not possible to disentangle in a clear manner. In the discussion below, I have tried to summarize the motivations of the demand-side actors but recognize that supply-side actors also influence the nature of the demand. I now take each of these angles in turn and conclude with some reflections on the gaps.

On the Demand for Evaluation Results

What is the enabling environment that defines the demand for evaluation results? The enabling environment, or the authorizing environment, as Mark Moore (1995) defines it, encompasses the various stakeholders (and their interactions) that are demanding, commissioning, or using, information about evaluation results. Among the demand stakeholders are commissioners of evaluation, who according to Mayne (this volume), often do not understand the complexities involved in evaluation (particularly impact evaluations) and therefore by demanding this type of evaluation generate unrealistic expectations of what can be delivered in the way of results. Commissioners of impact evaluations often demand to know about results that are not going to materialize for a long time (Gilchrist & Wilkins; Rieper, this volume). In other instances, the commissioners of evaluation, for example political actors, such as those described by Devaux-Spatarakis, Lindkvist and Bastøe, and Mazzeo Rinaldi (this volume), fund evaluations to "justify" that a particular policy, program, or project is delivering promised results. In these cases, evaluations are carried out, often using imperfect methods or imperfectly applied methods, without much regard to the evaluation results reported, because the politicians that commission the evaluations are not interested in using them for decision-making or learning. They are simply going through the motions to meet the demands of their constituencies, which may be more apparent than real (such as "warm-glow altruism" cited by Lindkvist & Bastøe, this volume).

In the French case, Devaux-Spatarakis (this volume) explains that the evaluation commissioners insisted on the use of experimental methods (RCTs) to evaluate the impact of a public social program, knowing full well that the results would not be forthcoming in a timely manner and would therefore not influence the political decision to proceed with extending the funding of that program – which was what the political authority intended anyway. That is, without the benefit of knowing whether the public program produced desired results or not. On the other hand, the evaluators commissioned to carry out the RCTs, i.e., supply the impact evaluations, did so with little reservation because this was well-funded work that kept the evaluation "consultancy" (and demand for publications) functioning. The politicians who commissioned the evaluation were opportunistic and did so solely to justify expanding a popular public program before there was any evidence of whether it actually worked. Another variant of this is the demand for advocacy evaluation, as in the case of climate change evaluation research discussed by Belcher, Young, and Suryadarma (this volume). This is also illustrated in the human rights approach case (Eliadis, this volume). The interest of the funders of this type of evaluation is to have information that can be used to advance their agenda, and allocation of funding for it. Because there is an inherent bias towards predefined objectives (environmental protection, social equity) there is an aura of suspicion that surrounds the legitimacy of this type of evaluation.

The EU case study illustrates the situation where the commissioners of evaluation do not set a defined evaluation agenda, but leave it up to those that receive EU funding to decide what the appropriate evaluation questions are, or what evaluations questions need answers. Evaluation choices are left to the recipient stakeholders. The rationale for this approach is that only beneficiary stakeholders can decide on the "culturally" appropriate questions and methods to be used and, Mazzeo Rinaldi (this volume) argues, the evaluation results produced in this way are more likely to be easier to understand, simpler and more "interesting." Whether they are more useful to policymakers is not determined. Indeed, Mazzeo Rinaldi indicates that EU policymakers and funders of evaluation have little choice but to rely on this approach because evaluation questions are not raised and are not instrumental at the time the policies get enacted.

The Irish case illustrates another demand variant. An outside body or organization influences government policy that demands evaluation focused on results, with the ultimate aim of affecting future policy and investment decision-making. The government has responded by strengthening the link between public expenditure and evaluation. According to Boyle (this volume), without the influence of an external force, this would have been unlikely.

The demand for evaluation results on impact as encapsulated above reflects the "realpolitik" that is embedded in demand and supply of results information.

There are many demand rationales but not a core demand concern – such as the pursuit of social or economic impact – that would provide a common thread or unifying theme behind such "demands."

On the Supply of Evaluation Results

As can be discerned from the above, on the supply side of evaluation results or information on impacts, the picture that emerges from the case studies and theoretical approaches addressed in this book is not any clearer. The various chapters describe or allude to different evaluation methods and their shortcomings. But as mentioned, these methods do not provide a unifying theory or approach to the pursuit of information about results. This is inherently a matter that can be traced to the multidisciplinary nature of the different demand and supply stakeholders. If the demand is about economic impact, or even value for money as in the Irish case (Boyle, this volume), then the methods revolve around some form of applied cost-benefit analysis. Boyle discusses that involving a group outside government, such as The Atlantic Philanthropies, has helped the Irish government's economic and social service to enhance the rigor of evaluation work and has highlighted what constitutes "good quality results information." If, on the other hand, the demand is about social impact, then the methods rely on social science, theories of social change, theory knitting (Lemire, Christie, & Nielsen, this volume), basic human rights (Eliadis, this volume) etc.

As in the case of demand, the supply of information is also often devoid of a single overarching theory that gives it a rationale. Information on prima facie "results" may be gathered through interview processes or surveys that are then analyzed and summarized (Lemire et al.; Belcher, this volume). These results are descriptive rather than quantitative, i.e., there is no unit of account that is used unambiguously to determine where the results fit in any logical impact scale or index, or whether they can be aggregated. The crux of the realpolitik of evaluation is that this ambiguity may well suit the desire of all stakeholders. It provides for weak accountability and one can conclude, perhaps cynically, that this is often what those who demand evaluation are after (Lindkvist & Bastøe, this volume). The problem is that when evaluation practice produces results that are not based on a particular unit of account, reported results will not successfully point to how policies, programs, and projects can be improved – there is no improvement metric. At the margin one could conclude that any evaluation theory is as good as any other. Theory knitting (Lemire et al., this volume), if it were fully comprehensive, i.e., addressed all aspects of impact, could provide useful conclusions. But its general applicability in the real world of evaluation practice seems highly unlikely.

In many cases, a more practical and useful approach might be to improve on the development of counterfactuals, i.e., what would be the impact of a program or project in the absence of an intervention. According to Mazzeo Rinaldi this was the evaluation method – a "Computable General Equilibrium Model" – that was deemed superior to other approaches by a thematic working group assembled to assess evaluation questions related to EU programs in Sardinia, although eventually it was not used. A counterfactual is the standard approach used widely in cost-benefit analysis. Cost-benefit analysis embeds theories of causality depending on the nature of the interventions evaluated; one could say that it builds in a theory of causality (change). Its advantage is that it is already widely used in the allocation of public resources by a multiplicity of stakeholder governments and organizations. It has respectable and widespread academic backing and improvements in methodology are always being made that produce useful results "closer to the truth." The major obstacle is that there are few experts in this field involved in evaluation practice and this has proven to be a powerful barrier to adoption.

Mayne raises the issue that evaluating impacts is only possible once impacts have happened and that could take many years. It is important then to recognize that if the demand for impact information is concurrent with the commissioning of evaluations, then the methods must be adjusted to reflect this. If, for example, policymakers are interested in the impact of a 30-year education investment that has been implemented but still has 20 years of useful life remaining, the evaluator should examine what has happened retrospectively and, in the light of that, reassess what is likely to happen in the remaining useful life, given that circumstances might have changed since the original investment decision was made. So, in the real world, this type of ex-post evaluation has both a retrospective and prospective component; one informs the other, and the resulting conclusions inform policymaking at the time the evaluation is carried out and that is as useful as evaluation can be. Nevertheless, one must consider, as in the CIFOR case study, that with respect to the impact of research on policy, often "tracing forward from project activities tends to overemphasize project impact while tracing back from observed project impacts tends to emphasize wider political processes."

In the French case (Devaux-Spatarakis, this volume), the decision was made to use RCTs to evaluate the impact of a politically driven social program. Decision-makers could not wait for the results, so they decided to expand that social program anyway. Notwithstanding the ethical problems with RCTs, these are truly long-term exercises that need to run their course to yield usable information. They are expensive and ultimately quite irrelevant to current decision-making (as the French case shows), despite their supply-side popularity. But they do feed a growing impact evaluation industry, especially in academic circles. In the Irish case, Boyle (this volume) concludes that while RCTs were generally welcomed, these took too long and were too expensive to yield useful and timely information on results for policymakers. The CIFOR case mentions RCTs as experimental counterfactuals that are very difficult to build into qualitative evaluations.

Another evaluation case that illustrates a long-gestation problem is the social services outcomes agreements or contracts (Gilchrist & Wilkins, this volume); these are plagued by issues of outcome specification or quantification and can take decades to deliver apparent results. Even then, the results are not easy to aggregate and therefore it is difficult to gauge impacts. In contrast, the evaluation of the Norway health reform program required comprehensive analysis but covered few issues and a very short period, when in fact the results would be expected to be of broader scope and take a long time to materialize.

The CIFOR case study discusses other evaluation supply considerations such as participatory evaluation where the emphasis is on stakeholder involvement and concludes that while this type of evaluation approach carries the risk of being perceived as biased, a less participatory approach runs the risk of missing or misunderstanding subtleties of the evaluated program. Ultimately CIFOR endorses a Theory of Change approach that lays out the causality pathways to the achievement of outcomes. However, it concludes that even if outcomes do not materialize in practice, this approach does not explain whether this is due to a failure of program intervention or to a multiplicity of other factors, and warns that constructing a counterfactual in complex environments is exceedingly difficult.

On the Gap between Demand and Supply

Indeed, it is generally exceedingly difficult to discuss the gaps between demand and supply of evaluation in practice. The considerations laid out above suggest that there are too many factors that explain the nature of the demand, and too many approaches to supplying results information that are reliable, timely, and affordable. There is no correct approach, only less than perfect ones. Ultimately what is suitable lies in "eye of the beholder," and this is explained by biases due to the various disciplines that underlie evaluation practice. In practical terms, on both the demand and supply sides, there is a need to explicitly expose, and be conscious of, these predetermined biases. The gaps will be closed only when there is a close match between the rationale for evaluations that yield the sought-after results information, and the approaches used that yield that information. For every demand and supply rationale there are constituencies, and – in the absence of a clear understanding of the underlying objectives of each group – demand and supply will only intersect in some abstract space.

Reference

Moore, M. H. (1995). *Creating public value: Strategic management in government.* London, UK: Harvard University Press.

Index

Page numbers in **bold** denote tables, those in *italics* denote figures.

For Product Safety Concerns and Information please contact our EU
representative GPSR@taylorandfrancis.com
Taylor & Francis Verlag GmbH, Kaufingerstraße 24, 80331 München, Germany

www.ingramcontent.com/pod-product-compliance
Ingram Content Group UK Ltd.
Pitfield, Milton Keynes, MK11 3LW, UK
UKHW022025061126
477531UK00002B/31
9780367434328